STUDIES IN COMMUNICATION

General Editor: John Fiske

ON VIDEO

IN THE SAME SERIES

ON VIDEO

Roy Armes

ROUTLEDGE   LONDON AND NEW YORK

First published in 1988 by
Routledge
11 New Fetter Lane, London EC4P 4EE

Published in the USA by Routledge
in association with Routledge, Chapman & Hall, Inc.
29 West 35th Street, New York NY 10001

Typeset by Hope Services, Abingdon
Printed in Great Britain
by Richard Clay Ltd, Bungay, Suffolk

British Library Cataloguing in Publication Data

Armes, Roy
On video.—(Studies in communication).
1. Video tape recorders and recording
I. Title   II. Series
778.59'9   TK6655.V5
ISBN 0–415–00717–8
ISBN 0–415–00718–6 Pbk

Library of Congress Cataloging in Publication Data

Armes, Roy.
On video / Roy Armes.
p.   cm.—(Studies in communication)
Bibliography: p.
Includes index.
ISBN 0–415–00717–8.   ISBN 0–415–00718–6 (pbk.)
1. Television—History.   2. Video recordings—History.
3. Motion pictures—History.   I. Title.   II. Series.
TK6637.A76 1988   87–34678
778.59'9—dc19   CIP

Recording has always been a means of social control, a stake in politics, regardless of the available technologies. Power is no longer content to enact its legitimacy; it records and reproduces the societies it rules. . . . But before the industrial age, this attribute did not occupy centre stage.

(Jacques Attali 1985: 87)

To JETTE

CONTENTS

GENERAL EDITOR'S PREFACE

This series of books on different aspects of communication is designed to meet the needs of the growing number of students coming to study this subject for the first time. The authors are experienced teachers or lecturers who are committed to bridging the gap between the huge body of research available to the more advanced student, and what the new student actually needs to get him started on his studies.

Probably the most characteristic feature of communication is its diversity: it ranges from the mass media and popular culture, through language to individual and social behaviour. But it identifies links and a coherence within this diversity. The series will reflect the structure of its subject. Some books will be general, basic works that seek to establish theories and methods of study applicable to a wide range of material; others will apply these theories and methods to the study of one particular topic. But even these topic-centred books will relate to each other, as well as to the more general ones. One particular topic, such as advertising or news or language, can only be understood as an example of communication when it is related to, and differentiated from, all the other topics that go to make up this diverse subject.

The series, then, has two main aims, both closely connected. The first is to introduce readers to the most important results of contemporary research into communication together with the theories that seek to explain it. The second is to equip them with appropriate methods of study and investigation which they will be able to apply directly to their everyday experience of communication.

If readers can write better essays, produce better projects and pass more exams as a result of reading these books I shall be very satisfied; but if they gain a new insight into how communication shapes and informs our social life, how it articulates and creates our experience of industrial society, then I shall be delighted. Communication is too often taken for granted when it should be taken to pieces.

John Fiske

INTRODUCTION
The need for
a new perspective

Our own technology cannot be assessed except in reference to the past. The cultural meaning of the computer becomes clear only in comparison with the meaning of the clock for its age and the steam engine for its age.

(J. David Bolter 1986: 16)

The argument of this book is that the understanding of video demands that it be seen within the whole spectrum of nineteenth- and twentieth-century audio, visual, and audio-visual media, including radio and photography, the gramophone, and the tape recorder. Video's very versatility and flexibility as a medium repulse any simple attempt to grasp its 'essence' or 'specificity', and continual technological development makes it increasingly difficult to pin down a fixed identity: video in the 1980s is a very different proposition from video in the 1960s, when the first portable black-and-white reel-to-reel systems were introduced.

Video is at one level merely a neutral recording device, with little more evident scope for creativity than a xerox copying machine. It can record and reproduce perfectly the systems developed within the film industry and the broadcasting institutions to depict reality and to create meaningful combinations of sounds and images. In its most prevalent form as a commodity – the video tapes universally available for hire or purchase – it has clear similarities to the gramophone record and cassette and, as music videos have become more popular, closer links have been established with the record industry. At the same time, video's method of electro-magnetic recording and its spread of often seemingly contradictory social applications echo those of sound tape. Moreover, as we shall see, most of the key issues relating to video are already anticipated in the nineteenth-century developments of still photography. Seen in a void video is a puzzling phenomenon, but viewed in relation to these other diverse media video's full range and potential become apparent.

One of the reasons for writing this book is to contest the tendency to see video as no more than a latter-day descendant of film and television. I myself came to the study of video after twenty years or more spent on critical and historical consideration of cinema. My initial difficulties in coming to terms with the new medium stemmed largely, I now believe, from attempting to define it in ways more appropriate to film – a view I held in common with many of my colleagues in the 1970s. There is now a very large body of valuable writing on many aspects of cinema, its history and economics, its technology and systems for creating meaning. The 1970s saw a resurgence of theoretical consideration of cinema – stemming particularly from the magazine *Screen* – and this work has shaped the perceptions of a whole new generation of students of film. But at least three aspects of this theoretical work make its direct application to video hazardous.

Firstly, the social definition of cinema as a new form of theatrical entertainment is very different from that of the other new media. The particular role of the feature film led 1970s theorists to stress the story-telling function of cinema, to ignore the diversity of filmic approaches, and to see film and narrative as inseparable. As early as the mid-1960s Christian Metz was describing the fictional feature film as 'the king's highway of filmic expression', while all the non-narrative genres – such as the documentary and the technical or educational film – were to be regarded as 'marginal provinces, border regions, so to speak' (Metz 1974: 94). While I for one would not wish to contest the centrality of the fictional feature film in any consideration of cinema as an institution, seeing film *exclusively* in terms of feature films has had certain regrettable consequences, especially a refusal to give any theoretical consideration to documentary.

Even greater distortions have arisen when the attempt has been made to apply categories derived from this narrative-based theorization of film either to the broadcast institution of television (where fiction, documentary, news, and entertainment have equal status) or to the recording medium of video (for which no one, to my knowledge, has ever proclaimed the centrality of narrative).

A second difficulty in applying to video the insights of film theory lies in the particular literary flavour of this theoretical work. It is a body of knowledge remarkable for its self-sufficiency. Over the years it has proved itself indifferent to contributions which might be derived from production activity, sociological study, film history, and the kind of formal analysis undertaken as a matter of routine in the study of art or music. In particular it refuses to see films as *social* texts, fully understandable only in relation to wider economic, social, and cultural contexts. As Dudley Andrew notes, it derives its impact almost exclusively from the application to film of metaphors drawn from other disciplines (Andrew 1984: 9).

It is the nature of these metaphors which causes the third problem in relation to video. All the successive metaphors which have dominated conceptualizations of film theory – the framed image, the window, the mirror – are purely visual (Andrew 1984: 12). They point to a tendency in virtually all 1970s film theory not merely to privilege the visual over the aural, but to concentrate exclusive attention on it – to deal only with the camera when considering the history of technology (Comolli 1977, 1986), or to offer schemes of analysis of the image track while ignoring totally the parallel sound track (Metz 1974: 108–76).

Television study, on the other hand, lacks virtually any coherent body of theoretical insights (Caughie 1984: 109). As long ago as 1970, in the introduction to his study of *The Effects of Television*, James Halloran gave his characterization of the three principal contending positions in the debate about television: those of the academic élitist – who 'may not even possess a set', the practical media man – who 'is usually ready to defend or idealize the operation of the medium', and the social scientist – 'a curious if cautious creature who is not known for his involve-

3

ment or commitment' (Halloran 1970: 10–11). Succeeding years have seen little real dialogue between representatives of these positions, and there is little explicit interconnection between the work which has been undertaken on television institutions and studies dealing with the television audience or with specific television genres. With the sole exception of John Ellis's book, *Visible Fictions* (1982), we lack any study of television's operation which invites meaningful comparisons with cinema, and there is hardly as much as an article which allows us to begin the task of relating the dominant audio-visual systems of film and television to video.

The present study adopts a much wider perspective than that offered by specific studies of either film or television. A necessary beginning for the process of estimating the potential impact of video is an evaluation of the influence which the new media of reproduction have had on us since the mid-nineteenth century. The varied histories and modes of application of reproduced sounds and images have profoundly affected the very bases of our lives, influencing our response to reality, reshaping our concept of language, and offering us new creative possibilities at the expense of subjecting us to covert (or at least unadmitted) forms of social and political control. The approach I should like to propose is very much in line with that adopted by Susan Sontag, since I feel that her analysis of photography can be extended to cover all the new media. What we need to consider is not merely the new 'image-world', but the whole sound-and-image-world of the twentieth century (Sontag 1978: 153–80).

Many writers on the media have stressed the ubiquity of recorded sounds and images: photographic reproductions adorn the advertising hoardings of our city streets, films are projected to us on aeroplanes, music is on tap for us when we drive a car, and a living-room without a television set is as inconceivable as a gathering of teenagers without transistor radio and record-player. Each year hundreds of millions of holiday snaps are processed, almost 4,000 feature films are produced world-wide, $6 billion worth of records are sold. The video cassette already has a multimillion-pound market (£260 million hire and £80 million sales in the UK in 1985), and everywhere radio and television channels come a step or two closer to fulfilling their technical potential of being multichannel, 24–hour-a-day, 7–day-a-week systems. Because we take this profusion of sounds and images for granted, the media have the capacity to shape our views of life in ways that generally escape us.

The nineteenth-century recording media were scientific 'wonders' in a very literal sense, offering replicas tied to their objects in such direct ways that the traditional neat distinction between copy and original lost its validity. The effect of sound waves causing a membrane to vibrate, like that of light emanating from a source to transform a photographic emulsion, creates a uniquely intimate link between copy and original. To possess a replica of this special kind is to possess something of the original: as Susan Sontag puts it, our feeling that the photographic process is something magical has a genuine basis. As our primeval ancestors used wall paintings in their caves as a way to understand and dominate their environment, so too we can use sound and image recordings to give us power over reality, a means of controlling it (Sontag 1978: 155).

However, along with this power goes a potential weakness – the danger of confusion stemming from a substitution of these sound and image replicas *for* reality. A home video can give us a version of a party or an outing which is uniquely 'real', but which can insidiously lose all sense of those aspects of the event which memory alone can preserve: smells and tastes, moments of private feeling. Marcel Proust's critique of photography for offering merely immediate sensations in place of a reality which comprises 'a certain connection between these immediate sensations and the memories which envelop us simultaneously with them' (Proust 1970: 145) applies even more strongly to the later media. Electro-magnetic recording in particular can take our most intimate situations and, while apparently preserving them, simply turn them into mere information flow, the very opposite of lived experience.

The credibility which we attribute to the photographic image we tend also to extend to all recorded and transmitted sounds and images. This can become problematic if, losing our awareness of the subtle complexity of our human senses, we bring ourselves to hear and see the world as microphones and cameras 'hear' and 'see' it. This is to forget that what these devices offer us is merely one single perspective on a reality that envelops us three-dimensionally in our own lives. With sound and video tape the dangers of uncritical acceptance may be enhanced, since these are systems which are essentially and inherently manipulable. The dyes used for Technicolor in the 1930s artificially changed the image in a way that already called into question the definition of photography as akin to a footprint or a death-mask. Taped sounds treated for noise reduction by the Dolby system and video images delicately recoloured through a studio control desk – though we tend to hail them as signs of progress in faithful recording – are in fact yet one stage further from being direct transcriptions of reality, although they still retain closer links than, say, writing or even painting.

Just as the new media reshape our ways of perceiving reality, so too they refocus our view of language. It is not merely that new forms of communication – each with its own particular verbal pattern and sentence form – have come into existence: the documentary film commentary, the 'on-the-spot' eye-witness report, the chat-show host's patter. It is not even that broadcasting's way of talking to its audience involves a new kind of speech, in which the absent listeners and viewers are apparently addressed directly and individually, although they can take no part in a two-way communication. The most important implications are much wider than these. Recording and broadcasting have helped to standardize the English language, reducing exaggerated class-based forms of expression and minimizing the role of dialect variations. Although the particular upper-class forms of expression beloved of John Reith now find their place only in World Service radio, the broadcasting institutions are imposing on us all a particular southern-English, educated brand of pronunciation. Similarly, the need for world sales in forms such as the feature film and the television drama has led inevitably to the development of a form of mid-Atlantic mediaspeak. It is the blend of these two which will shape the pattern of English in the twenty-first century, not the efforts of school teachers.

Equally crucial has been the new media's role in shifting emphasis from written to spoken language. Now that the bulk of the population receives its news, information, and entertainment in spoken form (through broadcasting, the telephone, records, and cassettes instead of newspapers, letters, and sheet music), the stabilizing effect of writing is disturbed. In place of the grammarians' rigidity we find a new flexibility in sentence structure, spelling, and inflection. This shift to spoken language has an impact on a whole range of our activities: teaching (the new emphasis on discussion, the use of oral methods in foreign-language teaching), political speech–making (a greater informality in place of old–fashioned florid rhetoric), even linguistics itself (the redefinition of language in terms of speech, the use of the tape recorder to analyse spoken forms).

It is not merely that information is now recorded and transmitted in new forms, the nature of the content which is conveyed changes too. What is lost is the notion of abstraction. The parliamentary reports in Hansard are cold and emotionless, with everything reduced to a single line, whereas broadcasting gives the full emotion of the debates, the emphasis of the words, the jeers and asides, which a written transcript ignores. The same is true of other media used for recording. No amount of photographs of factory sites can give us the abstract analytic concept of 'British industry', and a gramophone record is at one and the same time a concretization of the musical score and – inseparably – a particular individual interpretation of it.

Video needs to be seen as one element in this cluster of recording and transmission systems which together are changing our perceptions of the world in which we live. Video as art is merely the most recent of the new forms of artistic expression, and as such it follows still photography, cinema, radio and television drama, *musique concrète*, and certain studio–based pop recordings. These new forms have undoubtedly enriched our lives, but there are costs involved which far exceed the purchase price of equipment and recordings. Through these new media we become ever more deeply embedded in a consumer society: we buy individually pleasures once offered freely to society as a whole. Our broadcast news and information are far more tightly controlled by politicians than are newspapers or journals: radio and television have for this reason to be seen as new forms of social control. Battles for freedom of expression and against ever-encroaching censorship have to be fought afresh, and the social

7

effect of communication systems funded through advertising has to be assessed (Murdoch and Janus 1984). In the struggle for understanding of and control over the new media a particular importance attaches to those systems – still cameras, sound and video recorders – which allow us to act as producers as well as consumers and to create our own forms of sound and image expression.

Part one of the present study places video in its historical context, and its three successive chapters trace the overlapping pattern of development. Firstly, we consider the forms of recording which have their beginnings in the nineteenth century (the photograph, the gramophone record, and the feature film) together with the early electric communication media. The second chapter looks at the electronic revolution in communications which began with radio broadcasting in the 1920s and set the context for the explosion of television. Part One concludes with an exploration of the fresh impetus given after the Second World War by the development of sound and video tape, and the new structures of industrial organization which have been evolved to exploit recorded sounds and images. In Part Two the focus changes to the social context of video. The three successive chapters look respectively at the changing patterns of social application of the various media, at the differing ways in which production is organized in the three principal audio–visual systems of film, television, and video, and at the ways in which the audience is addressed. Part Three directs the attention to the ways in which video has developed as a form in its own right and looks at both the neglected area of sound in relation to video and the way in which video organizes its images.

The aim of the book is to enhance the understanding of video on the part of those engaged with video production, whether as teachers, students, or practitioners. While in no way a production manual or handbook, it does set out to explore those issues which need to be considered if video is to be used creatively. It has grown out of my work with students on the One Year Postgraduate Diploma in Video at Middlesex Polytechnic, which is largely a 'hands–on' practical course using video as its production medium. My debt to colleagues and to past students is enormous and self–evident.

PART ONE
VIDEO IN ITS HISTORICAL CONTEXT

For twenty-five centuries, Western knowledge has tried to look upon the world. It has failed to understand that the world is not for the beholding. It is for hearing. It is not legible, but audible.

(Jacques Attali 1985: 3)

The first need in attempting to reach an understanding of video is to define its proper historical context, and this means discarding the customary picture that emerges from the standard histories of cinema. In such histories, the origins of film are seen to lie solely in photography, and the primacy of the image is unchallenged, with sound merely entering at a single historical moment (the end of the 1920s) to supplement the visuals. Television – defined perhaps as 'the electronic image' – is fitted into this pattern in ways that ignore its radically new blend of sound and image, while video appears as no more than a kind of appendix or footnote – usually in the concluding paragraphs dealing with 'the future of the media'.

In fact video is the key final link in a complex chain of developments in both image *and* sound reproduction. It is true that still photography has a special place in the history of the communication media as the first system of *recording* to be perfected. But from the 1840s onwards there was a parallel development in the reproduction and *transmission* of sound – first the electric telegraph, then the telephone, and finally, at the end of the century, wireless transmission. Though arguably irrelevant to the initial invention of cinema in the 1890s, this strand of development is clearly a crucial part of video's ancestry. When we consider developments from the latter part of the nineteenth century onwards, we find that sound reproduction, far from being a 'poor relation', is more properly seen as the dominant partner. Sound reproduction has consistently preceded image reproduction and sound media have constantly shaped the subsequently developed visual media.

In the 1890s Edison invented a peepshow, the kinetoscope, and not projected motion pictures, because his thinking was influenced by the commercial success then being enjoyed by his 'talking machine', the phonograph, as an amusement-hall coin-in-the-slot entertainment. If the cinematograph was invented by a photographer, Louis Lùmière, it was the American and European pioneers of the phonograph, Thomas Edison and Charles Pathé, who industrialized it and gave it its commercial pattern. In any case, to see early cinema as a 'silent' medium and hence simply as the heir to still photography is a misconception. Music was always a vital accompaniment, even at Lumière's first showings of the cinematograph in the 1890s. Sound systems were sought from the earliest days and what so-called silent cinema lacked was not sound, but merely synchronized speech.

Viewed from an economic standpoint, the introduction of synchronous sound to the cinema in the 1920s was not the result of a collaboration between industrial equals, but a virtual colonization of the motion-picture business by huge electrical companies grown rich on the profits from the telephone and from radio. The Radio Corporation of America (RCA) was in fact the first of the transnational multimedia corporations which have subsequently come to dominate totally the sound and image industries. It was the structures and institutions developed by sound radio in the 1920s which determined those later adopted by television. Moreover, after the Second World War, the development of magnetic sound tape, which barely merits a mention in most film histories, revolutionized film editing, as well as transforming the record industry and creating a context for video.

The one recent technical advance in which a sound-and-image system preceded a purely sound one was, significantly, a commercial failure. The laser video disc introduced by Philips and Sony in 1975 was not a success, perhaps because there was no pre-existing experience on the part of consumers of buying pre-packaged material, such as films, for domestic viewing. The system had therefore to be relaunched a few years later, using only part of its potential, as a sound-only system, the compact disc. This found a ready market, despite the high cost of the CDs, because there was a public which regularly bought pre-recorded music and was used to paying large sums for advances in recording technology (from 78s to LPs to stereo, etc.). With the video cassette recorder having established itself since around 1979, first as a system of personal off-air recording and then for replay of hired or purchased material, there might be a possibility of reintroducing the laser video disc. Indeed at the moment of writing Philips and Sony are preparing the launch of a revamped version of LaserVision: the 12 cm diameter compact disc video (CDV) which contains 5 minutes of analog video with digital sound and 20 minutes of digital sound without video images. But video tape seems capable of keeping pace with any improvements in television technical specifications (for example, 1,000-line high-definition pictures and stereo sound), so the potential advantage of a 'hi-fi' system seems precluded. Furthermore, the reason why the laser disc is so attractive to the record industry – it is a replay-only system which precludes piracy – is precisely the feature which will make it least attractive to purchasers.

When we consider video it is not enough to show how it reproduces the image-sound systems developed by film and television. We also have to recall that it adopts a recording process analogous to that of magnetic sound tape, whose spread of application and production potential it exactly echoes. The full possibilities of the new medium of video can therefore only be properly understood if we reject the limitations of the customary film-television-video line of approach and see video within an overall history of sound and image reproduction which stresses the interconnections between the various systems.

1 EARLY SOUND AND IMAGE REPRODUCTION

> To an ever greater degree the work of art reproduced becomes the work of art designed for reproducibility. From a photographic negative, for example, one can make any number of prints; to ask for the 'authentic' print makes no sense. But the instant the criterion of authenticity ceases to be applicable to artistic production, the total function of art is reversed. Instead of being based on ritual, it begins to be based on another practice – politics.
>
> (Walter Benjamin 1973: 226)

There are three clearly distinguishable, if overlapping, stages in the history of sound and image reproduction: the cluster of media developed in the latter part of the nineteenth century, the electronic revolution that began with the creation of radio broadcasting in the 1920s and continued with the development of television, and the new phase inaugurated after the Second World War by the introduction of electro-magnetic recording. The present chapter deals with the tremendous burst of creative and commercial energy in the latter part of the nineteenth century, when three new media emerged – the still photograph, the gramophone record, and the film – and key initial work was undertaken on wireless and tape recording. Although the means of recording are totally different from those of video, the modes of industrial organization and forms of social application of these media had an enormous impact on subsequent developments, and to understand video we need to consider the context which they so largely shaped.

As we approach this history, there are a number of general factors which need to be borne in mind. We sometimes talk of technologies creating new societies – as in the title of Robert Sklar's social history of the US cinema, *Movie-Made America* (1975), or in such a phrase as 'the TV generation' – but in fact the relationship is quite the reverse. As Raymond Williams has demonstrated, it was wider social developments – the accumulation of capital and transformation of industrial production throughout the century – which led directly to the emergence at the end of the nineteenth century of the technologies underlying the new communication media (Williams 1974: 9–31).

This was a period of huge social transformation, with the rise to fuller power of the bourgeoisie creating new markets for goods and utilities to be produced by what was still a largely unregulated 'free-enterprise' industrial system. Overlapping with this was the emergence of the working class with increasing political strength (thanks to the extension of democracy), greater education and more leisure and purchasing power – a force to be feared, controlled, and exploited commercially. The late nineteenth century was also the height of European imperialism, culminating in the invasion of Egypt and the carving up of Africa in the 1880s. It was only at the very end of the century that the United States emerged as an overseas imperialist power, intervening to annex Hawaii and divert the liberation struggles in Cuba and the Philippines in 1896. This was an era of expansion in all forms of communication, with the spread of the railways prompting the growth of the telegraph, first ancestor of the electronic broadcast media of the twentieth century. At the same time growing literacy fostered the creation of the first news agencies and the emergence of the first popular press in Europe with the Parisian *Petit Journal* and the London *Daily Mail*.

The connection between technological development and social need is by no means as simple as might be thought (Winston 1986: 15–34). The history of communications technology shows that very frequently devices are invented as answers to short-term problems which fade into insignificance compared to the actual long-term applications which have been totally unforeseen. The classic example here is the cinema, which was invented in a form allowing one-minute glimpses of everyday life in movement – waves breaking on the beach or a train entering a railway station. Yet the superior marketing possibilities (and hence profitability) of narrative films designed for a lower-middle- and working-class audience soon became apparent. As a result, within twenty years the word 'film' had taken on a totally new meaning, as epic stories capable of sustaining a three-hour narrative (like D. W. Griffith's pioneering *The Birth of a Nation* (1915)) enthralled audiences world-wide and made a fortune for producers, distributors, and exhibitors alike.

Similarly, the process of invention is by no means simple and clear-cut. There is no unambiguous pattern of 'firsts' as individual great minds come up with instantly practical solutions to known but baffling problems. Often only part of the problem is solved initially. Daguerre, for example, offered a form of photography which allowed a sharp visual image but did not permit this image itself to be replicated (every daguerreotype was a unique object). Invention in the sound and visual media is more often a case of numerous theorists and practical men fumbling simultaneously in the dark, with fame and fortune going not necessarily to the most talented, but rather to those with access to capital, to workshop and laboratory resources, and to the high technical skills of dedicated craftsmen (this is true of Daguerre, Edison, Eastman, and Lumière).

Inventions have almost as often been independently duplicated as they have been knowingly duped or stolen. A striking example here is nitrocellulose film, which George Eastman developed and manufactured in 1889, but which had been quite independently patented two years earlier by the Reverend Hannibal Goodwin, the latter's heirs eventually being awarded $5 million in compensation after a very lengthy lawsuit (Jenkins 1975: 125–7, 332–4). On occasion, a development is made by means of equipment which everyone knows is transitional, but which has the virtue of being simple and reliable, and hence to some extent reassuring to those who entrust their fortunes to it. An example here is synchronized sound film which was introduced in 1926, via a Warner Bros subsidiary Vitaphone, through a system of sound-on-disc, although a superior, electronic, and less cumbersome sound-on-film system had already been brought to an advanced state of development by the Western Electric company (Ogle 1977: 201). Equally, some seemingly key advances are ignored for years. Halftone printing – the first method of reproducing photographs directly on the printed page without the intervention of an engraver – was used sporadically from around 1880 onwards. Yet the quality of the reproduction was initially coarse and uneven, and, given the graphic efficiency and economic competitiveness of the engraving and woodcut processes, there was no commercial incentive to improve the halftone process and to apply it widely until highspeed printing presses were developed at the turn of the century (Goldsmith 1979: 110–11). It will be clear from these preliminary remarks that nineteenth–century developments in communication technology were complex. Before, however, we turn to consider them in detail, there is a significant stage of prehistory which deserves at least brief attention.

Prehistory

Support for claims about the visual bias of our western culture – in which 'seeing is believing' and an eye–witness is to be believed while hearsay evidence is inadmissable – comes from the fact that the first western efforts were directed at the reproduction of the visible. These efforts, occurring some 400 years before the invention of photography, belong to the remote prehistory of the media, but they have a lasting interest. Significantly, progress on two related developments – the reproduction of reality and the mass production of images – was begun at almost precisely the same time in the early fifteenth century. As Rudolf Arnheim notes, it was the woodcut, the earliest preserved example of which is a *Madonna with the Four Virgin Saints* dating from 1418, which 'established for the European mind the almost completely new principle of mechanical reproduction' (Arnheim 1974: 284–5).

This advance was to be immediately reinforced by the invention of printing from moveable type before the middle of the century. There are Chinese precedents for the woodcut and for printing with moveable type, just as it is to the Chinese that we owe the invention of paper. But the second key fifteenth–century development – the codification of the rules for duplicating reality systematically – is an exclusively European phenomenon. The principle of the *camera obscura* – that light entering a minute hole in the wall of a darkened room throws onto the opposite wall an inverted image of a sunlit scene outside – had been known since antiquity. But it was only in 1435 (just seventeen years after the first known woodcut) that the optical laws governing this phenomenon were used as the basis for establishing the rules of central perspective by Leon Battista Alberti in his book *On Painting*. From this point onwards, western culture had a wholly distinctive and seemingly objective way of reproducing natural forms.

The European system of central perspective as codified by Alberti is interesting in many ways. Firstly, it is felt by those who use it to be an extremely realistic method of rendering optical space. Secondly, as Rudolf Arnheim observes, it is at the same time 'so violent and intricate a deformation of the normal shape of things that it came about only as the final result of prolonged exploration and in response to very particular cultural needs' (Arnheim 1974: 283). Whereas other systems of visual organization have been discovered independently in a number of different cultures, there is no parallel anywhere else for the European system. Thirdly, it provoked the use, as aids for draftsmen, of such devices as the *camera obscura* (the practical application of which to drawing was first described by Giovanni Battista della Porta in 1553). In this way it began the continuing interrelationship between western art and western technology. Fourthly, the portable *camera obscura* devices designed specifically for draughtsmen came to be equipped with lenses selected precisely because they produced an image conforming to central perspective rules (Scharf 1974: 19–26). In this way a self-proving system was set up (the rules were 'proved' by the lenses which were designed to produce just what the rules predicted), so that the 'truth' of perspective could become part of the west's unquestionable common-sense knowledge.

Photographic, film, and video cameras are merely devices for recording, by photochemical or electronic means, this long-established, predetermined way of seeing. Yet since central perspective is a system of organizing space in terms of a single

16

static eye, it opens up a gap between what we actually see and what the camera shows us, which continues to haunt the debates about the realism of photographic, filmic, and video images. For Arnheim, the discovery of central perspective was 'a dangerous development in Western thought', since it marked 'a scientifically oriented preference for mechanical reproduction and geometrical constructs in place of creative imagery' (Arnheim 1974: 284). From the standpoint of the present study, however, it opens up the fascinating area where art and technology, reproduction and representation coexist.

The timing of the two developments is also very significant. If we look at the wider context of society and culture in the early part of the fifteenth century, we find a major reshaping of western consciousness. This was the age of the Copernican revolution in science and of such technological advances as the discovery of gunpowder, the invention of canons and portable firearms, and the redesigning of sailing ships (Cipolla 1970). In this context the principles of the organization of central perspective (as a way of measuring, reproducing, and hence controlling the physical world) and the mechanical reproduction of woodcuts and books (allowing a new flow of images and ideas) contributed to the progress which, at the end of the century, was to lead to the onset of European world dominance.

When we take up the story of sound and image reproduction again with the invention of photography in 1839, it is precisely to the handful of dominant European nations, Britain, France, and Germany – now joined by an emergent United States of America – that we have to turn. These were the most advanced industrial countries of the nineteenth century, and it was in their factories and laboratories that the key nineteenth-century advances were realized. In their turn, the huge communication industries based on the successive discoveries of the reproduction and transmission of sounds and images have contributed to the reshaping of western consciousness.

Photochemical and mechanical recording

The nineteenth-century media of sound and image reproduction involved two separate but related requirements. The first was the duplication of some aspect of reality – the visual appearance of a landscape or the sound of a human voice, for instance. The newly acquired sound or image would need to be 'fixed' in some way and the choice of the carrier base on which it was recorded was of great importance. Some amplification of the aural or visual 'imprint' also had to be devised if the reproduction was to be made fully accessible to an audience. The second major requirement for the full commercialization of such duplications of reality was that they themselves should be able to be mass produced and marketed. The conventional still photograph, the feature film, and the gramophone record – which have their roots in nineteenth-century technology – fulfilled all these requirements and hence have been able to play such an important part in our lives.

The importance of the carrier base cannot be over-emphasized, as the analogy with the book shows. Writing in the form of engraved stones or impressed clay tablets had existed for thousands of years before the invention of the book, which emerged only when writing was applied to a pliant, light-weight, and easily portable substance. The early history of the book is the history of successive carrier bases – papyrus, parchment, paper – which both preserved words and allowed them to be distributed widely. The successive stages of the handwritten book also relate directly to the type of support: the papyrus roll (or *volumen*) succeeded by the parchment book (or *codex*). Paper is a prerequisite for the next stage, the printed book, which adds mass production to the book's earlier functions of preservation and distribution (Escarpit 1966: 19–20). In a similar way, celluloid is a prerequisite for popular photography and the cinema, supplanting glass plates for photography and paper rolls for projected images (Wollen 1982: 170). In this connection the enormous importance of sound and video tape to the preceding media of radio and television broadcasting can be clearly seen: they too allow sounds and images to be preserved, mass produced, and distributed in new ways.

In the initial form in which the new media of sound and image reproduction emerged, they used photochemical and mechanical means. Though developed simultaneously with the telephone, they existed separate from the developments in communications associated with electric power. As Raymond Williams has pointed out, there are two stages in the application of electricity to the problems of communication. During the first, covering the latter part of the nineteenth century and the beginning of the twentieth, electricity was applied to 'operational' communication, that is to say the conveying of specific personal or business messages from one individual to another. It was only after the First World War that the second stage began, the era of broadcasting involving an 'invasion' by the new forms of radio and television of the territory previously occupied by the film and record industries (Williams 1974: 20). For this change to occur, a specific development within the electrical industry was also required. The late nineteenth century is characterized by the use of electricity as a source of power, to drive machinery as well as to provide heat and light. Twentieth–century applications of electricity to communications depend far more on the new science of electronics, that is to say the use of minute quantities of electricity to control and direct messages (electric power in the old sense enters only to fulfil such functions as the amplification of the signal – through a loudspeaker – at its point of reception).

Photography

Historians generally take 19 August 1839 as photography's date of birth, this being the day on which details of the daguerreotype process were made public in Paris. But already by this time photography had its own specific 'prehistory' (Gernsheim and Gernsheim 1971: 17–26). As early as 1802 Thomas Wedgewood, an amateur scientist and son of the potter Josiah Wedgewood, had made photograms – that is, silhouette images of small objects created by placing them on a surface coated with silver nitrate, the uncovered parts of which turned black on exposure to the sun. But Wedgewood was not able to fix these images. In 1816 another pioneer, Joseph Nicéphore Niepce, apparently succeeded in recording and partially fixing a negative of the *camera obscura* image. But a further eleven years passed before he was able to produce, on a sensitized pewter plate and with an eight-hour exposure, the view from his window at Le Gras which is the earliest photograph to be preserved. Two years later, in 1829, Niepce went into partnership with Louis Daguerre, the showman owner of the Paris Diorama, but he died before their joint experiments were complete, so that Daguerre occupied the limelight alone in 1839.

The daguerreotype yielded an exquisitely detailed image on a silvered copper plate, but in its initial form it required a fifteen-minute exposure and an hour's work with potentially dangerous chemicals. One of the oddities of the very early daguerreotypes is that they turned crowded streets into empty townscapes, since traffic and pedestrians moved too fast to be recorded (Goldsmith 1979: 20–1). But developments in lens construction and greater light sensitivity for the plate were soon to remedy this exposure-time defect. Daguerreotype portraiture (with half-minute exposure) was possible from 1840 onwards, effectively supplanting miniature painting as the favoured means of portraiture and at the same time extending portraiture to new social strata. The daguerreotype was a great success in Europe, and in the United States it became a veritable industry. By the middle of the century well over a million daguerreotypes were being taken there every year, and already North America was the major market for the photographic business. But in terms of the needs of the developing capitalist economy, Daguerre's process was in fact a dead-end: a single-image system which did not allow individual daguerreotypes to be replicated.

The announcement in January 1839 of Daguerre's forthcoming disclosure seven months later spurred a number of other pioneers to stake their claims. Some of these were false, or the result of wishful thinking, but at least three deserve a mention since they fulfilled the needs of a capitalist system drawing profit from the combination of duplication of reality and replication of the image. William Henry Fox Talbot and Hippolyte Bayard had both independently developed negative/positive systems which gave less striking images than Daguerre's but which pointed the way forward for the commercial exploitation of photography as a whole. And as if to prove that the solution was 'in the air', the astronomer Sir John Herschel apparently solved the problems of photography on his own within a month of learning of Daguerre's forthcoming disclosure. It was Herschel too who coined many of the key terms we still use today: photography, positive and negative, snapshot (Gernsheim and Gernsheim 1971: 27).

The negative/positive system of photography on paper was patented as the Talbotype or calotype in 1841, offering an alternative method to Daguerre's, particularly for landscape photography. It was not only simpler and more flexible, but also allowed copies to be multiplied. Talbot himself used the process in 1844 to publish *The Pencil of Nature*, the world's first book illustrated with photographs (which had, of course, to be stuck in individually by hand). However, both the daguerreotype and the calotype were rendered obsolete when the wet collodion process was introduced in 1851, the year of Daguerre's death. This gave far greater light sensitivity, although at the cost of making photography if anything more cumbersome. The glass plates had to be prepared by the photographer immediately before shooting and developed immediately afterwards, necessitating the use of a whole mobile darkroom by those photographers wishing to shoot away from their studios – Robert Fenton in the Crimea, or Mathew Brady's team on the battlefields of the American Civil War, for instance.

With exposure times of several seconds still needed, photography remained a craft skill requiring professional dedication. But alongside the many formal and artistically striking works produced during the twenty-five-year period when the wet collodion process predominated, a whole range of cheap popular portrait processes was developed – the ambrotype, the ferrotype or tintype, the *carte de visite* set of portraits – allowing everyone to possess photographs of him- or herself and members of the family. The new mass public wishing to be photographed led to a continual expansion of photography as a business. It has been estimated that in France alone there were over a thousand studios employing half-a-million photographers by the beginning of the twentieth century (Freund 1980: 85).

The move towards the true democratization of photography, allowing all to participate as photographers as well as sitters, came only in the late 1870s and 1880s, when plates or flexible rolls of film with fast dry gelatine emulsions needing only a fraction of a second's exposure became available. Although the creation of a mass market took many years, the medium gradually became fully industrialized, with suppliers providing factory-made, fully prepared plates and films, and specialists offering their services to process amateur photographs. Equipment, too, developed towards portability and ease of operation.

George Eastman, who quickly acquired a monopoly controlling 80–90 per cent of the world's output of nitrocellulose film, revolutionized the amateur market with his Kodak camera in 1888. Marketed with the slogan 'You press the button – we do the rest', the Kodak was sold already loaded with 100-exposure film and was returned to the Eastman company for developing, printing, and reloading. The introduction of the daylight loading spool soon followed. Photography was now big business: Kodak's sales were $2.3 million in 1899, more than doubled to $5.1 million in 1904 and had almost doubled again at $9.7 million in 1909 (Jenkins 1975: 178). Alongside this growth of amateur photography, there developed a second mass market, that in photographs as consumer items. The postcard, permitted by law in Germany in 1865 and in France in 1872, depended on developments in the printing industry to become universally accessible and did not become widely popular until 1900. By 1910 123 million photographs had been printed in France alone (with 33,000 workers employed in the industry) and today world-wide annual sales are measured in billions (Freund 1980: 99).

By the turn of the century the range of applications of black-and-white photography was virtually complete, although colour systems were slower to develop. Louis Lumière, pioneer of the cinematograph in the 1890s, invented the first popular colour system – Autochrome – which became available in 1907, and numerous inventors followed his example. But it was not until the mid-1930s that modern colour systems based on multiple-layer emulsion coatings were developed with Kodachrome (1935) and Agfacolor (1936). Most modern systems are based on the German Agfacolor system which became available without patent protection after the Second World War, the only major exception being the Polaroid colour system for making instant direct positives which was introduced in 1963 (Gernsheim and Gernsheim 1971: 52–7).

22

The economic development of the photographic industry led by Eastman Kodak in the 1890s set the pattern for similar transformations in the sound and audio-visual media which would not be complete until the invention of sound and video tape. In the photographic industry of the late nineteenth century we can trace the shifts which will constantly recur: from European to US dominance (despite the strength of the German optical and chemical cartels), from craft industry to mass production, from a large number of competing single-owner businesses to a handful of huge corporations, and from local distribution to the control of world markets. The seemingly inexorable growth in the market for recorded images and sounds, and the steadily increasing share of this acquired by big business also have their origins in the 1890s. Reese V. Jenkins notes that while US industrial production rose annually by 4.7 per cent and that of the photographic industry as a whole by 11 per cent between 1889 and 1909, Eastman Kodak's domestic sales grew by 17.5 per cent a year and its annual world-wide sales by a staggering 29.8 per cent (Jenkins 1975: 178).

The full economic development of amateur photography demanded that it fill the two key demands of the capitalist economy: ease of access for the consumer and the potential of mass marketing for the producer. In specific photographic terms these demands could be met thanks to three crucial developments: the invention of dry gelatine emulsions, the choice of celluloid as a flexible base, and the use this allowed of roll film instead of single plates. Eastman's role was to bring these three together, introducing mass production and institutionalizing technological innovation (a trend which culminated in 1913 with the founding of the Eastman Kodak Research Labortory which had a budget of over $300,000 a year by 1920). Eastman's progress with the mass production of film materials for still photography proved invaluable to his success in capturing the new market for cine film which grew up in the early 1900s. By 1910, when sales of cine film equalled those of roll film for still cameras, Eastman controlled some 90 per cent of this new world market, in addition to his massive share of the still photographic industry (Jenkins 1975: 278).

Eastman's achievements are remarkable. He allowed universal

access to photography and aided the rapid development of cinema as a new form of popular entertainment. But there was a cost involved. Whereas in 1839 the French government had donated the secrets of photography freely to the world, from the 1890s onwards Eastman Kodak was protected by rigorously enforced patents covering every aspect of its operation. Increased access to the creative and leisure possibilities of photography therefore went hand-in-hand with increased monopoly control of photographic equipment and materials manufacture. A similar contradiction holds good today for readily accessible sound and video equipment. Here too a mass market has come into being thanks to the successful ending of the search to combine a flexible carrier base (in this case plastic tape) with a sensitive coating (ferric oxide). Yet once more this market has been dominated by a tiny handful of transnational corporations.

Sound recording

Photography was the result of bringing together and applying practically a number of earlier discoveries in optics and chemistry. No similar fusion was made in the nineteenth century between acoustics and electricity as far as the major developments in the recording of sound were concerned. Although Edison's first phonograph was patented just two years after Bell's telephone, the two sound systems remained quite separate. One device which might have created a bridge between acoustical and electrical developments – the tape recorder – was in fact devised and patented at the end of the century, but in the absence of workable microphones and amplifiers its application was inevitably extremely limited. The reproduction of sound therefore follows a double pattern in the latter part of the nineteenth century, with a clear distinction between the electric *transmission* of sound applied to business and person-to-person communication and the various systems of mechanical *recording* of sound developed for entertainment purposes.

Advances in the application of the principles of electricity paralleled the various investigations into optical phenomena in the decades preceding. Daguerre's breakthrough. As far as the electric transmission of sound is concerned, there are three key dates. In 1844 Samuel Morse was able to give a successful demonstration of his electric telegraph, the first to incorporate an electro-magnet, by sending by wire the message 'What Hath God Wrought' from Baltimore to Washington. Morse used the signalling code which he had devised in 1838 and which remains in wide use today. It was only thirty years after Morse's invention that the problem of transmitting the sound of the human voice by wire was solved. In his basic telephone patent of 1876 Alexander Graham Bell described a way of converting sound waves into electrical oscillations (which travel hundreds of thousands of times faster). These can be conveyed long distances by wire and then reconverted by a receiver into fully recognizable sound: the basic principle which is still in use today. Twenty years after Bell, in 1896, Guglielmo Marconi patented in London his wireless transmission system, by means of which he was able to send messages across the Channel in 1899 and across the Atlantic in 1901. It was Marconi's work which opened the way for the eventual creation of radio and television broadcasting. These three key achievements – devices which both worked and had an immediate and lasting social application – were merely the peaks of nineteenth-century electric communication technology and relied on the prior work of dozens of less celebrated scientists and engineers.

Perhaps the biggest paradox of Thomas Edison's career is that although he is widely celebrated as 'the father of electricity' and turned to the problems of sound recording soon after successfully devising a way of sending four signals (two in each direction) simultaneously along a single telegraph wire, the phonograph which he patented in 1878 was a purely mechanical device. Indeed it was not until 1925 that an electrical gramophone was marketed to play electrically recorded discs. As was the case with Daguerre in photography, Edison's successful commercial breakthrough conceals the fact that he was not the first to conceive of a potentially viable method of achieving the results sought. As early as 1857 Léon Scott de Martinville invented the 'phonautograph', a device which made permanent visual records of sound vibrations. This was a scientific tool for the study of sounds and could not be used to replay them. Twenty years later a Frenchman, Charles Cros, set out details of a method of sound recording *and* replay in a paper lodged with the Académie des Sciences in Paris in April 1877. But Cros could not obtain financial backing, and the successful transition to a working device was left to Edison, who could call on all the resources of his well-equipped research laboratory.

The 1878 phonograph was, however, far from achieving the same impact as the 1839 daguerreotype. The hand-cranked, tinfoil-covered cylinder device was fragile and gave only a faulty one-minute's worth of reproduced sound. Sir William Preece, Engineer-in-Chief of the British Post Office and subsequently a key figure in the development of British broadcasting, heard the device in 1878 and described it as giving 'to some extent a burlesque or parody of the human voice' (cit. Gelatt 1977: 31). Although some 500 examples of the phonograph were produced and sold, their only applications were as toys or show-business curiosities. Within six months the novelty value was exhausted, and Edison turned his attention to the problems of producing a workable electric lamp and with laying the foundations of the electrical power industry.

It was almost ten years before 'talking machines' made their reappearance when, in 1888, Edison was forced to devise an 'improved phonograph' in response to a new recording machine. This was the 'graphophone', which used wax cylinders and had been patented in 1885 and demonstrated two years later by Chichester Bell and Charles Tainter. Although both new machines were superior to the 1878 'toy', they still had only a limited range of sound reproduction and a mere two minutes of running time. The rival interests were on the brink of a patents war when they were brought together in a million-dollar enterprise, the North American Phonograph Company, by a financier, Jesse Lippincott. However, the latter, making use of the fact that the cylinder models could record as well as replay, tried to market them by rental as office dictating machines. The results were disastrous, and what were to be the dominant uses of the phonograph – first as coin-in-the-slot entertainment machine and then as consumer durable for the home – rose out of the ruins of Lippincott's bankruptcy.

In Europe the phonograph made little headway, except in France where Charles Pathé achieved a monopoly (and made his first millions) by the sale, for entertainment purposes, of cylinder machines based on the Edison model. The major drawback of the phonograph during its years of dominance in the 1890s was that the only way of duplicating pre-recorded cylinders was by pantograph, allowing perhaps twenty-five copies to be made from a single master recording. The singers and monologuists employed had therefore to record the same words and songs over and over again, a factor which inhibited major artists from appearing in front of the recording horn.

Although Edison's cylinders offered the best pre-1914 sound and he continued to issue them until 1929, his phonograph had already been overtaken in 1900 by the gramophone, a disc-recording machine patented by Emile Berliner in 1887. This was aimed unambiguously at the domestic market, and therefore depended on the mass produceability of records. These were stamped from etched zinc masters, first made of vulcanized rubber and then of shellac. But Berliner lacked marketing skills and in any case did not possess the capital necessary to develop the machine's technical capability. As a result, initially at least, the gramophone sound was markedly inferior to that of the phonograph. Eldridge Johnson, later to be a key figure in the early record business, described the sound in 1895 as 'like a partially educated parrot with a sore throat and a cold in the head' (cit. Gelatt 1977: 84).

The Victor Talking Machine Company, which Johnson founded in 1901, flourished, however, so that profits of almost a million dollars were made in the first year of operation. A pooling of patents in 1902 allowed just two companies, Victor and Columbia, to establish a total US dominance which was to last fifty years or more. In Europe, Pathé turned his attention to the cinema (becoming the major force in world production and distribution around 1908), and the market came to be dominated by a single company, The Gramophone Company, which was established in 1898 and came to own recording studios in London, a factory for pressing records in Germany, and branches in Russia, Austria, France, and Spain. It, too, was making a profit of $1 million a year by 1903. The Gramophone Company pioneered the recording of operatic arias, and its ten 1902 recordings of Caruso have been described by Roland Gelatt

27

as 'the first completely satisfactory gramophone records to be made' (Gelatt 1977: 115).

Throughout the next two decades the record industry continued to expand. By the early 1920s it was already a multi-million-dollar industry in the United States, selling a million gramophones and 100 million records a year. In Europe, The Gramophone Company now shared the market with the London branch of Columbia, and together these companies showed themselves more innovative in terms of classical repertoire than their US counterparts, pioneering orchestral recording after 1910. But it was in the United States that the new forms of jazz and dance music were recorded and began to offer a wider popular scope to listeners. Although it had grown huge in terms of profit, the international record industry had hardly changed in thirty years: gramophones were still mechanical and the records lasted a bare four minutes and were still acoustically recorded. Virtually no research was being carried on anywhere in the industry to improve sound quality. Only in the design of gramophone cabinets, now built to look like anything but what they actually were, was there real change after 1914.

In no way was the industry prepared for the electronic revolution which the 1920s were to bring. In 1924 Eldridge Johnson, still head of the world's leading recording company, could proclaim that:

> The radio is not a Victor competitor nor a substitute for talking machines. If the radio ever gets straightened out in America the Victor company will be greatly benefitted. The Victor company has no notion of becoming a dominant factor in radio.

> (cit. Gelatt 1977: 217)

However, the following year electric recording, developed independently in the Bell Telephone Laboratories, was forced on the reluctant record industry. While its profits were standing still in the mid-1920s, those of the radio companies doubled and redoubled. 1929 saw the end of an era when Victor was bought by the Radio Corporation of America.

Looking back on the first fifty years, we see that after a hesitant start sound recording found its dominant disc format and its domestic role. The gramophone became the first of the new media to be marketed for use within the home, but in the process the potential for individual recording contained in the cylinder machines was lost. In this sense the gramophone is the direct ancestor of such one-way systems as radio and television. (Anyone intrigued as to *whose* voice the little dog, Nipper, is listening to in the 'His Master's Voice' trademark, needs to know that the painting originally depicted an Edison cylinder machine.) Like all the nineteenth-century media, the gramophone concentrated on a single application, specializing in music, just as the telephone specialized in business and personal messages, photography in recording leisure and family life, and the cinema in story-telling. The gramophone's success was obtained without any of the constant technological innovation undertaken by Eastman Kodak or the creative expansion of the product characteristic of cinema. The lack of flexibility in recording, combined with a stultifying industrial monopoly, inhibited the full expansion of sound recording, which had to wait until the 1950s – and the advent of sound tape – to achieve the explosive development which photography had attained in the 1890s and cinema in the early years of the twentieth century.

Cinema

The development of cinema has fascinating parallels with, and differences from, that of the sound-recording industry. In the case of moving pictures, as with sound, initial developments were scientifically oriented. Both Eadweard Muybridge and Etienne Marey made important contributions to bringing photography and motion together, but since they were concerned to *analyse* motion, they could have no interest in efforts to *recreate* motion as an illusion. Yet their work is a key step in the immediate prehistory of cinema, offering invaluable research on which subsequent pioneers could draw.

The next decisive step was taken in the laboratories of Thomas Edison, who was familiar with Muybridge's and Marey's work. In 1888 Edison set his young Scottish-born assistant William K. Laurie Dickson to work, and within three years a feasible solution to the problem of recording and showing moving pictures had been found. Within two further years a working model of the new machine, the kinetoscope, was demonstrated, and in April 1894 the first kinetoscope parlour opened on Broadway. The kinetoscope employed the celluloid film patented by Eastman in 1889 and used a succession of still images run at speed to give an illusion of movement. But because of the success currently being obtained by Edison's earlier invention, the phonograph, the device which Dickson was instructed to make, and which he in fact produced, was a coin-in-the-slot peepshow.

Interestingly enough another inventor, the Frenchman Emile Reynaud, was simultaneously working on a system using hand-drawn animated images, the praxinoscope, which was demonstrated in 1892 after four years of patient development work. The two machines each anticipated the cinema in every respect except one: Dickson's kinetoscope used photographic images but not projection, while Reynaud's praxinoscope employed projected images which had not been obtained photographically. Reynaud can be seen as father of the animated film (which thus has a lifespan three years longer than cinema proper), but his use of paper as the support for his images proved to be a dead-end, whereas Dickson's advance opened the way for the final breakthrough to cinema.

Dickson and Reynaud were only two among a great many inventors working at that time to perfect a system of moving pictures. Strenuous efforts were made by both Georges Demenÿ, a former assistant of Marey, and William Friese Greene, whose tombstone in Highgate Cemetery wrongly claims that 'his genius bestowed upon humanity the boon of commercial kinematography of which he was the first inventor and patentee'. Because of Edison's uninhibited use of his patent rights in the United States, it was perhaps inevitable that the final breakthrough to *projected* moving pictures would be made in Europe, where the kinetoscope was not covered by patent restrictions. The first person to achieve this crucial step was Louis Lumière who, with his brother Auguste, ran Europe's largest factory producing photographic materials and so had the resources to develop and exploit his invention. After a number of demonstrations to learned societies, the first cinematograph screenings organized for a paying public took place in Paris on 28 December 1895, and the cinema was born. But already by the early months of 1896 other European inventors working quite independently – particularly the Englishmen Birt Acres and Robert William Paul – had come up with equally valid solutions.

Film was invented to record the world in movement, and during its early years it was little more than a curiosity, offering in a quite undifferentiated fashion everyday scenes and actualities, fragments of stage performance, conjuring tricks (the speciality of the magician Georges Méliès), and little staged outdoor scenes (the ancestor of which was Louis Lumière's *Watering the Gardener* of 1895). None of the founding fathers of the cinema – neither the failed visioniaries like Demenÿ and Friese Greene nor the successful practitioners such as Lumière, Dickson, and Paul – conceived of film as a story-telling medium (Metz 1974: 93). For them, film was a novelty which could fit easily into the entertainment schedules of the music hall and vaudeville show. Indeed, since Lumière's cinematograph combined the functions of camera, printer, and projector, the travelling operator was a kind of self-contained stage act, able to tour the theatrical circuits alongside the conjurers, comedians, and acrobats (R. C. Allen 1979).

At least until the end of the nineteenth century, there was little sign of the creative dynamism which would take the cinema from a one-minute novelty showing domestic scenes and outdoor 'views' to a three-hour spectacle of epic proportions by the middle of the First World War. This development – so different from the situation in the record industry, where the gramophone record barely changed between the early 1900s and the mid-1920s – depended on three factors. The first was the choice of the theatrical mode, which proved enormously popular in an age of increasing wages and leisure for the working class. The second was the fusion of film and narrative, which came about when showmen realized that audiences could be persuaded to return regularly to their local cinemas by films which told predictable but individually different stories. The third factor was the flexibility of nitrocellulose film, strips of which could easily be joined together to make longer and more complex works.

It would seem to be the spectacular growth of film as a product, combined with the enormous increase in the film-going public (particularly in the United States), which prevented film from being stultified by monopoly control as the record industry was. Nevertheless, although the definition of cinema as a theatrical entertainment soon gave it a quite new identity, its initial spread does echo in many ways the expansion of the two earlier media. This is because the pioneer industrialists used their existing business contacts to exploit film. Lumière, for example, drew on the network of outlets for his photographic products, while both Edison and Pathé adapted the strategies of exploitation which they had developed for the commercialization of the phonograph.

The early history of cinema is that of successive (failed) attempts to establish monopoly control, largely through the use of patents, in the manner which had proved so successful (for the companies if not for the development of the product) in the record industry. Lumière, who had a brief start on his rivals, attempted to maintain monopoly control by refusing to sell the cinematograph and insisting that his operators projected the films (in return for a percentage of the profits). This strategy failed, since Lumière had no way of preventing others from making and selling viable camera and projection systems. He was uninterested in the production of more complex films and within a few years he returned to his photographic work, perfecting one of the first colour systems for still photography.

Lumière's principal successor in France was Charles Pathé, who had made a fortune from the phonograph before turning his attention increasingly to film after 1901. Pathé was the first producer to industrialize cinema, but his system was one of simple mass production, with his studios churning out a succession of short films barely distinguishable the one from the other. This was a mode of production which was to become outdated as films developed towards feature length and so became individual commodities in their own right capable of meeting the public's demand for an evening's entertainment. But in the 1900s Pathé was the world's leading producer and distributor, controlling a third of the entire world film business by 1908. He had offices in Calcutta and Singapore as well as in London, New

York, Berlin, and Saint Petersburg, and for a time he was even able to sell more films in the United States than all his American rivals put together. However, film distribution developed very slowly in France, failing to find a popular mass audience, and gradually the Pathé product, which reflected Parisian bourgeois tastes and assumptions, proved unsuited to world markets. Although Pathé moved his main production base to the United States, his grip was already weakened before the outbreak of the First World War brought production in France to a sudden and catastrophic halt (Armes 1985: 19–33).

In the United States Pathé had a formidable rival in Thomas Edison, who had already used his impressive array of patents in an attempt to eliminate such local rivals as Biograph and Vitagraph at the turn of the century. In 1908 Edison was instrumental in setting up the Motion Picture Patents Company (MPPC) bringing together under his leadership eight US firms and two outsiders (Pathé and, a little later, Méliès). Initially this attempt at monopoly control through the use of pooled patents gave enormous profits, but even before it was judged illegal under US anti-trust law, it had proved unable, in an ever-expanding market for an increasingly complex product, to prevent the emergence of a number of highly successful independents, many of whom were in fact the very men who would go on to create what we know as Hollywood. An early coup by Edison in 1909 had been the agreement by George Eastman that he would supply film stock only to MPPC firms, and it was a sign that the monopoly was crumbling when, early in 1911, Eastman went back on this agreement and traded openly with the independents (Kindem 1982).

All attempts at establishing a monopoly control or an oligopoly (exclusive control by a small group of companies) depend on a successful strategy for keeping out newcomers. In the era of competitive capitalism before the First World War the use of patent rights to achieve this end could be successful in a fairly static market, like that prevailing in the record industry, but not in a rapidly developing one like the film industry. An alternative (and ultimately successful) way of instituting control in the film industry was pioneered by Famous Players-Lasky (later Paramount), which created a vertically integrated company (combining production, distribution, and exhibition) around 1920. The success depended on creating a distinctive product (through the use of stars now under exclusive contract), establishing a nation-wide (and later world-wide) distribution network, and building a number of luxury cinemas in prime sites which could be used for the highly profitable first-run release of the company's films (Gomery 1986: 4–5).

This strategy did not allow Paramount to control the market by itself, indeed no single company in Hollywood ever grew big enough to become wholly dominant alone. But it did allow a small number of companies to divide the bulk of the market between them and keep out outsiders. In 1925, on the eve of the transition to sound, there were just three major companies dominating the market. Events in the late 1920s caused a certain upheaval as far as individual companies were concerned, but the same basic strategy and pattern of organization persisted in the film industry until the breakup of the studio system in the 1950s.

This study began with a plea for a new historical perspective, arguing that video should not be seen simply as a latter-day descendent of film. The history of the early years of cinema, outlined here and set against that of the other nineteenth-century media, underlines film's uniqueness. It was the only one of the new media to be developed as a public entertainment and to adopt a theatrical, rather than a domestic mode. All subsequent developments in the reproduction of sounds and images have been directly home-oriented. This is obviously the case with video, but it is worth noting that the same applies now to the cinema itself: in the 1980s the production of feature films has come to depend increasingly on advances for the rights to subsequent home-video distribution. In other respects, too, cinema shares much with the other new media. For example, it occupies a mid-way position between the exclusive monopoly control of the record industry and the more open access afforded by photography. Although the feature film industry was closed to outsiders, amateur film systems were developed from the start (Acres patented his 17.5 mm Birtac in 1898). Although avant-garde and experimental work was rare in the early years of cinema, film technology was exportable. The west retained firm control over world film distribution, but feature films were made by local film producers throughout the non-western world from the 1920s – in a dozen or so Latin American countries, in India and China, in the Philippines, Korea, Turkey, and Egypt. Indeed by 1928 India was producing more films than Britain, and this geographical diversity of cinema has continued, so that for the past thirty years or more over half of the world's films have come from Asia (Armes 1987: 55–61).

Conclusion

The pattern of development followed by the photograph, the gramophone record, and the film from the late nineteenth century until the 1920s helps us to define certain key aspects of the context in which video is placed, since it shows clearly how sound and image media are used in our society. Four points are of particular interest in this connection.

Firstly, the development is only comprehensible if we take into account the broad economic and social context, in particular the shift in capitalism itself over this period from a system of unbridled competition between a large number of small, single-proprietor companies towards a market shaped and dominated by a handful of corporations acting in virtual unison. The reasons for the geographical shift in the centre of production from Europe to the United States after the First World War also lie in general economic factors: the transformation of the USA from a debtor nation to the world's most prosperous country. Just as the motor industry was revolutionized by Henry Ford's production line, so too the European inventions of photography and cinema were given a new identity by US mass production techniques (Eastman Kodak; the Hollywood 'majors'). In taking control of their own domestic market after 1914 the Hollywood film companies were merely following the example of dozens of other businesses. In social terms, the spread of the new media is part of a double overall movement in western society embracing both Europe and the United States: on the one hand, towards greater leisure (with cinema growing as entertainment alongside the music hall and the football game, and increased travel giving a new application to photography); on the other, towards a greater demand for consumer durables in the home (the still camera and the gramophone following the sewing machine, the vacuum cleaner, and the electric iron). Both of these, in turn, depend on the growing affluence of the lower-middle and working classes which constitute the base of the media mass market.

Secondly, the impulse behind this development is neither humanitarian, nor scientific, nor artistic – it is the search for ever greater profits within the capitalist system. As a balance is sought between unbridled competition and total monopoly control, the photographic industry moves from freely accessible daguerreotype secrets to Eastman Kodak patent control, while allowing increasing personal use of the medium; the record industry's development is blocked by a pooling of patents between just two companies at a very early stage of development; and the Hollywood companies impose a system based on a high-quality, high-cost product and ruthless control of key exhibition outlets, thereby imposing a single style of film – the Hollywood movie – world-wide.

Thirdly, the same impulse towards profit-making defines and limits the particular social application of those inventions which are developed. Standardization and simplification of technical procedures occur because the key to profitability is ease of replication. Systems like the daguerreotype, the cylinder recorder, and the praxinoscope are discarded, not because they are necesarily technically or artistically inferior, but because they do not lend themselves to mass production. It is by no means the case that the full technical potential of a given medium is necessarily employed in the eventually dominant application. The gramophone supplants the cylinder machine because the profit is seen to lie in the ease with which records can be mass produced. Still photography is made open to all because the highest return comes from the millions of cameras and hundreds of millions of rolls of film. But cinema, as a theatrical entertainment, becomes a closed monopolistic industry because most profit accrues to a company which combines a willingness to risk capital on high-cost film production with a tight control over distribution and exhibition.

Fourthly, all the nineteenth-century media are to some extent parasitic on earlier forms of art and entertainment: photography on nineteenth-century traditions of art, film on popular theatre and the novel, the gramophone almost completely on the classical and popular musical repertoire. Yet all three present themselves as systems of direct, unmediated reproduction. The idea that what they offer is a representation of reality, shaped to create pleasure and meaning, is hidden by the stress on such aspects as the detail of visual appearance in still photography, the fidelity of the reproduction of movement in film, and the record's increasing acoustic clarity. But in all three cases there is a tangible product, and the nature of the physical material on which this is recorded offers an invaluable means of understanding the medium's potential and limitation. As we shall see, this is no longer the case when we turn to the characteristic media of the early twentieth century: radio and television.

Further reading

On the relation between technology and society, the most useful sources are Aitken (1985a and 1985b) who deals with radio, R. Williams (1974) who focuses on television, and Winston (1986) who covers the whole spectrum of communication and information technology. For the paradoxes of perspective, see Arnheim (1974), Gombrich (1960), and Gregory and Gombrich (1973), while Cipolla (1970) offers a fascinating background account of fifteenth-century developments. The evolution of the book is the subject of Escarpit (1966) and Febvre and Martin (1976). There are numerous conventional histories of photography among the most approachable of which are Gernsheim and Gernsheim (1971), Goldsmith (1979), Jeffrey (1981), and Newall (1982). In addition, Jenkins (1975) offers an industrial history of Kodak, Scharf (1974) explores the impact of photography on painting, and Freund (1980) considers photography's social role. Comparatively little has been written about the record industry, but Gelatt (1977) offers a clear narrative account and Dearling and Dearling (1984) provide numerous factual details. No wholly satisfactory technological history of cinema exists, but Wollen (1982) gives a stimulating brief introduction, Fielding (1967) a useful anthology of technical articles, and Neale (1985) a useful discussion of a disappointingly limited range of topics.

The collection of papers in Lauretis and Heath (1980) reflects a theoretical position to which Salt (1983) offers a highly personal rebuttal. For a conventional history of movie photography see Coe (1981), while the range of debates about early cinema is reflected in the anthologies edited by Balio (1976), Kindem (1982), Fell (1983), and Kerr (1986). Early cinema's place in its cultural context is idiosyncratically discussed in Fell (1974), and developments outside the west are treated by Armes (1987).

2 THE BROADCAST REVOLUTION

> I think it will be admitted by all, that to have exploited
> so great a scientific invention for the purpose and
> pursuit of entertainment alone would have been a
> prostitution of its powers and an insult to the character
> and intelligence of the people.
>
> (John Reith, cit. Briggs 1961: 8)

The second stage in the development of sound and image
reproduction – the bringing together of the hitherto separate
threads of recording and transmission – did not follow immediately after the first. The invention of various components
demanded by an electronic system of communication had first to
be accomplished before a quite new and revolutionary concept
could be developed around 1920: broadcasting. The twin media
of radio and television, heirs to the electric telegraph and the
telephone as well as to cinema and the gramophone, are essentially
systems which instead of mechanically mass producing replicas of
the original, transmit reproductions instantly and electronically
to a large number of receivers.

Both radio and television were originally live media, able to
use gramophone records and feature films for transmission, but
not requiring a means of recording to come into existence. But
once they were in operation, both needed for their smooth
running more flexible systems of recording than the ones which
they had inherited. For initial local transmission there was no
inherent need to record sounds and images. But as nation-wide
networks were built up – particularly a country like the United

States which is both geographically huge and split into differing time zones – a facility allowing programme timings to be varied, and repeats and export sales to be achieved became necessary. Eventually – after the Second World War – this demand was to lead to the creation of new systems of electro-magnetic recording. Meanwhile, in the 1920s, there were important interactions with the film and record industries, both of which were transformed by fresh capital investment and the importing of new electronic technology from broadcasting.

The key steps in these readjustments were taken in the inter-war years when radio became widespread and the most important research work on television was successfully completed. These developments took place in a very different world from that of the 1890s. Four aspects of the broader political and social change are particularly significant. Firstly, after the First World War the United States had risen to unquestioned world dominance as the richest and most powerful nation the world had ever known. Secondly, virtually everywhere in the world state power and bureaucracy had much increased. From the beginning, broadcast systems have been tightly regulated by the state, although their commercial exploitation has often been granted to big business. Thirdly, the social application of broadcasting reflects the new importance of the domestic consumer market. Only for initial experimental transmissions in the USSR and Germany was a system of public reception of programming tried out. Elsewhere broadcasting became a key element of *universal* domestic consumption, with the radio (and later the television set) occupying a prominent place in virtually every home in the advanced western industrial countries. Fourthly, the better housing and rises in real wages which had led to a greater importance of the home for the bulk of the population provided the essential base for a mass market and a mass audience. Whereas the earlier media had been both aimed at specific groups of consumers and specialized in what they offered (either dramatic entertainment *or* news *or* music etc.), broadcasting brought news and entertainment, information and drama together through a single medium which, thanks to mass marketing and technological advance, could become increasingly accessible and inexpensive.

Radio

Whereas the late nineteenth-century media of sound and image reproduction were essentially the product of work undertaken by skilled engineers and visionaries whose scientific training was often negligible, the pioneers of the new broadcast media of the twentieth century were largely trained scientists. Two strands of nineteenth-century research had to be brought together to allow the creation of radio: the exploration of electro-magnetic waves and the elaboration of a theory of the electron, leading to the development of the vacuum tube. Significantly, the initial scientific research into both these areas was undertaken by Europeans, especially in Germany and England. Marconi, the first to turn this work into a practical, reliable system, also did his first important work in England. But enthusiasm for radio as a medium of entertainment was greatest in the United States, and the commercial radio industry which eventually came into being was an essentially American creation (Barnouw 1982).

As was the case with the pioneers of all the communication media we have to consider here, Marconi was only the best-known of a considerable number of key figures. Although he obtained numerous crucial patents, he had rivals in both Germany and the United States from the very beginning. Marconi saw the future of wireless exclusively in terms of messages from one transmitter-receiver to another. For him, the most profitable market seemed to be ship-to-ship and ship-to-shore communication, for which coded signals were sufficient. Marconi was a man of independent means, and this allowed him to wait patiently for the success he anticipated. Yet despite his business ability and his lead over all his rivals, it was years before his operations were able to make a secure profit. American Marconi, for example, the company which he founded in 1899, returned a deficit each year until 1910. Eventually, however, particularly after the publicity surrounding the last messages from *The Titanic* in 1912 (monitored by a young Marconi employee, David Sarnoff) and the new demand for wireless equipment created by the First World War (especially after US involvement in 1917), American Marconi began to fulfil all its founder's ambitions.

Marconi had no interest in – or indeed conception of – broadcasting. The broadcast applications of radio and television are so familiar to us today that it is difficult for us to realize that such a concept was quite unknown until the 1920s, and even then such a use of precious wavelengths for entertainment purposes was regarded by many in the wireless industry – and by its main customer, the armed forces – as a frivolous waste of time and resources.

The two principal US rivals of Marconi, Reginald Fessenden and Lee de Forest, were far less successful than he was as business men, but both were able to envisage the use of wireless transmission for broadcast purposes and both made key contributions to this aspect of radio. Fessenden was the pioneer of voice transmission, although many of his inventions were far in advance of what was feasible in engineering terms at the time. He made what is arguably the world's first radio broadcast on Christmas Eve 1906, when, from a shore station, he talked – and played a gramophone record – to ship wireless operators in a several hundred mile radius (Barnouw 1982: 13). De Forest made perhaps the single key breakthrough in radio with a device patented in 1907 which had immediate application: the three-element vacuum tube (triode or audion tube). This allowed the amplification of sound waves. In 1910 de Forest, too, became a pioneer broadcaster, with a transmission of an opera starring Enrico Caruso from the New York Metropolitan Opera House (Barnouw 1982: 15).

The period up to 1917 was a time of considerable growth in amateur radio activity, with over 8,000 US individuals holding licences to transmit. But with the entry of the United States into the war all this activity was ruled illegal, and the resources of the expanding wireless industry were poured into the war effort. With the end of hostilities, the amateurs – now estimated to number 100,000 in the United States alone – quietly resumed their transmitting activities. Their influence was enough to prevent an attempt by the US Navy to obtain for itself a wireless monopoly in 1918. The post-war mood was equally against foreign domination of the US domestic market. The Hollywood majors had taken over the US film distribution market unaided during the First World War, but it needed moves by the US government to achieve a similar result with regard to radio, through the Americanizing of the Marconi company in 1919.

The Marconi company's assets and patents were taken over by a new corporation, the Radio Corporation of America (RCA), which became a cartel through which the leading US electrical firms, including General Electric, Westinghouse, and AT&T, came together to pool their patents and assure themselves of a monopoly. This was quickly achieved with regard to those commercial activities formerly undertaken by Marconi, and the United States soon became the leading force in international wireless communication. However, the domestic radio market was much more difficult to control, although the cartel owned all the basic patents (some 2,000 in all). Part of the problem was the inability of industrialists (with the notable exception of David Sarnoff) to conceive of a system like broadcasting. It was only when confronted with the post-1920 burst of amateur radio transmitting activity that business men began to realize the potential of such a market. David Sarnoff, who remained the key entrepreneur of US broadcasting, beginning as office boy at American Marconi and ending as President of RCA, foretold the potential as early as 1916, but his advice was ignored at first. Sarnoff's detailed predictions of potential sales of radio sets (which he saw rising from $7.5 million to $45 million in three years) stirred little institutional interest, although in fact they were quite remarkably accurate, as was shown when marketing was undertaken (RCA's actual growth in sales was from $11 million in 1922 to $50 million in 1924 (Barnouw 1982: 36).

Even so, RCA initially cornered only a part of the market: its $11 million sales in 1922 represented less than a fifth of the total US expenditure on radio receivers. Similarly AT&T's subsidiary, Western Electric, which held all the basic transmitter patents, built only 35 of the first 600 radio stations to go on air in the 1920s. This situation soon brought members of the cartel into conflict, and for several years their unity was in doubt. It needed government intervention again in 1923 to bring order to the market and to allow the germ of a national network to emerge. This latter came in 1926, when RCA formed the National Broadcasting Company (NBC). 1927 was the key year, with a second network (which eventually became ABC) added by

RCA and a third, CBS, set up by the Columbia Phonograph Company. A ruling that the government intervention had been illegal threw the market into temporary confusion again, but the Radio Act of 1927 restored order. The Act affirmed the government's authority over the airwaves (wavelengths were licensed, not sold, to companies) and anti-trust provisions were strongly affirmed. Sarnoff guided RCA through both the boom years of 1928–9 (when the company made profits far in excess of those it achieved even around 1940) and the stockmarket crash of 1930. RCA emerged in the 1930s strong and independent, freed of its subordination to the electrical giants which had helped bring it into being.

Although Britain had been the original base of the Marconi company, it came to broadcasting later than the United States, perhaps because all amateur activity had been banned for five years from 1914 to 1919. The first transmissions by the Marconi company were made from Chelmsford in 1920, but after a few months they were banned by the Post Office on the grounds that they interfered with legitimate (that is, military) communications (Briggs 1961: 48–50). It was therefore not until 1922 that regular transmissions resumed, first from Chelmsford, then from London (the famous 2LO station sited at Marconi House). In order to establish a monopoly and avoid the market chaos prevalent in the United States, companies in the British wireless industry held discussions with the Post Office. The result was the British Broadcasting Company, set up in 1922 to control transmission and to receive income from annual licences and a royalty on receivers (the latter ended in 1924).

From the start, there was an attempt to reach every part of the country with broadcast transmission. Initially, in 1923, eight (subsequently nine) main transmitters were established, supplemented by eleven relay stations, so that by the end of 1924 some 70 per cent of the population could be reached. It had been expected that each of the main stations would originate its own programming, but the beginnings of a nation-wide network began to emerge as early as 1923–4, with increasing relay of programming which originated in London. This first transmission system was well suited to the crystal sets beloved of the amateurs. Although valve receivers were available, these were very expensive to buy and extremely complicated to use. Crystal sets, though lacking both amplification and the ability to separate transmission signals of comparable strength, were cheap, simple to use, and able to be assembled by the average handiman.

An international conference in Geneva in 1925, which was held to sort out the international problems of radio interference, led to a new generation of transmitters, with five regionally based high-powered stations in Britain, each capable of beaming two channels. This development led to the demise of the crystal set, and with valve sets still comparatively expensive, the early audience for radio in Britain was predominantly middle- or lower-middle-class, with none of the explosive growth of a popular audience characteristic of the United States. There was steady expansion, however. As the number of BBC employees rose from 4 in 1922 to some 650 in 1926, the number of licence-holders rose to over 2 million (Briggs 1961: 12, 18).

The period between 1922 and January 1927, when the BBC became a public service institution, the British Broadcasting *Corporation*, is a key period of transition in which all the principal features of the broadcasting system in Britain for the next thirty years were determined, including the context within which a television service would be brought into existence. The crucial figure was the General Manager of the Company (and subsequently Director-General of the Corporation), John Reith (Boyle 1972). From the start, the BBC in 1922 was a very muted example of capitalism, limited by Post Office ruling to a return of no more than 7.5 per cent on its capital investment and precluded from making a capital gain (Briggs 1961: 402). The wireless industry in Britain, like that in the United States, did not see itself as being in the business of producing programmes, and the initial phase of the BBC as a *company* was clearly seen as no more than a temporary holding operation, to prevent anarchy in the development of transmission. But it did result in certain key structural features which have remained into the present, most notably the separation of the radio industry (making its profits from the sale of sets) from the business of programme-making (to be funded from receiving licences).

At a time when the whole concept of broadcasting was little understood, it was Reith's vision of a public service corporation which, thanks to his forceful character and impassioned eloquence, eventually held sway. Although virtually everywhere (even in the United States) the state claimed control over broadcasting, the public service corporation solution can be seen as a uniquely British compromise. The British Broadcasting Corporation became a centralized, hierarchical organization with a notional independence from the state but dominated from the start by Reith's paternalistic attitudes and his conviction that the public should be given not what they might want, but rather what the Corporation thought they needed.

Reith himself was in no doubt about where the success of the BBC lay, attributing it to four factors: the public service motive, the sense of moral obligation, assured finance, and what he called 'the brute force of monopoly' (Smith 1973: 71). Writers looking at the BBC from within have often stressed the institution's independence from the government. The actual limitations of this were shown even before the Corporation was set up, when in 1926 the Company was faced with the choice of how to approach the General Strike. The organization found that in practice it had no alternative but to follow the government's line, and Reith noted bitterly in his diary in May 1926 that 'they want to be able to say that they did not commandeer us, but they know they can trust us not to be really impartial' (Hood 1980: 45). Subsequent treatment of national crises such as Suez, Ulster, and the Falklands War shows how little has changed in this respect.

Electric recording

One of the least remarked consequences of the lack of capitalist aggression and the dignified distaste for 'mere entertainment' exhibited by the BBC from the 1920s onwards, was its failure to move from work on radio transmission and reception into the areas of electric recording and replay for the gramophone. No pressure was therefore brought to bear on the two leading British record companies, The Gramophone Company (trading under the HMV label) and Columbia, both of which undertook their research into electric recording at a very leisurely pace. Neither was the BBC in any way involved in moves to provide synchronous sound systems for film, although work on this was undertaken elsewhere in Europe during the 1920s (particularly in Germany and Denmark). It was left to US companies to make the decisive breakthrough in both areas.

The unity displayed by the US electrical industry at the time of the founding of RCA in 1919 had long been dissipated. Under Sarnoff's leadership RCA had already acquired considerable independence from its parent firms before the formal separation took place in 1932, and AT&T (through its marketing arm, Western Electric) and General Electric (often marketing through RCA) had resumed their commercial rivalry. However, this was now rivalry of a corporate kind, not the bitter competitiveness of earlier years, and the pooling of patents between the interested parties remained in force. Since each of the electrical giants had its own research department, it was inevitable that other commercial applications for the new electronic sound technology developed for radio would be sought. The crucial breakthrough this time was achieved in the largest of these, Bell Telephone Laboratories, which was jointly owned by AT&T and Western Electric and spent over $300 million on research between 1916 and 1940 (Maclaurin 1971: 158).

Although work on electric recording had been going on since 1919, the record companies had shown little interest. The Victor Talking Machine Company (the name itself is redolent of nineteenth-century attitudes) took a year to reach a decision when offered the new system perfected by the Bell Laboratories on a royalty basis in 1924. The London-based Columbia company (separated since 1922 from its now ailing US parent) was more actively interested, but to gain access to a similar deal it had to buy US Columbia (for $2.5 million) and organize it as a branch of the London firm. This, too, was accomplished in 1925. As usual, the Bell development had a rival, and that same year General Electric began to market its own more cumbersome (and soon discontinued) recording system through Brunswick, a small-scale manufacturer of gramophones since 1916 and of records since 1920.

Electric recording and the new gramophone model (grandly called the Orthophonic Victrola) restored Victor's fortunes, and the company was sold for $40 million at the end of 1926. The following year it had a net income of some $7 million from the sale of almost a million gramophones and over 100 million records (Gelatt 1977: 246). With the growing sale of combined radio–gramophones, the prosperity of the record industry along-side radio seemed assured. Indeed it was a record company, the Columbia Phonograph Company, which set up the third US radio network, CBS, in 1927. But the equality was illusory, and when RCA took over the Victor company early in 1929, it soon showed itself more interested in utilizing Victor's factory capacity and retail outlets for its production of radios than for a continuation of the record business. This was particularly true after the Stock Market crash of 1929, which led Edison to cease production of cylinders and left Brunswick open to take-over by Warner Bros, the film company which had pioneered the synchronous sound film. The lowest point for the US recording industry was 1932, when only 7 million records (as opposed to 100 million in the mid-1920s) were sold. In Europe the decline was less severe, but the combined profits of The Gramophone Company (HMV) and Columbia had declined to a mere tenth of their 1929–30 level of £1.5 million when they were merged in 1931 to form a company which, initially, was to have a virtual monopoly in Europe, Electrical and Musical Industries (EMI).

The 1930s were a difficult period for the US record industry as it struggled to recover from the trough of 1932 in face of ever-increasing competition from radio. Recovery was initially slow and it was 1938 before sales reached even 30 million records a year (still a third of the mid-1920s figure), but thereafter growth was steady, to almost 130 million records by 1941. During this period both Victor and Columbia were revitalized by new management, and they were joined by a new and vigorous cut-price record company, Decca. A further important factor – stimulating growth and pointing to the postwar relationship between records and youth culture – was the spread of juke-boxes which from the mid-1930s became an increasingly important outlet for records. The entry of the United States into the war brought production difficulties (especially with the shortage of shellac, used at the time for record pressings), and a damaging dispute with the American musicians' union brought production to a complete halt for a year or more in the mid-

1940s. The postwar era began brightly, however, and a new peak of over 400 million records was reached in 1947, when the record industry found itself on the verge of a new transformation thanks to the introduction of magnetic sound tape.

The sound film

Given the success of the first (pre-Depression) move into the recording industry, the strategy adopted by the electrical companies for the transformation of the even more lucrative market of world cinema has a total logic. Synchronous sound systems of various kinds had been sought and claimed since the earliest days of cinema, and indeed the combination of phonograph and kinetoscope had been a dream of Edison's even before the birth of cinema itself in 1895. Even Sam Warner, a key member of the firm which eventually pioneered synch sound is often reported to have said that he 'wouldn't have walked across the street' to look at yet another talking picture system (Walker 1978: 6). In the mid-1920s a number of optimistic engineers had sound film systems on offer: the Tri–Ergon system in Germany (later commercialized by the Tobis company), two Petersen–Poulsen systems in Denmark (one optical sound–on–film, the other magnetic), and, in the United States, the Phonofilm system developed independently by Lee de Forest, the radio pioneer. But none of these – or of the dozens of other variants offered hopefully during the late 1920s – had the kind of reliability or the financial and industrial backing necesary to tempt the leaders of the highly successful film industry into a transformation that would vastly increase the costs and complications of production, render stocks of old movies commercially worthless, and cast doubt on the value of some of the highest paid and most reliable stars.

Yet the successful application of electricity to sound recording and to the operation of the gramophone offered the model for a system which would finally solve the age-old problems of synchronous images and sounds. It is certainly not by chance that Western Electric based their original thrust in 1925 on a system of sound–on–disc which explicitly echoed the new gramophone system and which left the image track unaltered in its dimension and aspect ratio. When they first approached the three 'first-tier' film companies – Famous Players (later Paramount), Loew's (MGM) and First National – Western Electric found them as uninterested as the Victor Talking Machine Company. But the situation was not static within the film industry, and the following year Western Electric was able to agree terms for its sound system with Warner Bros, one of the 'second-tier' companies, which was currenty undertaking an expansion on all fronts – production investment, the setting up of a distribution chain, and the acquisition of first-run cinemas – with financial backing from Wall Street banking interests.

The prevalent idea that Warner Bros was a bankrupt firm which gambled all on the conversion to sound (the corporate equivalent of the 'great man' theory of innovation) has been shown to be false (Gomery 1976a, 1976d). The company was pursuing clear financial objects at this time and for this reason was more interested than most companies in diversification. It set up two radio stations in 1925–6, established a touring radio transmitter for publicity purposes, and eventually bought the Brunswick record company. The investment in the Vitaphone subsidiary, initially intended to make short sound films of stage acts to replace the expensive vaudeville entertainment which customarily formed the first part of the bill in 1920s cinemas, was merely one part of the company's overall expansion plans. Moreover the conversion to sound was undertaken very gradually: it took a year to set up the programme of sound shorts and the recorded musical accompaniment for the feature film *Don Juan*, which was premiered in August 1926. A further year passed before *The Jazz Singer*, its first feature film with musical numbers, was released in October 1927.

If we ask ourselves why sound films became acceptable in 1927 in a way that they had not been in earlier years, the answer must surely be in part the fact that audiences were now becoming accustomed to electrically recorded sound thanks to radio and the new records. Whatever the exact reason, the immense success of sound films with the public gave Warner Bros a clear lead over its rivals and, combined with its other corporate strategies, allowed the company to take over First National in 1928 and to become one of the five 'majors' during the golden age of Hollywood in the 1930s and 1940s. In the process, Warner Bros' assets rose from $5 million in 1925 to $230 million in 1930 (Gomery 1986: 5).

The first of the other companies to follow the Warner Bros example was another of the smaller but rapidly expanding companies of the mid-1920s, Fox (Gomery 1976c). In collaboration with the independent Case Laboratories (but leasing some Western Electric patents), Fox developed the Movietone sound-on-film system. This compact, portable method, which initially recorded both image and sound in camera, proved unsuitable for studio production, where a separation of sound and image is preferable for greater control and precision. But it found a perfect application in the production of the Fox Movietone sound newsreels which were premiered in April 1927. The success of this strategy was a key element – alongside the purchase of a large number of first-run theatres – in Fox's rise to become another of the five majors of the 1930s.

The remaining companies, including the most powerful firms of the mid-1920s, decided on a more cautious approach, agreeing that decisions should be collective, so that a common standard could be adopted throughout the industry. After discussions with RCA, which in 1928 entered the market with the Photophone system developed in the laboratories of General Electric, the film industry negotiating committee opted for the Western Electric sound-on-film system. This became the industry's standard from May 1928, although Warner Bros continued to use sound-on-disc until 1930. RCA's particular system of sound-on-film was eventually to become the standard method in the late 1930s, but meanwhile, in order to find an outlet for it in the late 1920s, RCA brought together a variety of companies engaged in production, distribution, and exhibition so as to create RKO, the smallest (and least successful) of the five major companies of the 1930s and 1940s (Ogle 1977; Gomery 1977).

With this move, the pattern of the film industry for its twenty-year peak – the 'golden age' of Hollywood – became fixed. There were five companies that were vertically integrated (that is, combining production, distribution, and exhibition): Paramount, MGM, Fox, Warners, and RKO. These were backed up by three 'minors', which handled production and distribution but owned no cinemas: Columbia, Universal, and United Artists. Together these eight companies could take some 95 per cent of US box office receipts and dominate film markets throughout the world. Outsiders were kept from this select 'club' not by patent rights and restrictions, but by the level of investment required. To compete in this market outsiders would need to match the dominant companies' high level of investment in individual film productions. This figure – several hundred thousand dollars a film – was clearly not an insuperable obstacle in itself. But in making such an investment, the outsiders (whether US independents or foreign companies trying to break into the US domestic market) would have created a product which could *only* recover its costs if given a first-run release in the majors' tightly controlled prime-site cinemas, from which they were systematically excluded.

The impact of radio

The 1930s and 1940s are generally regarded as the 'golden age' of radio, and a number of nostalgic books have been published in Britain and the United States which look back on the programmes of this period in which wireless still occupied the focal point in many millions of homes. Whereas the gramophone had remained largely parasitic on existing musical performance, radio produced its own stars, who went on to make records and to appear in films (and later on television). While the BBC's monopoly protected British radio from the excesses of commercialization, it was US radio's popular mix of news and drama, soap opera and variety shows which set the pattern of content for later developments in radio and television in Britain as well as in the United States. In offering this fare, the US radio networks, drawing their income from advertising, became big business, with gross time sales in the United States rising from under $4 million in 1927 to over $50 million in 1936 and $300 million in 1945 (Maclaurin 1971: 117).

The same period was also a boom time for manufacturers – sales of radio sets in the United States alone rose from 3 million in 1928 to 6 million in 1935 and 13 million in 1941 (Maclaurin 1971: 139). Once the system had been established and the engineering requirements for building radio sets were known, the giant corporations like RCA found themselves outmanoeuvred in this growing consumer market. Smaller and more dynamic specialist companies – led by Philco in the United States – used advertising campaigns, design, and product innnovation (such as the introduction of portable radios) to increase their share of the market. Philco could match RCA in the sales of radio sets by the early 1940s, but because of RCA's patent pool such developments could occur only under licence (and with a payment of royalties to RCA). RCA therefore remained immensely profitable, with gross revenue rising constantly from the Depression years to reach over $150 million by 1941. The company had been bettered by Bell Laboratories in the development of electric sound for the record industry and by Western Electric in the conversion of the film industry to synchronous sound systems. However, its profits from radio were huge and allowed it to become the leading pioneer in television, in which it invested some $9 million for research in the 1930s (Maclaurin 1971: 206).

The period of radio's ascendancy was a time of overall growth in sales and profitability throughout the electrical industry, but in retrospect perhaps the crucial factor in all these developments is that, from the profits of radio, there emerged the beginnings of a generalized notion of an entertainment industry. The diversification of RCA into recording (Victor), film-making (RKO), and into television research set the pattern for the future. The new media had always been international: photography immediately found application world-wide, the sound empires of Edison, Pathé, Victor, and The Gramophone Company spread internationally, and film had been shown in the major capitals of Asia and Latin America, as well as throughout Europe and the United States, within six months of Lumière's first screenings. However, the initial impact was fairly limited in industrial terms. In film, for example, the Lumière operator travelled the world not as a media colonizer, but as an act able to slot into the programme of music-hall or vaudeville entertainment. Pathé set up branches world-wide, but many of these had considerable local autonomy and indeed some became the eventual focus of national opposition to French (and later US) dominance. Only with the Hollywood companies of the 1920s did the exploitation of world film markets become systematic.

Similarly, the media born in the nineteenth century had from the first been closely related phenomena. The extent to which they were part of a single impulse is shown by the involvement of individuals in two or more media: Samuel Morse, inventor of the telegraph, was a pioneer daguerreotypist; both Edison and Pathé moved from phonograph to cinema; Lumière invented the cinematograph and perfected the first viable colour system for still photography. Even the failed visionaries dabbled in both sounds and images. Before failing to get backing for the sound-recording system which would have anticipated Edison, Charles Cros had independently deduced the principles of the subtractive colour method for still photography (only to see Ducos du Hauron granted a patent two days before the publication of his results). Despite this spread of shared interests and involvements, the nineteenth-century industries evolved quite separately: Eastman never became involved in film production, the Victor company was uninterested in radio, cinema quickly separated itself off from photography to become a theatrical entertainment, and the Hollywood producers refused initial Western Electric terms for sound conversion which would have involved them in equipment manufacture. A major Hollywood company might have 100 or more subsidiaries, but all of these would deal directly with some aspect of film production, distribution, or exhibition.

RCA, the prime mover in US radio, was a company of quite a different kind – as revolutionary in its way as the very concept of broadcasting itself. Through RCA, with its links to the industrial giants AT&T and General Electric, the entertainment media entered the world of big business and into close ties with government. The US media companies were already very substantial: Victor was sold for $40 million in 1926 and by 1930 the five Hollywood majors had assets of between $100 million and $300 million each (although some 90 per cent of this was investment in real estate: the valuable first-run cinemas in prime urban sites). But from the beginning, RCA, with gross revenues of approaching $300 million and profits of over $35 million in the boom years of 1928–9, was operating on a completely different scale. To get production capacity and a distribution network for its radios, it simply bought Victor. Pushed into second place by Western Electric in the drive to bring synchronous sound to Hollywood, it set up its own Hollywood major, RKO. When the struggle to convert European cinemas to sound became a battle between Western Electric and Hollywood on the one hand, and Tobis-Klangfilm, backed by the German government and electrical cartels, on the other, RCA carved out its own stake in the market, partly by buying a substantial share in the German AEG electrical company. It would take a long time for the transnational, multimedia conglomerates characteristic of the era into which video was born to come into existence, but the first step was taken with RCA in the late 1920s and 1930s (Gomery 1980a: 80–93).

Television

The invention and social application of television follows the pattern set by the earlier media, especially radio, to the extent that we find a similar combination of visionary anticipation and dogged endeavour, dead-ends and striking breakthroughs, and predictable intercompany disputes and a few genuine surprises. As before, the focus shifts in the course of development from a number of independent European pioneers to the US industrial complex. Indeed, the development of television needed far greater resources than had been anticipated. The breakthrough expected at the end of the 1920s was variously delayed until the late 1930s, and then the outbreak of war led to further years of suspension, so that it was only in 1946 that full-scale television transmission got under way in Britain and the United States (Winston 1986: 35–102).

The early work on components of the television system dates back to the latter part of the nineteenth century, so that it is not surprising that one strand of development work sought *mechanical* answers to the basic problem confronting all television research: how to break down a sequence of images into units of information capable of being transmitted by wireless. What is surprising, however, is the extent to which some pioneers – particularly the dedicated but obstinate British pioneer, John

Logie Baird – kept to mechanical systems long after their limitations had become obvious. The lead in this direction had been given by a German engineer, Paul Nipkow, who patented (but did not produce) a mechanical scanning disc in 1884, and by Lazare Weiller, who devised a revolving-drum system using small deflecting mirrors some five years later. Much of the initial practical work on television adopted mechanical means: the German Fernseh system, the work of the Hungarian Denes von Mihaly and the Americans Charles Francis Jenkins and Herbert Ives, as well as Baird's work in Britain.

Initially, while research remained at the level of 60 to 100 lines, mechanical systems could hold their own against the more complex and expensive electronic scanning devices. Baird was able to accumulate a remarkable collection of 'firsts', including the first transmission of an intelligible television signal across the Atlantic in 1928. But the standard of 240 lines for 'high definition' television set by the British Selsdon Committee in 1935 was the absolute limit of what could be achieved by any mechanical system. Already by that date such systems were outclassed by the ambitions (and increasingly by the achievements) of those employing electronic methods in all respects except the transmission of film images. Because of their comparative lack of sensitivity, mechanical systems could cope better with the direct illumination given by a film projector than with the reflected light from even a brightly lit scene (a situation which led the ever inventive Baird to explore infra-red television even before he could achieve clear, stable pictures from a conventional studio set-up).

Jenkins (who had done pioneering work on the film projector) and Ives (working in the context of the lavishly equipped Bell Laboratories) both explored the television transmission of film images. But this strand of development reached its culminating point in Germany with the Fernseh 'intermediate-film' system, in which images were recorded on film, processed immediately in an attached developing tank, and then scanned mechanically. This was one of the two alternative methods (the other was a derivative of RCA's work) which were adopted by the German authorities for their coverage of the Berlin Olympics in 1936. Contrary to received opinion, it was the Germans who, in

March 1935, had begun the world's first regular public service transmission (of 180-line pictures), anticipating by a year and a half the BBC's first (240-line) transmissions of November 1936 (Winston 1985: 260).

These BBC transmissions at first matched Baird's work against the fully electronic system perfected by EMI-Marconi, but already from the start it was evident that there was in fact no contest, and that the future belonged to electronic television (the Baird transmissions were dropped in February 1937). The line of development leading to electronic television is quite separate from that using mechanical means and, despite patriotic claims that Baird is the 'father of television', it is one in which the British pioneer played no part. There is, in fact, an interesting parallel between Baird and William Friese Greene, who is often equally wrongly designated as the 'inventor of cinematography'. Both Baird and Friese Greene were striking figures who fit the popular image of the lone, eccentric inventor. Their lives give rise to a host of good stories – Baird turning to television after the failure of 'Baird's Undersocks' (designed to keep the feet warm in winter and cool in summer), and Friese Greene dying at a meeting called to discuss the crisis of the British film industry and found to have just the price of a cinema ticket in his pocket. Such mythic portraits disguise the fact that media developments have consistently come from the well-funded research laboratories of large companies which have institutionalized the process of innovation. Television as a viable system stems not from the contraption built out of 'worn-out electric motors, biscuit tins, a hat box, darning nedles and bicycle lenses' (Swift 1950: 30–1) which Baird used for his celebrated demonstrations in Selfridges store in 1925, but from the $9 million which RCA invested in television research between 1930 and 1939 (Maclaurin 1971: 206).

Given the very different technological potentials of the two systems, the preference for electronic over mechanical scanning was no doubt inevitable. It was to have one unforeseen but long-lasting consequence: television came to be seen as an essentially live medium. Electronic television in the form of EMI's emitron cameras did not cope well with film (where the mechanical systems excelled), and telecine systems which allowed film images to be scanned and transmitted were not developed until the late 1940s (Phillips 1986: 33–5). When television resumed after the war in 1946 unions were able to insist on a total banning of recorded programmes and repeats. Relationships with the film industry were basically hostile, and even today, in the late-1980s, the BBC has still to initiate production of films designed for both cinema and television release. As a result of these factors, by the time that video tape was introduced around 1958, television had established itself as a live medium, basing its output on variety shows, quizzes, and outside broadcasts (a quarter of total output in 1954 and comprising mostly sporting events). Even some television drama, notably the celebrated *Z Cars* series, was transmitted live, while news programming was firmly under the control of broadcasters from radio, who conceived it as a purely spoken live report. If cinema can be said to have been shaped by the flexibility of celluloid as a carrier base for its images, television was equally defined by its initial *lack* of an adequate means of recording.

The second – electronic – strand of television development has its origins not in Nipkow's device, but in the research work of other German scientists: the cathode-ray tube developed by Karl Braun in 1897 and the photoelectric cell developed by Julius Elster and Hans Geitel in 1905. Much further development work was needed on both these fundamental inventions, however, before a properly functioning, high-definition television system could be manufactured. In the USSR in 1907 Boris Rosing patented and carried out initial work on a system of television using a mechanical scanning device in the camera and an electronic, cathode-ray-based receiver. The following year, and apparently quite independently, a British Scientist, A. A. Campbell-Swintin, wrote an article in *Nature* proposing a fully electronic system, using cathode-ray tubes for both camera and receiver. But this article received little attention and Campbell-Swinton did not follow up this line of thought.

If one man deserves to be seen as central to the invention of television, it is the Russian-born Vladimir Zworykin, who studied with Rosing in Saint Petersburg, before emigrating to the United States after the Revolution. In the 1920s he worked in the Westinghouse laboratories on a number of projects, including a caesium-magnesium photoelectric cell and electronic television. His key patents were a first system with increased sensitivity thanks to the temporary storage of the charge (1923) and the 'iconoscope' camera (1928), which was the basis of RCA's dominant hold over television development after Zworykin's work was transferred to its laboratories in 1930.

Already in the 1920s, however, Zworykin had a rival in the unlikely figure of Philo Farnsworth, a farmer's boy from the Midwest, whose home did not have electricity until he was 14, but who had designed a completely original electronic television system at the age of 15, just before he left school. Though virtually self-taught, Farnsworth received backing from private sources (and for a couple of years from Philco), and this enabled him to take out his 1927 television patent (the first of some 165 in radio and television). In all, Farnsworth's research cost over $1 million up to 1938 (compared with $9 million – including $2 million spent on patent expenses – invested by RCA). With the introduction of commercial television in the United States continually delayed, it was not until the Second World War, when it did important war work for the government, that the Farnsworth Corporation became financially secure.

The importance of the Farnsworth 'image-dissector' camera and his work on other aspects of television circuitry is shown by the fact that RCA took out a cross-licensing agreement with him. This broke basic RCA policy (which was to buy outright everything it needed) and there are stories of the RCA patent attorney weeping as he signed (Winston 1985: 262). The only comparable exchange of patents for RCA in the 1930s was with EMI, a company in which it had a considerable, if not controlling, stake. This exchange concerned the 'emitron' camera developed at EMI by a team under Frank McGee. This seems to have been based on the principles of Zworykin's iconoscope, which it turned into a reliable 405-line system, far in advance of anything realized by that date in the United States. It was the emitron camera which was the basis of the BBC's first successful transmissions and its advances were incorporated into the 525-line system eventually adopted in the United States.

The delay there seems to have been caused partly by government anti-trust concern about the monopoly position

RCA had built up. The Federal Communications Commission (FCC) in its 1941 report, noted that RCA 'bestrides whole industries, dwarfing its competitors in each', so that it 'occupies a premier position in fields which are profoundly determinative of our way of life' (cit. Guback and Varis 1982: 18). As a result, RCA was required to sell its second television network (which became ABC) when the FCC gave authorization for public broadcasting to begin in 1941. By this time, both Soviet and British television had been suspended because of the war and although, oddly enough, the Germans continued transmitting until 1943, the infant US system, too, had ground to a halt by 1942.

Broadcasting began again in 1946, but development was comparatively slow until the early 1950s, when the period of explosive growth began. While most historians of television see 1953 as the key year when television found its audience, the occasions chosen as starting-points for the new era throw clear light on the differences between British and US experiences. For British writers the key date is 2 June 1953 – the coronation of Elizabeth II – watched by an estimated 20 million people, although only 2 million sets were in use at the time (Black 1972: 49). For the US historian, Erik Barnouw, on the other hand, the corresponding date is 19 January 1953 – the day on which Lucille Ball gave birth to her son and her screen *alter ego*, the heroine of *I Love Lucy*, did likewise, watched by 68.8 per cent of the US television audience (Barnouw 1982: 148).

In Britain, although the BBC's monopoly was broken by the introduction of commercial television in 1955, the system has been characterized by elaborate checks and balances (for example, in the ownership of the news company, ITN, and the second commercial channel, Channel Four), and as late as 1986 the idea of funding the BBC through advertising was rejected. In the United States control has been much laxer, with power granted to big business advertisers, giving rise to frequent excesses but also dazzling expansion. To give a few comparative figures: in Britain the number of licences went up from 0.7 million in 1951 to 9 million in 1958 and 19.5 million in 1980; in the United States the rise was from 1 million in 1949 to 10 million in 1951, 100 million in 1975 and 140 million in 1980. This phenomenal growth has been a world-wide phenomenon: only 5 countries had regular television transmission in 1950, but this had risen to 69 in 1960 and 148 by 1969. With the growth of broadcasting has come an increase in figures for ownership of television sets: from 273 million world-wide in 1970 to over 500 million in 1980 (*Statistics on Radio and Television* 1978; *Cultural Statistics and Cultural Development* 1982).

The nature of broadcasting

Space does not allow us to trace the detailed history of radio and television, but we do need to examine briefly the nature of broadcasting and the ways in which it differs from earlier systems such as the film industry and from the subsequent tape media. Cinema fits precisely into the framework of professional entertainment as it emerged in the nineteenth century – in attendance at football matches or the music hall. The spectator pays for the opportunity to view a specific performance which makes few if any demands on him or her apart from the price of admission: there is no need for special skills (such as literacy), or financial resources (such as those required for the purchase of a radio), or particular living conditions (the 'home' required for all domestic consumer durables). As far as the technology is concerned, television could have been developed on a similar economic model, with the purchase of the 'right to view' certain specific programmes at some place of public assembly serving to fund both the system of transmission and the costs of production. In such a model, prodution would play a predominant role, with some programmes being more popular (and hence more profitable) than others, the results being directly apparent in the box office receipts.

But as we have seen, radio and television developed in a very different way, with transmission and reception in the abstract being conceived before attention was given to production. The impetus for both radio and television came from equipment manufacturers to whom the profits from the sale of receivers went. This obligated the provision of a transmission capacity, but it in no way either defined what should be transmitted or funded its production. The latter could be financed by licence fee, by persuading the advertisers to pay (through direct sponsorship or purchase of air-time) or, potentially at least, by some pay-as-you-view system. The decision of manufacturers to market both radio and television sets to family units rather than to devise a system of communal or theatrical viewing was a key factor in making broadcasting attractive to advertisers. None of the nineteenth-century 'out-of-home' entertainments (spectator sport, music hall, cinema) was particularly attractive to advertisers. Only in the case of the newspaper – delivered daily to the home – did advertising come to play a major part in the economic well-being of the medium (until television, by bringing spectator sport into the home, made that of interest to sponsors and advertisers, too). The involvement of advertisers in the funding of production makes the purchase of a television set a far more complex (as well as costly) act than the purchase of a cinema ticket.

The situation in the early days of broadcasting, whereby programmes were only produced as and when it became apparent that the ever-widening time would have to be filled somehow, is echoed even in the 1980s. The many expansions of transmission (breakfast-time viewing, Channel Four, cable and satellite plans) are conceived not as responses to an excess of product needing an outlet or to a new definition of the product demanding new distribution strategies, but as decisions to be taken prior to any discussion (let alone organization) of production. One reason why television can operate in this way is that its own original production occupies only a fraction of the transmission time (witness the thousands of films and tens of thousands of records broadcast annually). Whereas a 'film' is, in common parlance, a piece of dramatic fiction of one dominant kind produced specifically for cinema exhibition, a 'television programme' may be factual or fictional, news or entertainment, live or recorded (on video, on film, or on a mixture of both), a self-contained entity or part of a series or serial, studio-based or shot on location, made specifically for television or produced originally for cinema showing or cassette sale.

Here we have a further major distinction between television and cinema. The latter can reasonably be seen as the sum of a number of discrete works – the body of films made since 1895.

These vary greatly – from Lumière's fifty-second actualities to Jacques Rivette's twelve-hour-forty-minute *Out One* – but all have a concrete, individual identity. They can each form an object of study, and collectively they constitute the basis for a history or a theory of film. But since television takes over so much of its content from other media, its programmes have a very different status. It is impossible to argue that television is the sum of its programmes, since many of these owe nothing to the specificity of the medium. In fact, the real equivalent in importance to the individual film in cinema is not the programme but the time-slot, the marketable segment of the basically undifferentiated broadcasting potential. This key distinction is also a factor which allows us to distinguish clearly between television production and video-making, even if both are recorded on the same material. The new electro-magnetic recording media consist of individual works – tapes – in exactly the same way that the nineteenth-century media comprise specific photographs, films, and records.

Further reading

For the interaction of science, technology, and business in the electrical industry, see Reich (1985). The standard histories of broadcasting are Barnouw (1966, 1968, 1970) for the United States, and Briggs (1961, 1965, 1970, 1979) for Britain. Both authors have also written one-volume histories: Barnouw (1982) and Briggs (1985). Specific histories of US radio, both stressing technical and organizational matters rather than programming, are Aitken (1985a, 1985b) and Maclaurin (1971). For the ideology governing broadcasting see Hood (1980) and Garnham (1973), as well as the biography of Reith by Boyle (1972). The basic documents on British broadcasting are collected in Smith (1974). Winston (1986) offers much useful material and a forceful argument. Crisell (1986) and R. Williams (1974) are helpful introductory texts for radio and television respectively. For developments outside the industrially developed west see Katz and Wedell (1978). The issue of the conversion of cinema to sound has been widely discussed. A popular introduction is

Walker (1976); more scholarly are Ogle (1977) and the numerous articles by Gomery (1976 to 1980). For the organization of the studio system, see Gomery (1986) and for the classic Hollywood style: Bordwell, Staiger, and Thompson (1985).

3 THE IMPACT OF SOUND AND VIDEO TAPE

> The principle is simple: take a sound – any sound – . record it, and then change its nature by a multiplicity of operations. Record it at different speeds, play it backwards, add it to itself over and over again, subject it to the influence of frequency filters, acoustic variations, combine one segment of magnetic tape with another, unrelated, segment; by these means, among others, we can create sounds which have never been heard before and which have a unique and indefinable quality of their own. By a lengthy technical process we can compose a vast and subtle harmonic pattern using only one basic sound – say, the noise of a pin dropping.
>
> (Donald McWhinnie: 85–6)

Although television came to the fore as a dominant part of western culture only after the Second World War, all its elements had been devised and tested by the end of the 1930s. In this sense the war held back progress, just as it kept Hollywood companies away from some of their richest export markets and caused problems of supply in the record industry. Yet at the same time the war stimulated technical development in such areas as radar, code-breaking, gunnery, bombing systems, and the atomic bomb, and this activity was to have a major impact on communications technology from the mid-1940s onwards. In a similar way, such postwar developments as the cold war and the space race had an important effect on the electronics industry.

Developments in communications immediately after the Second World War were strongly influenced by the fact that while Europe was in ruins, the United States had reached new levels of power and wealth. The aid distributed under the Marshall Plan was used to good advantage by US firms, and Hollywood in particular – presenting itself as the flag-bearer of the American way of life – was a covert beneficiary. Profiting from tacit acceptance of its monopoly position in the domestic market and encouraged to operate as a cartel in its foreign dealings, Hollywood remade the shattered European film industries on its own terms after 1945. Its foreign dominance was thereby maintained, even though the film industry itself was in decline with the coming of television.

In a period characterized throughout Asia and Africa by nascent nationalism, successful liberation movements, and growing awareness of a distinctive non-western, Third World identity, US communication media exerted an ever-increasing impact (Nordenstreng and Varis 1974; Tunstall 1977; Varis 1985). In virtually all the new sound and image media the United States had developed (and has maintained) the largest domestic market in the world. Through a variety of strategies – each appropriate to the particular medium concerned – this market has been kept under the control of US firms and used as the base from which to dominate world markets. Figures are of necessity approximate, but by the end of the 1970s the United States had some 140 million of the 500 million television sets then in existence and almost half of the 1,100 million radios. The US photographic industry, which had kept in the forefront of technical development, was selling some 20 million cameras a year, and US citizens were shooting an estimated 10 billion exposures. The mushrooming US record industry was selling $4 billion worth of records and cassettes a year, supported by the existence of 75 million gramophones. If the film industry had declined in terms of the number of films produced, these maintained a disproportionate hold over world markets, and the high production cost of individual films was made possible by annual domestic ticket sales of around 1 billion a year.

Within this pattern of continued US dominance of an ever-expanding market, two other developments occurred. In the early 1960s Japanese companies began to emerge as world leaders in the production of electronic communications hardware. The basic strategy adopted by the Japanese throughout the spectrum of electronic goods is exemplified by video: entry into the market at the low-cost end, the establishment of a reputation for choice and reliability, and then a gradual take-over of the whole range of products (in 1980 the Japanese had 100 per cent of US domestic video and home-radio sales, as well as a major portion of the market for CB radio, television sets, electronic watches, and hi-fi equipment). The estimated Japanese share in the world market for consumer electronics was put at around one-third by this time. Parallel to this shift in equipment manufacture came a fresh concentration of power among the manufacturers of films, tapes, and records, so that the various media all came to be dominated by transnational companies – mostly US-based – which saw marketing in world terms. Most of these companies had close links with firms manufacturing equipment and materials. Often, in areas such as video, there were links with Japanese manufacturers too (Guback and Varis 1982).

Just as most of the key technical breakthroughs in television had been made in the United States, so too it was there that the computer – the key technology of the new age – was born. The world's first major digital computer, the giant ENIAC housed in the University of Pennsylvania which came into operation in 1949, was still a valve system, with no less than 18,000 hand-made vacuum tubes. But a prototype of the transistor had already been developed in the Bell Laboratories by this date (it was to lead to the first pocket radios in 1954). In 1958 the second major breakthrough was accomplished with the integrated circuit (or silicon chip), itself exploited commercially with pocket calculators and digital watches in 1971.

The need – particularly in the United States – to find commercial applications for wartime technologies and to use profitably the capacity built up in the wartime electronics industry can be seen to be responsible both for the development of the two major postwar technologies (television and the computer) and for the climate of opinion necessary for the successful launching of so many technical innovations in the field of communications (Winston 1986: 52). Television got under way in 1946 and sound tape was first introduced into radio the following year. 1948 brought the black-and-white polaroid camera (the most innovative photographic system for decades) as well as the introduction of the 33⅓ rpm long-playing record and the 45 rpm single. In 1950 reel-to-reel tape recorders were put on the market for the general public. Fast tri-X film came in 1954. The first broadcast-standard Ampex video tape recorder was demonstrated in 1956 and brought into use by the BBC about two years later. In 1958 the first fully automated still cameras were introduced, and also the first stereo records (which had ousted mono recordings within a decade). 1958 also saw the production of the light-weight professional Nagra tape recorder, to be backed up in the early 1960s by other key elements of the *cinéma-vérité* style of filming: light-weight 16 mm cameras (Arriflex BL and Eclair NPR) and the Angénieux zoom lens (1962).

1963 was a year which combined the polaroid colour system, the Kodak 126 instant-loading cartridge camera and the first demonstrations of the Philips sound cassette. 1965 brought both Super 8 film and the introduction to the west of the Sony portapak (the first black-and-white reel-to-reel portable video system), as well as demonstrations of colour video tape for broadcasting. In 1966 the Dolby noise-reduction system for sound recording made its appearance. By 1970 Sony had demonstrated its three-quarter-inch U-matic VTR, and the first true domestic video cassette recorders followed in 1972. That same year the Polaroid company introduced the SX-70 system (eliminating the protective peel-off covering). 1975 brought the Philips/Sony laser video disc, followed in 1978 by the compact disc, which was fully launched in the early 1980s. Sound and video tape were thus introduced in a climate of constant technical innovation.

The media industries

At this point it is perhaps appropriate to consider the organization of the media industries as they have emerged in the postwar era to form the context for the introduction of sound and video tape-recording technology. In absolute terms, the corporations which control the media industries are not large. Benjamin M. Compaigne (1979) points out that in 1978 General Motors had a greater revenue than all the US media industries, including book and newspaper publishing, combined. Already by 1977 only two media corporations appeared in the listing of the top fifty US industrial companies ranked in terms of revenue: Eastman Kodak ($5.9 billion), which ranked 29th, and RCA ($5.8 billion), which followed closely in 34th place. No other media company was ranked in the top 100, unless we include a corporation like Gulf and Western, which ranked 59th (with revenue of $3.6 billion), but whose film interests – the old Paramount company – contributed barely 9 per cent of this total.

Size is not, however, the sole measure of significance. Firstly, it must be remembered that the control of world markets by a handful of (mostly US-based) corporations is long-established, going back to the early years of the century in some instances. Secondly, the pattern of exploitation is broadly similar for all the media, so that the impact of one reinforces the others. The same strategy is constant, with products which have recovered their costs in the American market being sold world-wide at prices below those of any local production, but still making virtually 100 per cent profit for the transnationals. Thirdly, the pattern of production and flow of material characteristic of entertainment is echoed by that of information. The US and British dominance in the export of television fictional drama is exactly paralleled by the dominant role of US and British newsfilm agencies (Smith 1980; Mowlana 1985). Technical innovations mesh together to reinforce this system, so that satellite links and video tape can combine to allow the daily exchange of news items internationally, without the problems of air freight, customs, etc.

The media industries form part of the general pattern of western industrial development and commercial exploitation, but they also foster the consciousness that sustains this system (Enzensberger 1972). They share a common role, but there are nevertheless significant differences between the various media industries. The most striking instance of continued market dominance is that of Eastman Kodak, which still dwarfs its rivals in the photographic industry. Kodak's 1977 revenue of $5.9 billion was bigger than that of any individual broadcasting company, roughly equivalent to the world market in records, and about double that of the dozen biggest US film companies combined.

In view of its traditional failure to innovate or even to keep abreast of technology, it is hardly surprising that the record industry is now dominated by companies with major interests elsewhere, principally in broadcasting and electrical hardware. In the early 1980s just five transnational corporations dominated and were collectively responsible for some 60 per cent of the world market: CBS and RCA (subsidiaries of the US broadcasting companies), WEA (part of the US Kinney group), EMI (owned by the British Thorn Electrical) and Polygram (jointly owned by two European electrical giants, Siemens and Philips) (Wallis and Malm 1984: 74–119).

What was perhaps surprising was the extent to which they became profitable in the period after the war, particularly in the 1960s and 1970s. One path to prosperity during these years was the final breakthrough to genuine stereo hi-fi (although even this has now been taken a step further by the compact disc). But the major new consumer group discovered by the leisure and fashion industries during this period was that comprising young people in their teens and early twenties, who now had both leisure time and disposable incomes larger than ever before (Frith 1983: 7). By making itself a key element in the new youth culture, the world record industry rose to new heights of production and profitability. As a result, EMI which had been the world's largest record company when it was founded in 1931 and has remained an industry leader, had a mid-1970s revenue of about $1 billion. This figure was equalled in 1978 by Polygram, which had been formed by the merger of Deutsche Grammophon and Philips/Phonogram. In the mid-1970s CBS records contributed $485 million towards the parent company's overall revenue of $1.9 billion. Much of this huge revenue can be attributed to the popularity of individual stars who, having begun recording for the independents, quickly signed up with one of these major corporations. Thus Elvis Presley made no less than 31 million-selling records for RCA between 1956 and 1962, and the Beatles (with estimated world sales to 1980 of 100 million singles and 100 million LPs) gave new prosperity to EMI.

To show the extent of the operation of such corporations we may take the example of EMI, which has taken over such well-known names as The Gramophone Company, French Pathé Marconi, German Odeon and Electrola, American Capitol, etc. In the mid-1980s the company's activities covered the recording, manufacture, and distribution of records, tapes, compact discs, and music videos and embraced both pop and classical music. With headquarters in London and Los Angeles, EMI also had branches in well over thirty other countries, and licensees in twenty further states. The combination of transnational hardware and software companies – Thorn/EMI, Siemans-Philips/Polygram – already represents a considerable economic power. But there are further combinations which result from innovations needing the collaboration of Japanese electronics companies. Thus EMI participated with its sister company Toshiba in the 1982 Japanese launch of the compact disc, which had been developed by Philips in collaboration with Sony (its absence from the subsequent European launch was caused by a dispute over the royalties demanded by Philips).

Perhaps the most radical restructuring has been that of the film industry, where the traditional vertically integrated companies specializing solely in film but combining production, distribution, and exhibition were broken up by anti-trust rulings in 1948. Thereafter the companies controlling film theatres developed quite separately from the parent production companies. In this way, the Paramount theatre chain became part of the ABC television corporation, and Loew's, owner of the exhibition side of MGM, became a diversified company to which the film interests contributed a mere 1.3 per cent of a total revenue of $3.2 billion in 1977. The industry had to cope simultaneously with the impact of television and went through a period of great uncertainty. Eventually many of the film production companies, vulnerable after the loss of the exhibition outlets which had formed some 90 per cent of their assets, were swallowed up by huge entertainment and leisure service conglomerates.

Those that remained largely film companies – Columbia, say,

or Twentieth Century Fox – were in the $300 million–$450 million class in terms of revenue by the mid-1970s. Yet even where the old name persisted, film was often only a minority interest: contributing just 47 per cent of MGM's revenues, only 31 per cent for Warner Communications, and no more than 19 per cent for Walt Disney Productions, now largely a tourist and leisure-park concern. Some previously independent film interests found themselves submerged in huge conglomerates. While Universal was still able to contribute 58 per cent of MCA's revenues in 1977, United Artists made up just 12 per cent of the revenues of its parent company, Transamerica Corporation, and Paramount no more than 9 per cent of those of Gulf and Western. Films were now only part of the commercial interests of corporations which embraced such activities as hotels and restaurants, car parking and gambling, other forms of entertainment and leisure, and so on. The result was a total redefinition of film as a product, since cinema receipts were now only part of an overall package which included the sale of rights for network and cable screenings, subsidiary rights to noveletization, books about the making of the film, television spin-offs, sound-track recordings and cassettes, commercially retailed video tapes, as well as merchandizing tie-ins such as T-shirts, toys, games, comics, etc.

Such a reorganization of cinema as an industry is typical of the general drive to expand markets and to maximize sales during this period. A central feature has of course been the spread of television and its establishment as a dominant aspect of domestic life throughout the western industrialized world, together with the steady expansion of broadcasting in the Third World (Katz and Wedell 1978). With the exception of Eastman Kodak, the largest companies concerned directly with the sound and image media are the three US network corporations. RCA (owner of NBC) is easily the biggest, with assets and revenue equal to those of the other two networks, CBS and ABC, combined. All three are diversified companies, with interests in such areas as television production, records, and publishing. They have often been instrumental in providing the technical advice and training necessary for the establishment of broadcast systems in the Third World. One activity crucial to the flow of information world–wide (though marginal to these companies in terms of revenue) is their involvement in the production and distribution of newsfilm. In addition, the contracts for network screening which only they can offer are vital to the nature of US television, although the actual production of dramatic entertainment has generally been left to the Hollywood-based companies. Since the 1920s the latter have had a global distribution system which has proved as useful for the flow of television programming as it has traditionally been for films.

The pattern of growth has been constant, aided by the companies' willingness to diversify. For the US film industry and the transnational record companies this has meant partly setting up distribution companies specifically to exploit markets – such as, say, West Africa – previously considered too small to be of interest. For radio, when it was displaced by television as the focus for the whole family, continued growth and profitability meant finding new listeners – hence the proliferation of specialized radio channels, each with its own target audience (and hence its potential for advertising revenue).

Despite the new importance of Japanese electronics companies in the manufacture of communications hardware, the picture is basically one of remarkable continuity. The old names – Warner, Disney, MGM – still appear, Nipper continues to advertise HMV records, Eastman Kodak and RCA still occupy the commanding heights. Just as certain seemingly viable innovations – such as laser video – have been virtually discarded, so too several promised revolutions have failed to occur (Winston 1986). A key example here – at least outside the United States – is cable television. But at the time of writing a further revolution in television seems imminent: satellite television. This could well inaugurate a new era of fundamental change, destroying the old economy of television in the UK, based on a shortage of channels, and bringing in powerful new interests from newspaper publishing, such as the Rupert Murdoch and Robert Maxwell empires.

To date, however, the existing structures have proved remarkably resilient and capable of controlling the flood of technological innovation. Postwar developments hitherto are strongly reminiscent of the change undergone by photography at the end of the nineteenth century. There is a continuing interplay between greater individual access and increased external control. We can see this split in the mid-1970s with the simultaneous development of CB radio on the one hand and laser video and compact discs on the other. The same tendencies are to be found throughout the period. After the Second World War there was a concentration of industrial power into monopolies and networks of interlocked and collaborating corporations. In this sense there is an increasing separation of producer from consumer. A resulting trend has been the imposition of a standardized, commercialized culture world-wide: along with coke and hamburgers, the same pop records and television series are present everywhere, threatening to obliterate local cultural traditions.

At the same time, the postwar period has seen a democratization of the media akin to that allowed by celluloid for photography in the 1890s, with individual control, access, and even creative production increasingly available. While commercial film production has been dominated by the $40 million blockbuster, the advent of television also fostered developments in 16 mm film technology (fully adequate for the image requirements of the new medium), and one result has been a massive growth of independent film-making throughout the west. Sound tape has had the same impact on the recording industry, fostering the establishment of dozens of independent, low-cost recording companies. More recently the sound cassette – an accessible and comparatively inexpensive technology – has allowed even small countries to develop their own music recording industries. Video is a key continuation of this democratizing tradition, as a system which allows personal recording and creative production as well as the consumption of pre-recorded, pre-packaged material.

Sound tape

Although tape recording was introduced commercially only long after the gramophone, a first system – the telegraphone – was in fact patented in 1898 by a Danish engineer, Valdemar Poulsen, who demonstrated it with some success at the 1900

74

Paris Exhibition. However, Poulsen's device had a number of problems which prevented it from becoming widely developed. The steel wire used was not an ideal recording substance, the adoption of telephone receivers and transmitters meant that only speech (and not music) could be recorded, and there was no possibility of amplifying the signal output. As a result, progress was extremely slow until the 1920s and the tape recorder was confined to use as an office dictating machine. It is worth noting that the developments in housing and employment which led to the emergence of the home as the centre for audio-visual entertainments also saw the evolution of the office as a direct consequence of the growth of business corporations. As a result, the late nineteenth century saw a parallel burst of office innovation: the modern calculator (1875), the telephone (1876), the shift-key typewriter (1878), and so on (Winston 1986: 125).

Although it was eventually to prove a dead-end, work using metal as a recording substance continued in England. In 1929 Louis Blattner was the first to record on a thin steel band, producing a machine with half-an-hour's recording potential and targeted at film and record companies as well as office users. A highly polished tungsten steel strip was used in the tape recorder developed by Kurt Stille in collaboration with Marconi in 1934. This machine was in use at the BBC from the mid-1930s, although the thin steel strip had to run at very high speeds and was not an ideal recording substance. The Marconi-Stille recorder was considered so dangerous that the attendant had to be housed in a separate room, and when the tape broke, it had to be arc-welded together again (Mackay 1981: 25).

Poulsen's 1898 patent had speculated on the possibility of using paper coated with magnetized metal dust, and this was the line of development followed by Fritz Pfleumer in Germany. In a 1928 patent Pfleumer proposed paper tape coated with iron oxide, and when this paper base was replaced by plastic, electro-magnetic recording could be commercialized, with tape made in 1934 by BASF (a subsidiary of Siemens) and the recorder – the magnetophon – built by AEG, another of the major German electrical companies. First marketed in 1937 as an improved office machine, the magnetophon was subsequently developed as a broadcast-standard recorder from the early 1940s. Like the

Agfacolor system developed by I. G. Farben, electro-magnetic recording became part of the spoils of war, and a device on which all the pioneering work that had been undertaken in Europe was brought to full commercial development – without patent problems – after 1945 in the United States by the 3M company, makers of 'Scotch' tape, and by Ampex.

Far from being welcomed by the radio industry in the 1940s, sound recording was opposed by the networks, who still saw radio as what it had always been, an essentially live medium. They were reinforced in their views by the fact that current disc-recording techniques gave a demonstrably poorer sound quality than live transmission. Instead of backing research into new recording systems, however, the networks simply required that shows be repeated, live, for audiences in the different US time zones. Pressure for recording came, therefore, from the performers, and it was a dispute over the issue of recording which took Bing Crosby, then a top radio star, from NBC to ABC in 1947. Crosby's needs were met by Ampex which, late in 1947, produced a reel-to-reel tape recorder which matched radio requirements. Other broadcasters followed Crosby's example, and sound tape quickly established itself as an adjunct of broadcasting, first in the United States and then elsewhere. By the beginnings of the 1950s tape recorders for the domestic market had been developed and put on sale.

The key step in the development of the tape recorder was the combination of a non-magnetic plastic base and an iron-oxide coating (analogous to celluloid and emulsion in photography). This has allowed constant progress towards 'high-fidelity' recording, as the coating has been constantly refined and improved: ferric oxide, chrome dioxide, 'ferri-chrome', etc. The electronic aspects of the recorder have also been constantly improved: amplification, equalization, noise reduction (first through the addition of a 'bias' tone at a frequency above that which the human ear can detect and then, since the mid-1960s, by the Dolby system). But sound and video recorders both retain aspects of nineteenth-century technology in that their mechanical systems remain equally important. Unlike computers which can operate at incredible speeds because they lack moving mechanical parts, tape recorders need systems to keep tape speed steady and uniform when recording and replaying, and to keep the tape away from the heads in fast-forward or rewind modes. The mechanical solutions to these fundamental problems would have few surprises for a nineteenth-century engineer like Poulsen.

Applications of sound tape

The advent of plastic tape in the late 1940s had the same explosive impact on sound recording as the development of the celluloid base had had on photography some sixty years earlier. Sound tape found application in the needs of the broadcasting institutions – the ability to pre-record awkwardly timed events, to repeat successful programmes, to maintain archives in a simple way, and in general terms to turn programming into a flexible commodity. But its impact has extended far beyond radio – to the film industry, the record business, and even to the definitions of western music itself (with the creation of electronic music and *musique concrète*). There was a double pattern of impact. In its original reel-to-reel format, tape had some personal and domestic application for home recording, but contrary to initial expectations it did not become the key medium for the consumption of pre-recorded music. However, reel-to-reel machines did have an enormous and lasting impact on all the industries using recorded sound. With the introduction of the Philips sound cassette in the mid-1960s a second and perhaps even wider-ranging impact was achieved, allowing easier production and marketing of pre-recorded music, giving far greater access and control to the consumer, and fostering new attitudes to the whole business of listening.

Radio has always been a speaker's medium, giving a key role to presenters who link items and introduce records or outside broadcasts, and to story-tellers able to devise ways of utilizing the essential intimacy of the medium so as to create a uniquely close link between the listener and an imaginary world free from the physical constraints of real time and space. Reel-to-reel recorders altered nothing of this fundamental quality, but did allow a new informality and control for the creative use of sound within radio.

Disc and steel-band recording were cumbersome, studio-bound and difficult to edit, whereas reel-to-reel machines were portable and highly flexible. They allowed radio programmes to be compiled out of a fast-flowing collage of commentary, comment, and interview. This in turn fostered the emergence of fresh forms of documentary programming, which could draw on popular speech recorded on location, instead of the educated, upper-class, studio-recorded tones so beloved of John Reith. Charles Parker's pioneering *Radio Ballads* series for the BBC, which began in the 1950s, is one supreme achievement in this vein, combining the words of ordinary people recorded in informal situations with ballads by Ewan MacColl and Peggy Seeger. Parker's fate – fired by the BBC in 1970 despite the universal acclaim of his work – points clearly to the political potential of sound tape and the importance of the specific opportunities it offers. To give working people space to offer their own views in an otherwise middle-class dominated, hierarchical medium is already a radical step, a political act which the authorities may well find intolerable.

Parallel to this fresh potential for documentary was sound tape's contribution to radio drama, which it enabled to become a powerful writer's medium (McWhinnie 1959). Tape did nothing to diminish the immediacy of the human voice on radio or the medium's possibilities for evoking distant or futuristic worlds. Rather it made a key contribution to augmenting the impact of sound drama through the new control over pacing and rhythm which it offered to producers, the ease with which editing could be undertaken, and the new range of sound effects which could be created by mixing and manipulating various sound sources. The work of such writers as Dylan Thomas, Harold Pinter, and Samuel Beckett exploits to the full these potentials.

Sound tape also had a revolutionary effect on cinema, although this is ignored in most standard film histories. The studio production methods of the classic Hollywood era from around 1930 to the early 1950s were largely determined by the need to get adequate results from cumbersome sound-recording equipment. Systems such as playback (re-recording a pre-recorded music track simultaneously with the dialogue), back projection (refilming pre-shot location footage as a background to dialogue scenes shot in the studio) and post-synchronization (substituting studio-recorded voices for the actual sounds recorded in the studio or on location) were all designed specifically to counter problems of sound recording (Altman 1980a: 5–7). Tape recorders allowed both greater control within the studio and also freedom to record on location. This was a key factor in the move away from the studio movie in the 1950s, for three-quarters of the industry had already abandoned optical recording for tape by 1951 (Fielding 1967: 216).

In film editing, too, tape brought a new flexibility. Transfer to magnetic tracks (sound tape sprocketed like film stock) allowed sound and image to be run side by side on an editing machine and prompted experiments to set one against the other. Ways were quickly found to cut and join tape so as to allow sound edits to pass imperceptibly in the cinema. Moreover, it was also discovered that the Scotch tape used to join cut lengths of sound tape in the editing was ideal for joining celluloid too. Whereas the old cement joins used for film editing had meant a loss of two frames at every cut, the new tape splices were easy to adjust, again prompting a more innovative approach. By the mid-1950s the technical basis was there for both the more adventurous forms of documentary and the radically modernist experiments with time and narrative in the feature film, which are so characteristic of the New Wave period (Vaughan 1974: 73–85.

The development of the Nagra – a fully professional tape recorder just the size of a small suitcase – by Stefan Kudelski in 1958 made flexibility of synchronous sound shooting a real possibility, especially when the Nagra was used with one of the new light-weight Eclair or Arriflex 16 mm cameras developed at the same time. The result was an image-sound combination fully adequate for television showing and a new observational style – *cinéma vérité* or direct cinema – was born around 1960. The feature film industry itself, though converted to tape for recording, continued with more elaborate sound procedures involving dubbing and mixing, and optical sound tracks were retained for exhibition purposes. Indeed in the late 1970s some producers began to adopt the sophisticated methods employed by that time in the recording industry: radio microphones, multitrack recording, twenty-four track mixing and Dolby noise reduction (Altman 1980a: 9–11).

Initially, in the 1940s, tape was thought to offer a considerable challenge to the record industry. Tapes matched the best sound that discs could offer and in addition they were compact, durable, able to run continuously for half-an-hour, and easy to repair if damaged. At first there was no system of mass producing pre-recorded tapes, but clearly this would soon be developed. To make matters worse, retail record sales were falling (from over $200 million in 1947 to around $157 million in 1949 in the United States). As a result, the record companies were galvanized into action in the biggest transformation of the industry since the 1920s. In June 1948 Columbia launched the LP record, made in unbreakable vinylite and playing at 33⅓ rpm – the product of years of research by a team under Peter Goldmark. The LP offered new potential (in continuity, reduced surface wear, cost-effectiveness, and accessibility) to classical recordings, and eventually became a creative medium (the LP 'album') for ambitious pop performers. At almost the same time – January 1949 – RCA Victor brought out the 45 rpm 'single' with the same running time as the old 78 rpm records (the extended-play 45 rpm was not produced until 1953). This, too, was made of vinylite, and the new format – light and unbreakable, easy to handle and to transport – made it ideal for mass distribution and for use by disc jockeys within radio. It made a decisive contribution to the creation of the new, immediate yet casual relationship with the listener which is characteristic of pop music (Belz 1972: 54).

With these changes the gramophone easily held off the reel-to-reel recorder as the medium for playing pre-recorded music (a superiority which lasted until the advent of the Philips cassette in the mid-1960s). But the creative recording potential of tape was fully exploited. Various takes of classical music performances could be invisibly edited together and wrong notes eliminated. As multitrack facilities were developed, the studio could become a creative environment for pop groups. Yet tape also meant that recordings could be made away from the central studio as well. The early 1950s saw the emergence of a whole mass of new independent record companies, making profits from records by artists of more limited audience appeal (including the so-called 'race' records, recordings of black artists intended solely for black audiences). With the old monopoly control in temporary abeyance and new areas of music steadily becoming available, the stage was set for the huge upsurge of pop music which began in the 1950s. Between 1954 and 1957 record sales doubled – from $213 million to $460 million – and this rate of expansion continued through the subsequent decades to reach $4 billion in 1980. Rock music, drawing on elements from black musical culture, became the first form of popular music for which the record is the key element – the 'original' as it were.

The sound cassette, introduced in the mid-1960s and becoming widespread in the 1970s, has had a fresh impact on the recording industry in precisely those areas least affected by reel-to-reel recorders, namely the marketing of pre-recorded music to consumers and full user-access to home recording, thereby continuing the sales momentum in the industry. Combined with the easily portable transistorized recorder, the cassette gave an alternative outlet for new releases. It also prompted the re-release of recordings deleted from the catalogue. This is part of the industry's constant striving to re-use existing recorded material (transfers from 78s to LP, digitalized sound, reissues in compact-disc format, etc).

The new cassette system also proved more universally utilizable than the electric gramophone and discs sensitive to heat and damp. From the 1970s onwards it became possible for villagers in remote parts of the Third World to hear pop music before they could have access to electricity or piped water. The impact on distance teaching methods has also been enormous. Anthony Bates notes, for example, that 'audio-cassettes have been the Open University's most sucessful media innovation' (Bates, 1984, 206). Hand-in-hand with this increased availability of pre-recorded material has gone greater access to recording itself. Disc production has always been a specialized, high-cost industry, located predominantly in the highly industrialized countries. But mastering on tape and distributing through mass-produced cassette copies is a far more accessible technology, and in the 1970s and 1980s small countries in the west and developing countries in the Third World could begin to counter the flood of music from the transnationals with at least some locally produced material. In this way the sound-recording industry has become as widely diffused as film production, offering local artists at least a possibility of becoming more widely known (Wallis and Malm 1984).

The cassette recorder functions as a two-way machine, allowing home recording from disc, radio, cassette, or microphone – as well as replay. With this technology it is a small step from legal individual home taping to large-scale commercial piracy: in a country like Tunisia 90 per cent of cassettes on sale are calculated to be pirated, and for Singapore the export of pirated cassettes is an important contributor to the national economy (Wallis and Malm 1984: 288–9). The triple market of independent production, home taping, and piracy opens up a huge market for the sale of blank cassettes, akin to that for photographic materials. Philips seem to have recognized from the start that the sound cassette recorder opened up a new era in sound recording, since it offered the rights to the use of its patented system freely to all other manufacturers. Certainly the sound cassette, like the xerox copier and the video cassette, is a form of technology which breaks down the old barriers of copyright. However, we need to be susipcious of the claims by the transnationals that they need to be compensated (by a levy or tax on blank cassettes) for the losses caused by piracy and home taping. Certainly artists lose out on royalties because of these activities, but the major companies normally own or are closely linked to companies manufacturing the equipment and materials which make such copying activities possible.

Video tape

By the time that video came into wide use, film's range of applications had come to be reflected in a clear, fixed hierarchy of formats: 35 mm for the feature film industry, advertising, and film theatre release; 16 mm for television, documentary and avant-garde and student production, and for non-commercial and educational distribution; 8 mm or Super 8 for domestic shooting and viewing ('home movies'). Video has an even wider range of formats: reel-to-reel and cassette, two-inch, one-inch, three-quarter-inch, half-inch, and even quarter-inch systems. Although these can be broadly distinguished in a hierarchy of cost and image-sound quality in relation to production, there are far more overlaps than with film. There are two main reasons for this. Television demands only the visual equivalent to 16 mm film, so the range is narrower. Moreover, the past thirty years have seen enormous developments in video technology – far greater than during any similar period of film-making – so that half-inch casette systems have been used for both domestic and fully professional production.

The advent of the home video recorder has clouded issues still further, since, at the point of commercial distribution and sale, material originally produced on any film or video standard is reduced to the lowest (domestic) level. When tapes are viewed, the hierarchical distinction between a multimillion-dollar feature film and a domestic recording of a family wedding is erased. There is no clear marking-off of domestic production, and this level must be taken into account – alongside the more professional applications – in any comprehensive approach to the medium. Just as historians of photography have to consider the snapshot as well as the most sophisticated studio product (Beloff 1985: 179–204) so too any study of video must cover the whole range from two-inch quadruplex to domestic half-inch cassette.

Despite these confusions and overlaps, the clearest approach to video remains in terms of levels of application. It was in 1956 that Ampex demonstrated the first broadcast-standard video recorder. This two-inch, reel-to-reel machine used four video heads (hence the name 'quadruplex'). Though expensive to buy and install, these recorders were comparatively cheap to use in a broadcast context and quickly replaced the old film-plus-telecine systems, which gave a poorer image quality at higher cost. The fact that recorders giving high-quality recordings on two-inch tape became the broadcast standard has had important consequences for video. Because this led to the development of outside-broadcast units which are as cumbersome as the old (pre-tape) film location units, film and television drama continue to have their location sequences shot on film. Purely video production remains inhibited by industrial inertia and understandable union doubts over lowered crewing levels.

Although one-inch, reel-to-reel systems were introduced in the early 1960s for industrial use, the next real breakthrough came almost a decade after the Ampex innovation, in 1965, when Sony introduced the reel-to-reel, black-and-white portapak, which used half-inch tape, helical scanning, and a transistorized recorder. With other Japanese companies – such as Hitachi and Panasonic – producing similar machines for industrial use, the problem of compatibility arose, and was solved, temporarily at least, with the introduction of an intercompany standard: EIAJ (Electric Industries Association of Japan). However, a decisive advance was already being prepared by Sony, which in 1970 demonstrated its U-matic format, three-quarter-inch cassette system, introduced into Britain some two years later. Editing video tape recorders and portable battery-charged cameras were added to the system, and this format became for a time the industrial (non-broadcast) standard. But technical progress and change have been constant, and almost immediately work began on systems designed to bring industrial portable recording closer to broadcast standards with the development of both the 'high-band', U-matic format and the Sony Betacam half-inch cassette system.

The third video market was opened up in 1972 by the first Philips video cassette recorder, a half-inch cassette machine designed specifically for the domestic market so as to allow 'time-shifting' (the recording of awkwardly timed broadcast programmes and their replay at leisure). Philips eventually lost their control of this market to two mutually incompatible Japanese systems, Sony's betamax and the even more popular VHS format, both introduced into Britain in 1978. By the beginning of the 1980s home recorders were equipped with a whole range of features related to off-air recording: digital timing, fast-forward and rewind 'search' functions, freeze-frame and slow-motion facilities, remote control, etc. As they began to be installed in ever greater numbers a new market – for the sale and hire of pre-recorded cassettes – was opened up.

Applications of video

In considering the applications of video it is useful to distinguish between three very different areas: the use of video in broadcasting, the spread of the domestic video cassette recorder, and the creative use of video as a medium in its own right. Within broadcasting, video's role largely parallels that of sound tape in radio. It has served to turn news items and television programmes into commodities to be bought and sold between networks and across national boundaries. Within the studio and for much outside broadcasting (particularly sport, where the ability to provide instant replays via magnetic disc recordings is a major advantage) video has been adopted as the normal recording medium. However, for several reasons – particularly the effectiveness of professional 16 mm, synch-sound film systems, the adoption of video as a production medium for location drama and documentary shooting has been slow. Where it has been used, however, it has often proved highly effective (one thinks, for example, of four episodes of *Boys from the Blackstuff*) (Millington and Nelson 1986: 109–21).

The very effectiveness of video as a means of recording multi-camera studio or outside broadcast unit output has paradoxically led to its being overlooked. It is so efficient that it becomes invisible (there is no way of distinguishing formally a live broadcast from one which is 'recorded live' and transmitted later). At first sight, therefore, the videoing of programme material would seem to offer video no more scope for creativity than a xerox copying machine. Certainly, just as we can separate the 'tape music' of Stockhausen and Berio from music which is simply 'taped', so too we can distinguish specifically video production from this mere video-recording of broadcast output. But no recording medium is wholly transparent, and although the application of video initially had little impact on programme forms, it has gradually begun to change the look and texture of television broadcast output – through the use of replays in multi-camera sports reporting, the application of video editing to pop programming and commercials, and the link with other electronic systems in computer-generated and video-recorded credit titles.

It remains true, however, that outside of broadcasting, all the dominant commercial applications of video exploit little more than its simple recording ability. In common parlance, a 'video' may be several things:

1 A feature film reproduced on video tape for sale or hire in an alternative (domestic) market.
2 An educational or instructional tape – on cooking or keeping fit, for example – which will probably have been shot in a multi-camera television studio and merely recorded on video.
3 A pop promo, which may well have been transferred to video and processed for its special effects with video equipment, but which will almost certainly have been shot on film stock.

None of these examples of a 'video' is – significantly enough – an expression of the specificity of video production.

Despite these handicaps there has been an enormous and growing use of video in the non-broadcast sector. This has been largely in the corporate sector, where video has proved itself to be a flexible and effective medium for information, promotion, and training. There has also been a wide application to such areas as social and community work. However, the more overtly creative use of the medium has been more limited, and although video's potential has been seized on by some artists, the body of video art cannot at present be said to match the achievements of electronic tape music. These aspects of video as a specific production medium will be dealt with in greater detail in a subsequent chapter, but meanwhile the domestic applications of video need to be considered since these form an important influence on video production.

Sales of domestic video recorders have been particularly buoyant in Britain, which now has one of the highest densities of any country in the world, with some 8.5 million video recorders sold by the end of 1985 (that is, sets in over 40 per cent of the nation's households). The most widely quoted impact of video has been its contribution to the further decline of the cinema, particularly in Britain, where annual attendances have fallen from their 1951 peak of 1.3 billion to barely 50 million by the mid-1980s (there is some dispute about exact figures). With broadcast television showing around 1,000 feature films a year (951, for example, in 1983) and the majority of hired or purchased video tapes also being feature films, the film theatre has been displaced from its central position in the national entertainment spectrum. A 1984 survey found that almost two-thirds of those questioned thought that the best way to watch a film was on television or on a video cassette recorder, compared with just under a third who preferred to visit the cinema (Docherty, Morrison, and Tracey 1986: 81–5). In view of this, it is not altogether surprising that by 1984 the 2.5 million sales of pre-recorded cassettes and the 175 million hire transactions far outnumbered the 54 million cinema admissions (Wade 1985: 22–8).

While, for devotees of cinema, this may signify a cultural decline, in global terms it is more appropriate to see it as a convergence of the products of the sound and image media which parallels the earlier described convergence of economic power in the relevant industries. The shift which has made the home the focus of leisure and entertainment in the twentieth century is not conditioned simply by technological changes within the communications industry, but by broader social developments within western industrial societies (new patterns of work, remuneration, housing, family organization, leisure). These developments were not fully under way in the late nineteenth century, so that while the gramophone focused largely on the home, and photography built its mass market on domestic life and personal travel, the cinema was able to flourish as a theatrical entertainment. Since the 1920s the broadcast media have developed in ways which strengthen this focus on the home. Initially this existed solely in terms of transmission, and tended to displace rather than incorporate earlier forms of sound and image recording (records and films). But with the development of the tape media, the advantages of individual access, control, and recording – previously characteristic only of photography – have been added to the scope of the sound and image media within the domestic context.

Just as the radio companies, by electrifying the gramophone and bringing synchronous sound to cinema, created new fusions between previously divergent media, so too the tape media have brought wider choice, in terms of when broadcast programming is consumed and which pre-recorded material is acquired. The result has been a triple growth in the market: in terms of equipment, pre-recorded products, and recording material. Capitalism needs to keep creating new and improved domestic consumer durables, hence the moves in television from 405 to 625 lines and from black-and-white to colour, and in recorded sound from the gramophone to the hi-fi system and now to the laser-read compact disc. The reel-to-reel tape recorder did not fully fit this requirement in terms of the domestic market, but sound and video cassette recorders have proved to be products which consumers can see as usefully supplementing (not replacing) their radios and television sets.

Perhaps the only safe prediction to make about the future is that things will change more slowly than manufacturers claim. At the time of writing the sound and image media are embarking on a new wave of innovation which may or may not produce lasting changes. The compact disc has been successfully launched, but whether it will replace the vinyl LP record within the predicted three years remains to be seen. Yet already, before it is fully established, a rival is on the horizon in the form of digital audio tape (DAT) which will give compact disc quality from a small cassette and provide both record and replay facilities. The system has been several times announced by Japanese manufacturers, but has yet to be launched. A similar upheaval is threatened in the video cassette market – the real success story of the 1980s – with the initial marketing of the new 8 mm video format (about the size of current audio cassettes) which is planned to replace the existing incompatible Betamax, VHS, and Philips V2000 systems. But will customers be willing to replace recently purchased expensive VCRs?

One thing that is certain is that when a new channel is established, a new market for original pre-recorded sounds and images is created and a new value is given to existing material in the archives. First television, then the video cassette recorder (and potentially cable and satellite systems too) give a fresh life to old films which have exhausted their commercial worth in the film theatres. The LP persuades sound enthusiasts to discard their old gramophones and collections of 78s, and so too the compact disc, as it establishes itself, may lead to a similar replacement of expensively purchased LPs (half-a-million CD-players had been sold in Britain by 1986). In addition, even people with large collections of LPs who are satisfied with the sound they can achieve at home are persuaded to duplicate their collections with cassettes for the car or portable recorder. The third and often unconsidered market – that for recording material (blank video cassettes) – can also be hugely profitable, as the example of the photographic industry shows, and complaints – as with sound cassettes – about piracy from corporations which market both blank and pre-recorded video cassettes need to be regarded with some scepticism.

The concentration on the home might seem an extreme limitation for the entertainment industry, and certainly first-run cinemas (establishing the commercial worth of a film), discos, and juke boxes continue to have their place. But the crucial centre of the whole commercial operation is the domestic market, now complex and multifaceted: a main TV set in the living-room, but also portable TVs for the children or in the bedroom; the main hi-fi system for the adults, but also cheap record decks for the teenagers and Sony-walkman devices for jogging or riding in the tube; no longer a radio in the living-room, but inevitably a transistor in the kitchen for news and music, and a radio and cassette deck in the car. Perhaps the best way of looking at the domestic video recorder is to consider what it adds to existing systems in terms of scope and diversity: it offers a control over the output of the television set with which it shares the screen, a supplement to the gramophone and sound cassette player in choice of pre-recorded material (now images as well as sounds), and an equivalent to the home-movie system in its ability to play personally produced material (such as wedding tapes).

Further reading

For the growth of the media industries, see Compaigne (1979) and Tunstall (1977). A popular history of postwar British television is Black (1972), and Tunstall (1983) surveys the whole post-1945 British media scene. There are a number of Unesco studies of the multinationals and the one-way flow of film and television material: Nordenstreng and Varis (1974) and Varis (1985) are particularly useful. For the flow of news and information see Smith (1980) and Mowlana (1985). For the postwar transformation of the music industry a useful guide is Frith (1983); for developments outside the dominant west see Wallis and Malm (1984). Developments in electronic music are covered in Mackay (1981). Little has been written about the impact of sound tape on cinema – Neale (1985), for example, ignores it totally – but Vaughan (1974) gives a vivid (if brief) picture of the impact of tape on film editing, and Doane (1980b) is helpful. Even less has been written about specifically video developments, but Marshall (1979) offers a brief history, and Wade (1985) provides much helpful statistical information on the industry.

PART TWO
VIDEO IN ITS
SOCIAL CONTEXT

With the development of the electronic media, the industry that shapes consciousness has become the pacemaker for the social and economic development of societies in the late industrial age. It infiltrates into all other sectors of production, takes over more and more directional and control functions, and determines the standard of the prevailing technology.

(Hans Magnus Enzensberger 1972: 99)

As we have seen, the media reproducing sounds and images are all products of western industrial society and therefore develop historically in relation to the changes undergone by industrial production: the transformation wrought by the application of electricity and electronics and the steady shift towards the transnational, multimedia corporation. The reproduction of sounds and images also reflects the west's dominance of world trade: films, records, cassettes, and television programmes, as well as equipment, all follow a one-way flow from the highly industrialized countries to the less developed societies of the Third World. In industrial terms our examination of video within the context of the other media which have developed over the past 150 years shows that its actual place is far more central than that of film, which so often overshadows it in discussions of media developments.

In Part Two, which considers the social context of video, we need to continue the approach adopted in Part One, that is, to see video in relation to the other media. Video is not an isolated phenomenon but the end product of a century and a half of commercial endeavour. Chapter 4 looks in greater detail at the ways in which the various media have been applied in society. The interaction of economic, social, and cultural forms is inevitably highly complex. Although the pattern of industrial development which formed the subject of Part One is crucial to the understanding of the new media, it would be wrong to see it as a process which *determines* the social application of these new media in any simple way. These media are products of the wider developments, but all bring something new and unexpected to the society in which they are born. Similarly, many of the key issues of the twentieth century find their reflection in the new media – the shifting relations of industry and state, for example, or the constant battle to assert individual freedom in face of the imposition of political and social control – but recorded sounds and images play an ambiguous role in these shifts and struggles.

The next task, which forms the subject of chapter 5, is to untangle the entwined and overlapping production systems of film, television, and video, so as to define just what is characteristic of each and just what it is that video brings which is new. A production system is akin to what Thomas Kuhn in his book on *The Structure of Scientific Revolutions* calls a 'paradigm'; that is to say, it is a cluster of aims, attitudes, assumptions, unquestioned views, projects of capital investment, types of personnel recruitment, work practices, contractual requirements, union agreements, and so on. These come together *to make a system that works*. This in turn becomes the learned practice of the institution, enshrined in the various technical manuals, where the elements of the system are depicted as natural 'rules', which need no stated origin or source of their authority. Video, as the third of the major systems of sound-image reproduction, has inevitably had its own specific approach cluttered with practices and assumptions inherited from its predecessors.

As a further stage, in chapter 6, we shift our emphasis from the ways in which images and sounds are recorded to the ways in which they function as systems of representation, that is to say, the manner in which the spectator interacts with the fictional and non-fictional 'worlds' constructed in the produced work. If the moment of production can be defined as the encounter between the maker and his or her materials (the recording equipment on the one hand, the sets, locations, performers, etc. on the other), the world constructed in and by the work needs to be measured and assessed within the context of the spectator's response. How is the spectator addressed? What assumptions are made about his or her situation, attention, identification? What operations are involved in the interaction of spectator and text in the translation of elements drawn from an observed or enacted reality into systems which represent human activities, aspirations, and dreams? The best starting-point for a consideration of these issues is the spectator.

Here, as elsewhere in Part Two, we can draw much from the analysis undertaken by film theorists during the past decades. Once more, however, we shall find that the fictional feature film, which has so regularly been assumed to be the key audio-visual system for producing meaning and pleasure is in many ways uncharacteristic of the sound and image media in general. The reasons for this lie in film's development as a theatrical entertainment, which gives it particular characteristics not found in systems devised for domestic consumption. Despite the fact that fictional feature films are the most costly and highly wrought of all audio-visual artefacts, documentary production – which most film theorists have ignored and deemed marginal – can be seen in many ways to be far more typical and revealing of the overall pattern of sound and image production.

4 SOCIAL FORMS

> Every new medium of the past century has been greeted
> with euphoria, and also dire prediction. Each has been
> seen by some as leading to a more richly informed
> public, the fulfilment of democracy, and by others as
> leading to increased social control, a diminishing of the
> individual.
>
> (Erik Barnouw 1982: 491–2)

In considering the new media in society, we need to bear in
mind the whole set of new principles which they introduce into
western culture: not only their impact on business and commerce,
but also the fundamental changes they have caused to the existing
definition of the relationships between art, entertainment, and
society. The capitalist economic system has a structure whereby
the producer is separate from the consumer, but the two are
brought together through a transaction by means of which a
commodity created by human labour is bought and sold:

   producer – commodity – consumer

This finds its echo in the dominant system of western art, at least
up to the middle of the twentieth century. The artist is separated
off from the community at large (reduced to a 'public', or
simply 'spectators' and 'listeners'), just as the artwork produced
is clearly differentiated from natural phenomena. In this way a
new but parallel relationship is formed:

   artist – artwork – public

Even before the birth of the new recording media a kind of
bastardized variant had developed linking commerce and art, for
example in the music hall. This variant is modern entertainment,
in which a specialist professional entertainer produces a per-

formance designed for – and marketed to – an audience which pays for its pleasure:

entertainer – performance – paying audience

The new media reproducing sounds and images were of necessity contained within this three-part structure: we date the birth of cinema as 28 December 1895 because this was the first day on which moving pictures were shown to a *paying* audience (there had been several earlier projections). But the new media did not simply record the artist's or entertainer's performance and so turn it into a commodity able to be mass produced and marketed more widely. It is a measure of their fundamental novelty that they brought all aspects of the three-part structure into question.

Consider, for example, the crucial relations and distinctions between artist and public, entertainer and audience. An early challenge to these barriers came from photography, although at first the new medium assumed a traditional social mode, with professional photographers producing portraits for sale to their clients. Eventually, however, photography was democratized in the 1880s and 1890s through its application to the leisure activity of all. With the Kodak camera everyone could take their own photographs and since, in an important sense, all photographs are equal and equivalent, everyone was now – potentially at least – a portraitist, a reporter, even an artist. At present, sound and video recording have something of the same potential.

By the 1920s – moving in quite the opposite direction – film had redefined and totally mystified the performer–audience relationship. Whereas the music-hall stars, for all their real popularity, could be said to be serving their public, the new stars of cinema, such as Charlie Chaplin, Douglas Fairbanks, and Mary Pickford, became universal celebrities of a quite new kind (Schickel 1976: 97). Adoring crowds flocked to greet them everywhere on their travels. They had access to the palaces of royalty without ever, for that reason, losing their common touch: Chaplin was known to, and loved by, king and peasant alike. Thus in a transformation echoed, and to some extent amplified, in the record industry from the 1960s onwards, the stars became mythical beings, while their audiences were reduced to the status of fans or adoring slaves. The personal magnetism of figures like Chaplin and Elvis Presley can go some way towards explaining this phenomenon, but broadcasting gave stardom a new twist by turning those filling the apparently most banal roles – the television presenters and newscasters – into million-dollar-a-year celebrities.

Silent films, records, and radio all offer quite new experiences of performance: on the one hand, the visual spectacle turned into a ghostly parade deprived of all its inherent and incidental sounds (although this was from the start partly concealed by the use of accompanying music); on the other hand, sound without an apparent source, separated from vision and from the human body. It is perhaps difficult for us today to recapture the initial impact of these amputations of experience, since we are so familiar with them in our everyday lives. But Maxim Gorky's account of a visit to the cinematograph in 1896 does help capture some of the novelty of Lumière's invention:

> Yesterday I was in the kingdom of the shadows. If only you knew how strange it is to be there. There are no sounds, no colours. There, everything – the earth, the trees, the people, the water, the air – is tinted in the single tone of grey: in a grey sky there are grey rays of sunlight; in grey faces, grey eyes, and the leaves of the trees are grey like ashes. This is not life but the shadow of life, and this is not movement but the soundless shadow of movement.
>
> (cit. Taylor 1979: 2)

As far as music was concerned, the processes of sound recording and of reproduction without a human presence represented a break with tradition as momentous as the separation of western music from its earlier religious context in the sixteenth and seventeenth centuries (Durant 1984).

Radical mutilations of this kind were perhaps needed to make possible the decisive step of turning recorded sounds and images into marketable commodities (as well as being necessitated by the limitations of pre-electrical nineteenth-century recording technology). But the subsequent history of sound and image reproduction can be seen as a series of steps towards achieving newer, easier, and more flexible reintegrations of the divided elements. Sound films, television drama, and pop videos all offer a synthesis of sound and image, but at the expense of fragmenting the performance. The new electro-magnetic recording systems give the fleeting sounds and images of the broadcast media a repeatable (and marketable) existence, but their methods of reproduction – being inherently manipulable – take them far from nineteenth-century notions of simple recording, with a shift in the balance of performance and record. Perhaps the most extreme reversal occurs with pop-music records created in a sophisticated, multitrack sound studio. In concert appearances, the players find themselves unable to reproduce these sounds and simply mime to the record. In this way the live performance is devalued to such an extent that it is reduced to no more than an imitation of its own recording.

In addition to commodifying performance, the new media simultaneously blurred the conventional division between the artwork and natural phenomena. The camera's principle of mechanical reproduction offered a fundamental challenge to the art of the representational painter, since photographic images were able to claim a unique authority from seemingly being produced automatically, without the intervention of the human hand. As a result, photographs swiftly eliminated the more utilitarian applications of the painter's art, such as the production of portrait miniatures. When the daguerreotype was replaced by the negative/positive system a second challenge to tradition emerged: photographs were pictures of a kind quite different from paintings, since they were not individually unique, but existed in a virtually limitless series of identical replicas, all of equal status (there is no original of which all the others are mere copies). It is worth noting, however, that tradition has in time been able successfully to counter this particular challenge, with original nineteenth-century prints – as rare objects – now selling for many thousands of pounds in the auction rooms.

An equally radical shift was occasioned by the nineteenth-century media of electric transmission of sound. The telephone and wireless transmission provided a successful alternative to the print communication of information, reducing distance to nothing and drastically shortening the time required for business transactions. The subsequent step – the shift to the electronic storage of sounds and images – marks a radical break with the traditional print-based systems of information. The published play text and the transcript, the reporter's written account and the printed notation of music are increasingly discarded in favour of the direct recording of dramas and news items, interviews and musical performances. From the production of recorded sounds and images designed simply as a *supplement* to existing forms (photographic illustrations for books and newspapers, discs as records of live concert performances) we have moved towards a situation in which the electronically stored and instantly retrievable sounds and images *replace* print forms.

With these generalizations borne in mind, we can now proceed to look briefly at the cultural dimension of the various individual media, since the social definitions given to photographs, records, films, and broadcast programmes, help shape the current approaches to sound and video tape.

Photographs

A good insight into how photographs were seen in the mid-nineteenth century is afforded by Charles Baudelaire's review of the 1859 exhibition by the French Society of Photography:

> If photography is allowed to supplement art in some of its functions, it will soon have supplanted or corrupted it altogether. . . . It is time, then, for it to return to its true duty, which is to be the servant of the sciences and arts – but the very humble servant, like printing or shorthand, which have neither created nor supplemented literature. Let it hasten to enrich the tourist's album and restore to his eye the precision which his memory may lack; let it adorn the naturalist's library, and enlarge microscopic animals; let it even provide information to corroborate the astronomer's hypotheses; in short let it be the secretary and clerk of whoever needs an absolute factual exactitude in his profession – up to that point nothing could be better. Let it rescue from oblivion those tumbling ruins, those books, prints and manuscripts which time is devouring, precious things whose form is dissolving and which demand a place in the archives of our memory – it

will be thanked and applauded. But if it be allowed to encroach upon the domain of the impalpable and the imaginary, upon anything whose value depends solely upon the addition of something of a man's soul, then it will be so much the worse for us!

(cit. Newall 1982: 83)

It will be evident from this statement that our view of photography has changed radically over the past 130 years. Art has been transformed to such an extent that photographic reproduction could in no way be seen as a challenge to it. Indeed photography is now widely recognized as a major art form. We are also far more aware of the enormous dynamism of the new media and realize instantly that any attempt to confine a modern medium like photography (or video) within the role of a 'very humble servant' is doomed to failure. For example, in one of its major applications – advertising – photography has indeed encroached on the imaginary, even if with questionable results. In a justly celebrated piece of analysis John Berger has shown how the imagery of glossy coloured commercial photographs is in many ways a continuation of the tradition of European oil painting (Berger 1972: 129–54). Yet, whereas painting was traditionally used to celebrate a world of the present characterized by ownership and private possession, advertising tells us of an imaginary future which will be ours if only we will make the necessary payment: buy the product, purchase the holiday package, put down the deposit on the car.

Rather than take Baudelaire's polarity of art (from which photography must be excluded) and documentation (where it is agreed to exccel), many contemporary writers on photography, such as Susan Sontag, see the crucial spectrum – again shared with video – as extending from serving power to expressing private experience, from surveillance to self-observation (Sontag 1978: 1–24). Photographs – from mugshots and passport photos to the advertising images of our supposed dreams – are one of the means by which government and capital exercise social control over us. A key instance of photography's complicity with the state came with the short-lived Paris Commune of 1871, just a dozen years after Baudelaire was writing. Confident of victory, many of the communards allowed themselves to be photographed, smiling proudly and defiantly, on the barricades. A few months later, when the Commune had been crushed, the police used these photographs to identify and hunt down the state's opponents (Freund 1980: 108). A second series of photographs ensued, depicting the executed communards publicly displayed in their open coffins. Despite this, photographs continue to be a deeply intimate, indispensible form of personal expression: to get married without having the event photographed is, in a very real way, not to get married at all; to fail to take, possess, and carry with you photographs of your children is to reveal yourself as a totally inadequate parent.

Although advertising images talk to us of a hypothetical future, most photographs tell us about the past. Despite the vaunted visual bias of our culture, the extent to which we believe what photographs show us, and accept them as irrefutable evidence is striking (we are much more sceptical about sound tapes, for example, as the Watergate Affair showed). It is true that in general an event has to happen in order to be photographed and that photographs are therefore a record of what happened and where it happened. But although we are all aware that events can be faked or staged, that the photographer's intervention is crucial, and that darkroom and laboratory procedures allow photographic images to be cropped, manipulated, and distorted, we still, paradoxically, accept the truth of the photograph (Scharf 1965: 31).

Two reasons can be advanced to account for this acceptance: our familiarity with photography and the nature of the medium. Although the scope of photography's images is truly universal – everything that exists can be, and perhaps has been, photographed – we are all able to participate fully, as photographers, in this most democratic of the arts. Moreover, we seem always to sense that photographs, because of the nature of the photochemical process, are inextricably tied to the objects they depict – in a way that no paintings (and certianly no words) ever could be. The analogies drawn by writers on photography are with such phenomena as the death-mask, the footprint, a tracing in the sand (Sontag 1978: 154). Certainly we feel this link particularly intensely if we are joined in some way to the person depicted: to throw away an old photograph of someone you have loved is to do the person a real injustice, to aggress the memory.

However, despite the closeness of image and object, other aspects of the photographic experience imply distance and separation. In some ways photographs cut us off from experience. Tourists taking incessant snapshots are allowing the camera to come between them and a true experience of alien reality 'out there', and a second amputation is likely to come when, back home, the resultant photographs become a substitute for the lived memory. Photographs posit that the immediately visible is the true, and in so doing they separate objects from the flow of time, from the tradition within which they are placed, and from the wealth of our other senses: sound, smell, awareness of movement, tactility. We go along with photographs – accepting their truth – although as Bertolt Brecht pointed out long ago, a photograph of a Krupp or an AEG factory tells us virtually nothing about the truth of capitalism. The very credibility of the photograph is in retrospect perhaps the medium's greatest bequest to the subsequent media of film and video, conditioning us to accept without real questioning both moving pictures and electronically generated images.

Records

The ten ways in which Thomas Edison, writing in 1878, predicted that his new invention of sound recording would benefit mankind, cover a wide spectrum:

1 Letter writing and all kinds of dictation without the aid of a stenographer.
2 Phonographic books, which will speak to blind people without effort on their part.
3 The teaching of elocution.
4 Reproduction of music.
5 The 'Family Record' – a registry of sayings, reminiscences, etc., by members of a family in their own voices, and the last words of dying persons.
6 Music boxes and toys.

7 Clocks that should announce in articulate speech the time for going home, going to meals, etc.

8 The preservation of languages by exact reproduction of the manner of pronouncing.

9 Educational purposes; such as preserving the explanations made by a teacher, so that the pupil can refer to them at any moment, and spelling or other lessons placed upon the phonograph for convenience in committing to memory.

10 Connection with the telephone, so as to make that instrument an auxiliary in the transmission of permanent and invaluable records, instead of being the recipient of momentary and fleeting communication.

(cit. Gelatt 1977: 29)

Most of these applications have been explored at some time or another, although some needed the successful invention of the tape recorder to become commercially feasible (Dearling and Dearling 1984: 21–5). But it is noticeable how little emphasis is placed by Edison on the major application of the phonograph and its successor, the gramophone: the recording and reproduction of music.

We have seen that our approach to photography is shaped by the close connection we feel to exist between the photographic image and what it depicts. But photographs are in no sense total replicas – they always remain two-dimensional representations of the appearances of objects, scenes, and people, and as such they can never be confused with the originals. To reproduce a set of appearances is not to reproduce the object – things do not have 'sights' that can be separated off from them. But objects and people do create sounds – particularly musical sounds – which are separable and reproduceable, and the whole history of sound recording is best understood as the attempt to replicate these.

Early sound recording with the acoustic horn did not give a fully adequate version of any sounds, not even the human voice (the contrast with early photographs of the human face is striking). The advent of electric technology in the 1920s improved range and quality, but limitations remained. The aim of virtually all improvements in sound-recording techniques was – and still is – to deny the difference between, say, a live singer and a recording of his or her voice. Equally important, we as listeners, it would seem, wish to go along with the technical innovators and to perceive no distinction between a sound and its reproduction.

Nevertheless, recorded sound is always quite distinct from the sounds we hear in real life: it is shaped, filtered, constructed. The contrivance is inevitable. Whereas early photographers were free to leave the confines of the studio (which had been so convenient for portraiture) to explore virtually any aspect of the visible world, sound recordists still often find themselves confined to a studio. They are troubled even today by the problem of how to eliminate from a recording the kinds of extraneous noise which our ear can easily ignore in real-life situations, but which become obtrusive when we listen to recorded or transmitted sounds.

A further area of problem with the gramophone record, at least until tape recorders became common in the 1950s, concerns the material used for the master recording and for the saleable commodity. Wax was an inflexible medium for manipulating recorded sound and the shellac disc format inhibited the development of the long-playing record. As a result, for fifty years the gramophone record remained just that, a record not a fully creative medium, failing to make the leap to an independent artistic identity which the cinema contrived within a couple of decades of its invention. Until tape was introduced, there was virtually no music written specifically for, or dependent on, recording. Instead the gramophone continued to be largely parasitic on the existing repertoire of classical and popular music.

This repertoire had already been turned into a marketable commodity – through sheet music – before the gramophone came into wide use. *A Bird in a Gilded Cage* sold 2 million sheet copies in 1900 and *Meet Me Tonight in Dream Land* sold 5 million in 1909 (Fell 1974: 235). But the gramophone – reinforced by the radio – changed the whole experience of listening to music, separating it off not just from active music-making, but also from the sight and presence of the music-makers. The gramophone has the advantage of bypassing the constraints of conventional musical notation, and so allows us access to a fantastically wide range of musical experience. In return it imposes on the listener a single version of music which, to come fully alive, needs to be re-created and reinterpreted anew at every performance. More importantly still – and this is particularly important for the reception of sound and video tapes – it has taught us to equate music with the particularities of recorded music, which is filtered through microphones, amplifiers, and speakers, and adapted to the acoustical demands of our domestic interiors.

Films

An article on the cinematograph published in a French scientific magazine in October 1895 gave its predictions for the application of the new invention:

> It will be a precious instrument for recording the movement of troops, diverse military manoeuvres, charges. . . . It will be of service to travellers and explorers. . . . But in our opinion it is the teaching of arts and crafts which will benefit most from the cinematograph.
>
> (Deslandes 1966: 280)

Such documentary applications of the cinematograph – the kind envisaged by its inventor, Louis Lumière – have indeed been a part of the story of film's development. However, like virtually all contemporary critics and journalists, the author left out of account the factor which would do most to shape film as a form, namely its application to narrative. Today, if we go to see a film, it is almost invariably to be told a story, just as we put on a record when we want to listen to music. It is clear that the huge advances made by cinema, both in the growing complexity of the works produced and in the spread of movie-going worldwide, depended on three factors: the flexibility of celluloid film as a material support for the images, the competitive situation in the film industry during its formative years, and the storytelling function adopted in the first decades of the twentieth century.

At first sight the use of films to tell stories is a little surprising,

104

since this is a function which photography rarely takes on. Of course photographs were used from quite early on to *illustrate* stories, but the actual unfolding of the narrative was generally left to words. Even the various forms of photo-story we can find today are more a by-product of cinema than an outgrowth of photography itself. The crucial difference between photography and film lies in the change which movement brings to the photographic image (Barthes 1977: 44–6). Photographs are closely linked to the past – they show us what happened at some time in the past, how people and places looked *then*. There is always a time-gap between the taking of a photograph and our seeing it: even an instant polaroid snap shows how things were a few seconds ago, not how they are now. For this reason, the application of photography to the preservation of records – as well as the role which photography plays in memory and hence in our sentimental life – is a predictable development which grows out of the nature of the medium.

But films are different. Although the depicted events must logically belong to the past (since they have been photographed), the way in which they unfold on the screen is in the present. A clip of a newsreel film showing a ship sinking slowly in a naval battle fifty years ago is a document, a record of what happened. But when we project it, the sequence of events unfolds in real time, in the present, so that we relive the disaster as it happens. As Christian Metz has pointed out, movement is not, strictly speaking, reproduced in the cinema (Metz 1974: 7–9). It is re-produced, that is to say, produced anew, each time a film is projected. Film has, therefore, its own particular paradoxical combination of past and present, forming a unique kind of historical present which is ideally suited to narrative. It captures crucial aspects of the oldest of all modes of story-telling: the group gathered in the darkness around a campfire to listen to a story-teller who speaks of things which have happened (otherwise they could not be narrative events), but tells them as they happen (prompting the incessant questions, 'And then?', 'What happens next?').

Films are linked as closely to story-telling as records are to music, but the important difference is that film quickly developed its own brand of narration and so *created* its own stories, instead of merely reproducing existing ones. Even a film which closely adapts a novel or play is a unique form of the story, existing in its own right and quite distinct from the original. Film's development of its distinctive form of narration is due in large part to the fact that it developed, historically, as one of the last new forms of public entertainment. Its immediate ancestors, such as the lantern lecture and the peepshow, were types of entertainment occurring outside the home, and the Lumière cinematograph was ideally suited to take its place as an item in a music hall programme or as an attraction in a travelling fair (R. C. Allen 1979: 13–18). The viewing context had important consequences for the growth of films from fifty-second actualities to epics capable of sustaining audience attention for two hours or more. As films grew in length and complexity, so too the movie theatres became more luxurious and elaborate, with larger screens and better projection (Gomery 1979). Hollywood corporations now sought a reliable flow of products which would ensure regular, dependable returns – hence the gradual creation of the various formulas of genre, story, and star which characterize what we know as the Hollywood movie.

The result is a highly-wrought and extremely economical form of story-telling. In the conventional film or television drama, reality is turned into a succession of narrative events, time is shaped into drama, and space becomes a location for action. Although the discontinuities are disguised by the conventions of editing, the viewpoint offered to the spectators is constantly shifting. While in no way equating to real perception, this viewpoint fulfils enough of the conditions of perception to satisfy us. Above all, it allows us an essential freedom. Like listening to music, viewing a film involves anticipation and retrospection, surprise and suspense, tension and resolution, symmetry and disorder, pattern and chance.

Broadcast programmes

The key founding document of broadcasting is the letter written in 1916 by David Sarnoff to the general manager of his employers, the American Marconi Company, in which he set out his vision of a novel mode of commercial exploitation for radio-telephony:

> I have in mind a plan of development which would make radio a 'household utility' in the same sense as the piano or phonograph. The receiver can be designed in the form of a simple 'radio Music Box' and arranged for several different wavelengths, which would be changeable with the throwing of a single switch or pressing of a single button. The 'radio Music Box' can be supplied with amplifying tubes and a loudspeaking telephone, all of which can be neatly mounted in one box. The box can be placed in the parlour or living room, the switch set accordingly and the transmitted music received. . . . This proposition would be especially interesting to farmers and others living in outlying districts removed from cities. By the purchase of a 'radio Music Box' they could enjoy concerts, lectures, music, recitals etc., which may be going on in the nearest city within their radius.
>
> (cit. Barnouw 1970: 78; Smith 1973: 49)

This prophetic statement, which was backed up with some quite remarkably accurate predictions as to potential radio sales, is striking for a number of reasons. Firstly, it proposes a radical departure in the application of electric communication technology. All the previous systems – the telegraph, the telephone, radio-telegraphy – had used the two-way potential whereby each receiver was itself a transmitter. Here Sarnoff proposes the one-way system which is the distinguishing feature of broadcasting: one transmitter which does not receive feed-back and a large number of receivers which cannot transmit, either to the source transmitter or to each other. Secondly, following the example of the telephone, the camera, and the phonograph rather than that of the cinema, Sarnoff proposes a domestic market for his 'radio Music Boxes', implying a vision of society in which the bulk of the population has both the affluence to buy consumer durables and leisure time which needs to be filled. On this basis, Sarnoff foresees the potential for an industry which will draw its profits from manufacture and sale, but which will not be concerned with programme-making.

Indeed the most striking omission in Sarnoff's vision is of any awareness that an institution will be required to produce broadcast programming: his system is wholly parasitic on existing events, which would simply be transmitted unaltered. The question of finding a source of finance for production is therefore also ignored: it is certainly not seen as part of the responsibility of manufacturers. Interestingly, this split between equipment manufacture and programme production, which does not exist in any of the preceding sound and image media, has persisted virtually everywhere, with programming funded either through licence fees or by advertising and sponsorship. Where the latter is the case, a fascinating example of the working of the capitalist market occurs: the customers who purchase a commodity (a radio or television set) are turned into commodities themselves, an 'audience', to be sold by the thousand as potential customers to advertisers.

Seeing radio as likely to have the same links with music as those enjoyed by the gramophone, causes Sarnoff to ignore the future involvement of broadcasting with current affairs (in 1916 solely the province of newspapers). Thus, just as story-telling was unforeseen by Lumière with regard to the cinematograph, so too there was no initial anticipation that radio (and later television) would eventually become society's prime disseminator of news. Combined with the equally unforeseen concentration of influence through nation-wide networking in the 1920s, this led Sarnoff to ignore, too, the fact that broadcasting would everywhere become a concern of the state.

Apart from these developments and a change in vocabulary, remarkably little has changed in the seventy-odd years since Sarnoff's prophetic formulation. It is true that radio has lost its central role of serving the whole family group as a single unit and has diversified, both in terms of the range of outlets (portable transistors, car radios, the Sony walkman, etc.) and the multiplicity of specialist channels (for London listeners: the four BBC programmes, Capital Radio, LBC, Radio London, etc.). However, its previous role has been taken over more than adequately by television which, despite its recent spread into pubs and other public places, remains essentially a domestic medium catering for the whole family (Morley 1986). Television reception has none of the compulsive power of the cinema screen. The domestic interior is not obliterated by its images and sounds (perhaps so as to provide the necessary drab, present-day counterpart for the advertisers' idealized imagery of our potential future?), and a variety of studies have shown that its impact is muted by the interaction among the group of viewers, by breaks for food and drink, by tinkering with the remote control, and so on. As a domestic entertainment, television puts few demands on its audience, whose attention-span is in any case not expected to last beyond about three minutes at any one go.

The paradox of broadcasting is that although vast effort is put into the selection and scheduling of largely pre-recorded programmes, the prime characteristics of broadcasting are that it is live (in terms of presentation) and that its channels are as indifferent to content as those churning out musak. How then can we define the essence of a broadcast programme? The answer would seem to lie in the extent to which the programme itself becomes an 'event' for its audience, a compilation of material from various sources held together in real time by a presenter who appears not as the final (visible) link in a complex production chain involving dozens of co-workers, but as a god-like organizer of a world of infinitely varied sounds and images (Hall 1976: 247). In this perspective news programming is central for both radio and television: during the Second World War the wireless *Nine O'Clock News* became a key feature of national life, and today its television successors like *News at Ten* continue to draw huge audiences.

The apparent authenticity of news programming depends on its restrained tone as well as on its appearance of offering an immediate 'window on the world', but the same format is to be found in entertainment programmes. In radio there is the pop programme, in which a disc jockey fuses together the very latest list of 'Top Ten' records through a welter of jokes and chat, creating an atmosphere in which other items (news, weather reports, traffic information, sports results) can be handled as if they too generated the same immediate excitement. In television, we have a programme such as *Grandstand*, which makes a complex, smoothly edited assembly of live and recorded events, off-the-cuff comments, formal interviews, and on-the-spot reports, using the full resources of the broadcast system to move back and forth in time, in and out of the studio, all thanks seemingly to the imperturbable, highly professional presenter. Not all programming follows this mode of presentation – broadcasting remains even today parasitic on other forms – but it is here that the unique qualities of the broadcast system are most clearly revealed (a fact borne out by the way in which presenters, disc jockeys, and newscasters become highly paid media personalities).

Tapes and cassettes

The heritage of the earlier systems of reproduction is crucial to the identity of the new tape media. Despite the use of electro-magnetic recording techniques, the video image inherits some of the credibility which has traditionally been attached to photography. Similarly, we accept video sound as 'real' because our ears have long been accustomed to the filtered, inherently artificial sound of records and radio. Although video-makers may wish to address different audiences in different situations, their work cannot fail to be influenced by the cinema's tradition of narrative economy and documentary precision – even if this influence is expressed through a conscious rejection of certain specific filmic effects. From its association with broadcasting, video, like sound tape, has an air of immediacy lacking in the nineteenth-century forms of film and gramophone record, although again the broadcasters' particular forms of direct address to listener or viewer may be largely irrelevant. These are not qualities inherent in tape work, nor are they inevitable outcomes of electro-magnetic recording, but they are crucial factors in how we – as an audience – approach sound and video tapes.

The introduction of plastic tape, first to record sounds and then sounds-and-images could not quite match the immediate dazzling breakthrough achieved by celluloid film stock (revolutionizing photography and allowing the birth of the movies) some sixty years before. Tape was not launched with manifestos and programmes for action: it crept out ino the world as a by-product of broadcasting, and even today its role in reshaping the sound-recording and film industries remains largely disregarded.

For its original industrial application, the reel-to-reel system was perfectly adequate, but more recently the accessibility of the cassette format has become a key feature of marketing strategy. In this format, feature films and pop videos are accessible in the home to all who own or rent a video recorder, while portable sound recorders allow us access to pre-recorded sound wherever we may find ourselves and however mobile we may be. But the tape media have an exciting creative potential, and the way this has been explored with regard to sound points clearly to video's future.

Sound tape was developed in the 1940s specifically for the radio industry, merely as a replacement for the current (and cumbersome) disc recording facilities. Yet as soon as sound tape was introduced within the broadcasting institutions, it attracted the attention of avant-garde musicians (Mackay 1981). In Paris, Cologne, and elsewhere, sound workshop facilities were made available to composers. Many of these – Edgar Varèse, Karlheinz Stockhausen, and John Cage among them – had already sought to incorporate new kinds of sound (formerly dismissed as 'noise') into their music, and some had even made attempts to manipulate sound from records. Now they responded enthusiastically to the opportunities offered to them, first by broadcast organizations and later by major educational institutions.

It is important to distinguish the 'tape music' produced by the avant-garde from 'taped music', by which is normally meant music recorded live in a straightforward conventional way. Already in the early 1950s two broad streams of tape music became apparent. In Paris, Pierre Schaeffer and Pierre Henry developed what they called *musique concrète*. This involved the manipulation (by change of speed, editing, repetition, super-imposition, filtering, etc.) of pre-recorded real sounds, including the human voice and even conventional musical instruments. Simultaneously, in Cologne, a second trend was brought into being by composers such as Pierre Boulez and Karlheinz Stockhausen. This was pure electronic music, using only electronically generated source material as the basis for composition. Although the distinction between the two trends is useful, it very quickly became blurred in practice, as musicians in Europe and the

United States uninhibitedly explored the whole range of new possibilities which sound tape opened up.

Common to all tape music is the opportunity it offers to the composer of creating directly, without the need to write down a score and have this performed by other musicians. For the composer the scope is virtually unlimited. Tape music can be rigidly controlled and programmed – by systems akin to the serial techniques developed by composers like Webern and Schoenberg – or it can be, as so often with John Cage, a matter of chance combinations and improvization around a set of given procedures. It can create a whole symphony out of a single initial sound, combine different varieties of tape music, or fuse tape sound with live performance. It is designed primarily for domestic consumption (through broadcast or recording) but it can also be given a concert performance. In the latter case, it may use just one or two loudspeakers, positioned on the platform where the musicians would usually sit (giving the audience the problem of where to *look* during the performance), or it can use a whole battery of speakers located throughout a defined performance space so as to create a new, three-dimensional kind of listening. But always it possesses that particular inhuman, futuristic quality which many composers have felt to be particularly suited to express the concerns of a post-nuclear age, characterized by space travel, satellite transmission, and computerization.

The potential range of video tape, which we must keep in mind as we turn to consider the nature of video production, matches the scope of sound tape far more closely than that of film stock. Video, too, can be employed simply as a straightforward recording system, can be used to compile and manipulate given sounds and images (especially off-air material, as in 'scratch video'), or can embrace purely electronically generated imagery (as with the computer-aided graphics now so common in television title sequences). Although video was seized upon by certain avant-garde artists when portable machines became available in the mid-1960s, it has as yet failed to generate quite the same level of creativity as sound tape: there is no body of video art to equal the achievements of electronic music.

Conclusions

Looking at the cultural identity of the various forms of sound and image media which have established themselves over the past 150 years, several general points become clear. Firstly, and most obviously, all are part of our modern industrial civilization: development is commercially motivated and in every case profit is seen to derive from the possibilities offered by mass production and wide distribution. Although the time–span involved means that there are relics of earlier approaches (such as the threatrical development of film), all the sound and image media have come to focus on the home. The ideal pattern would seem to be a three-fold pattern of profits (from the sale of a consumer durable, pre–recorded products, and recording materials): the triple market created at the turn of the century for cameras, postcards, and photographic materials is echoed in the 1980s by the combination of domestic video recorders, taped movies, and blank cassettes. Wherever the full pattern is blocked in some way (as with replay–only systems such as the gramophone and CD player), the profit motive behind this form of industrial organization is very apparent. Along with the focus on the home goes an increasing integration of systems once segregated (in both industrial and equipment terms): the current 'midi' sound system combining radio, record, CD, and tape replay and recording is merely a step on the way to the full 'home entertainment centre' including television and video as well as sound in a single package.

Secondly, the eventual social application of the new media is in most cases quite different from that anticipated or envisaged by the pioneers. This is important, because it shows clearly that the new communication media were not responses of any simple kind to a known and clearly defined social need. Their initial development may (as with the daguerreotype, the cylinder recorder, and the cinematograph) have been a response to a particular expression of public taste for novelty. But in their long–term development the interaction of the profit motive and changing social conditions and needs will have led to quite new and unanticipated identities: the role of amateur photography, the record industry's place in youth culture, the fictional feature film. The establishment and spread of broadcast systems themselves have often been motivated by immediate response to momentary – even frivolous – events. The role of the 1953 Coronation in the spread of British television is well-known and has been constantly echoed in the Third World: an initial television system was introduced into Senegal and Indonesia to allow coverage of sporting events (the Olympic Games and the Asian Games, respectively), while the conversion to colour was made for a meeting of the Organisation of African Unity in Uganda and for a Miss Thailand beauty competition in Thailand (Katz and Wedell 1978: 10–12). Such responses to events of transitory interest leave expensive communication systems whose incorporation into the national life and economy has been unplanned.

Thirdly, it follows from this that arguments based on some variation of technological determinism and ignoring changes in wider social relations have little relevance as explanations of media developments. Brian Winston rightly pours scorn on those futurologists who propose imminent revolutionary changes in the technological basis of our society without indicating the social transformations which would make these possible. As Winston observes, their vision does 'considerable violence to every aspect of our culture', supposing 'the end of productive work, the institutions of representative democracy, the school and the shop'. But their technologically determined stance leads them to assume that one institution will stand unchanged: 'the engine of upheaval – the modern corporation' (Winston 1986: 365). The factors which have had the most marked impact on the speeding of technological change have been external ones, namely the ending of the two world wars, which left industrial productive capacity without immediate application and released trained technicians on to the labour market. As a result, the end of the First World War gave a stimulus to developments in radio, while the conclusion of the Second World War initiated the inexorable spread of television world-wide. Perhaps a halting of the nuclear arms race would have a similar invigorating impact on the communications media – otherwise technological innovation is likely to be comparatively slow. In any case, those

114

new technical systems which are adopted tend to reinforce the given cultural identity of the media rather than forge new social applications. Since the innumerable technical improvements to still photography made in this century have hardly changed its cultural identity as established in the 1890s, it is hardly surprising that the thirty-year history of video has yet to make a major impact on the basic audio–visual forms of fictional story-telling or factual reporting.

Further reading

For a general consideration of the historical meaning of the much misused term 'revolution' see Porter and Teich (1986); Winston (1986) forcefully questions its application to the specific field of communications and information technology. The writings of Berger (1972; 1980) offer clear insights into the ideological implications of visual forms, and Attali (1985) makes a spirited defence of the role of music in society and history. Particularly useful on specific media are Sontag (1978) and Beloff (1985) on photography, McWhinnie (1959) and Lewis (1981) on radio, Cavell (1971), Heath (1981), Andrew (1984), and Ellis (1982) on film and television, Durant (1984), Frith (1983), and Mackay (1981) on various aspects of the music industry, and Marshall (1985) on video.

5 SYSTEMS OF PRODUCTION

> For those who are excited by the radical social possibilities of the video portapak it is easy to forget that the development of this particular consumer commodity was underpinned by a vast investment in new commercial, military and managerial technology, such as commercial information storage and retrieval, computer visual display units, internal television and video systems, data banking and military and commercial surveillance.
>
> (Stuart Marshall 1985: 66)

There are a number of factors which make video difficult to define as a system of production: the novelty of the medium, the diversity in the level of complexity of the various video formats, and the flexibility of video as a means of recording. But perhaps the most crucial is the general fluidity between the three major audio–visual systems of film, television, and video. Film can be transferred to video tape and video to film, television can transmit live, filmed, or video–taped material indiscriminately, film can be used to record the output of a television studio (indeed before the application of video tape in the late 1950s it was the only such recording system available). In particular video, the third of the systems to come into existence, is able to reproduce perfectly the production patterns of the earlier ones to which it is heir. Nevertheless, despite these overlaps, it is possible to make clear and revealing contrasts between: firstly, the production system adopted almost universally for the making of feature films and film documentaries; secondly, the production system essential to television studio broadcasting;

and thirdly, the specific system of video which, in addition to its ability to copy, has features missing in both the others.

The starting-point for an examination of these distinctions is the basic point stressed in preceding chapters: the particular nature of the sound/image reproduction. Film and video use different recording substances and therefore inevitably have different qualities and potentials. More fundamentally still, while film and video are systems of recording which result in concrete, tangible works, television is in essence a channel of transmission to whose principles of operation recording as such is secondary. On this basis we can trace differences between the various systems of production on a number of levels: in the role of the studio as well as in the principles of shooting, editing, and sound work.

Before we proceed to examine each of these three production systems in turn, it is worth noting one characteristic which they all share, namely that their pre-production stage involves the preparation of a detailed script which then serves as a guide to the subsequent production. In historical terms it is striking that the introduction of the detailed continuity script coincided with the industrialization of film-making in Hollywood during and immediately after the First World War (Staiger 1979a, 1979b). This industrialization took two forms. Firstly, there were new approaches to exhibition which drew lessons from the distributive trades (such as the Woolworth chain) (Gomery 1979). Film exhibitors of the 1920s showed a concern with building a balanced evening's entertainment out of a mix of live acts, shorts, and features which strikingly anticipates the scheduling of an evening's viewing which is of such concern to television executives.

Secondly, as far as the industrialization of production was concerned, the key to any factory system is the division of labour (Braverman 1974) and the 1920s were the period when the specialized roles involved in film production came to be defined (J. T. Allen 1980). The resulting fragmentation of the workforce led to new managerial problems which could only be resolved by placing a fresh emphasis on the script. The detailed continuity script, to which the director was contractually obliged to adhere, allowed the crucial separation of the conception (and hence costing and timetabling) of the film by the management – the producers – from the execution of the film by the studio's paid employees – who included the director. Only in this way was it possible to ensure the control over budgets, recourses, and scheduling necessary to guarantee a steady flow of economically costed products from the studios.

Similar methods of organization have been adopted by the subsequent media. The detailed continuity script is characteristic of production at all levels – broadcasting and feature film-making as well as independent production and amateur realization – and the difference in the type of script will depend far more on the type of production (drama or documentary, for example) than on the particular medium adopted. The importance of the script to individual video-makers is self-evident: it allows them to organize their thoughts before embarking on the much more expensive stage of realization on set or location.

Film production

As we have seen, the birth of the cinema is dated very precisely as 1895, that is, the moment when a particular recording base (a strip of perforated 35 mm nitrocellulose film stock) was applied to the provision of projected moving pictures for a paying audience. Other earlier 1890s forms of moving pictures for entertainment purposes – slide shows, peepshows, systems using the projection of hand-drawn images – are universally seen as no more than precursors, as the final steps in the cinema's prehistory, whereas the carrier base which Louis Lumière used in 1895 – film – has given its name to the work recorded on it.

At least in the first ninety years of its existence, cinema has found no viable alternative to film stock as its preferred mode of distribution for the theatrical presentation of its images and sounds (although big-screen video projection is already almost there as a viable technological alternative). Until this is widely adopted, definitions of cinema and film remain perfectly straightforward, with the 'object of study' for critics, historians, and theorists narrowed down from the whole range of nineteenth-century optical entertainments to just those which specifically use photographic means of reproduction on film stock for the projection of moving images to a paying audience.

While there are accounts of cinema which deny the centrality of films to any consideration of cinema (Ellis 1977: 56–66), it is in fact precisely the ownership of 'strips of celluloid in cans' – and of all the rights pertaining to them – that makes distribution the key economic sector of the film industry, the point at which capital accumulates and ultimate power resides. Any study of Third World film-making underlines this importance of distribution (Armes 1987: 35–49). It is the Motion Picture Export Association of America's ability to deliver or deny 'strips of celluloid in cans' to exhibitors throughout the world which is the source of Hollywood's monopoly power and enormous profits. Difficulties in physically transporting films, as well as their vulnerability to tariffs and import controls, play an important part in determining who sees which films in the movie houses of the world – and who makes a profit.

The qualities of the celluloid base and the increasingly light-sensitive emulsions applied to it determined the nature of film production from the very beginning. The fact that a film studio and a television studio have marked similarities in respect of physical space (the shared notion of a light-proof, sound-proof box equipped with facilities for controlling lighting and sound recording) has led some critics to see them as essentially the same. In fact the use of a studio has a very different function and history in the two media. The early years of cinema show an alternation of studio and location: Edison's kinetoscope films were shot in a studio, Lumière worked only on location, Georges Méliès took film back into the studio, and so on. While Méliès's studio was highly elaborate – containing all the mechanical devices necessary for a magician's trickery – most early film studios were very simple structures, using natural light (often filtered through gauze).

In no sense was the studio a prerequisite for cinema, and the eventual move into electrically lit studios for interior scenes was secondary, a step taken initially to enhance the credibility and 'realism' of the images by making them more visually expressive through control of lighting. From the late 1920s, the need for a studio was increased by the difficulties of obtaining a clear, clean

119

sound track outside it. All the subsequent improvements in the sensitivity of film stock and the effectiveness of sound-recording equipment have lessened the dependence on studio contrivance. Indeed, far from being essential to the film process, the studio in its traditional sense can be seen in retrospect as a kind of historical detour, necessitated by the impossibility of obtaining – with the available technology – the kind of aural and visual perfection demanded by producers without the control which a studio alone allowed. By the 1960s technical improvements in filming and recording had made the film studio an anachronism, except for special effects work.

In any case, the principles of film shooting are identical in the studio and on location. Although on occasion in the history of cinema multi-camera systems have been used, the single camera is more normal. One of the things fundamental to the way in which film structures its relationship to reality so as to create meaning is the visual organization of the elements before the lens. Material, whether overtly staged or ostensibly natural, is organized for the single camera, so as to enable the camera-person to take a shot or, more usually, a series of shots. The retaking of any or all of these shots several times is standard practice. Even in documentary this is not strictly speaking the recording of an event: it is in effect a construction in its own right. There is absolutely no need for the event actually to occur in its entirety at the time of shooting: a film sequence can easily construct, for example, a conversation between two people who were never, in reality, in the same room at the same time. In this construction of sequence, filmic reality, and meaning, the single camera occupies a privileged position – a situation which film theory echoes.

In film, the integrity of the camera image is assured, since the laboratory develops and prints the film as shot. All creative decisions regarding particular visual effects to be included in the eventual film – such as fades, dissolves, or superimpositions – are made on the basis of an examination of a work print of the original camera material. But the realization of such special effects work is secondary in time. Although decided by the director and his or her editor during the cutting, and indicated on the work print, such effects are carried out only later, at the second laboratory phase concerned with the making of the release print. This second laboratory phase – like the initial developing of the camera negative – is a stage from which the director and members of the creative team are excluded. In the ideology of conventional film-making, such effects work is regarded as a purely technical operation – hence not requiring the creative participation of the director, although the latter may in fact return to the production at a slightly later stage, to be involved in the grading (for colour and tone) of the release prints to be screened in cinemas.

In film-making, editing of necessity constitutes a second, separate stage subsequent to the shooting, since the camera material needs to be processed and printed before it can be assembled at the editing bench, and the sound recorded on quarter-inch tape needs to be transferred to sprocketed magnetic tape in the same format as the film images. The fact that sounds and images are separate in this way means that bringing the two together ('synching rushes') is a key initial stage in the editing process. Likewise the maintaining of synchronization during editing – as shots are changed in order and length – is a continual concern. At the same time, the separation of sound and image on parallel tracks, and the ease with which either can be continually adjusted simply by cutting and joining with splicing tape, encourages the kind of complex interaction of sound and picture which is characteristic of cinema since magnetic recording was introduced in the 1950s. It is also worth noting that all this editing is very much a manual activity, with reels of film and magnetic tape physically cut and joined by hand.

The editing process comprises two basic procedures as far as the images are concerned. The first is the selection of the most appropriate of the various takes of any shot, and the second is the piecing together of these selected shots so as to create a sequence offering a coherent rendering of the continuity of the intended narrative event. Just as the image has primacy at the shooting, so too it is the visual continuity and flow which has priority in the assembly of a film, with the sound track cut and manipulated to support the action and to disguise shot changes and visual discontinuities. While, in editing, the picture continuity will constitute a single roll of film, which is pared down and polished as the editing proceeds, there will normally be a steady build-up of several rolls of synchronized sound track, each containing one portion of the three major types of sound: speech (dialogue and/or commentary), music, and sound effects.

The last stage of film-making deemed to be fully creative (that is, requiring the presence of the director) is the sound-dubbing session. Here the various rolls of sound track, which have hitherto been kept separate for ease of manipulation, are brought together with any added effects and are then mixed, balanced, and filtered, so as to create the single master magnetic track. The subsequent laboratory stages: the cutting of the original negative to match the edited picture continuity, the transfer of the master magnetic track to an optical format, and the matching of the two to produce a combined print, are normally carried out in the laboratory without any of the film crew being present.

To summarize the characteristics of film-making as a production system, we may note that, visually, a film's representation of reality is doubly removed from the event it represents: firstly, by the organization of space, lighting, and action for the single camera; and, secondly, by the editing of a succession of shots so as to create a film event, which need never have happened in its entirety. In this process the event will almost inevitably acquire its own dramatic compression ('life with the dull bits cut out', in Hitchcock's memorable phrase). At the moment of shooting the sound will be just as organized for the microphone as the action is for the camera. But the sound track itself will be far more elaborately shaped during the sound editing, with the addition of many new elements, most notably the musical accompaniment. While the integrity of the image is largely preserved, the sound track will be both subordinated to the picture through synchronization (which makes the image seem to *produce* the sound), and also manipulated (in terms of level, tone, balance, etc.) so as to ensure maximum clarity. There is a clear separation in time between shooting and editing, and between production and exhibition to the spectator. Similarly a conventional distinction is drawn within the film industry between the creative stages (shooting, editing, dubbing), which very much involve manual skills and at which the director is present, and the laboratory stages (developing, printing, negative cutting, sound transfer), which are seen as purely technical operations.

Television production

The situation with regard to television production is very different from that of film. As we have seen, video tape is in no way a prerequisite for the invention of television, and a television channel making no use of it is perfectly feasible. Indeed, even if we ignore the 1930s experiments, television had been in full operation for a dozen years before video tape was introduced in 1958. Broadcast networks, like closed-circuit television and video surveillance systems, operate in exactly the same way whether or not video recorders and video tape are used as part of the chain from producer to viewer. Video tape therefore cannot be used to delimit the field, as film stock can for cinema. The distinction we make within the electronic production of sounds and images so as to single out 'broadcast television' is not based on the consideration of some carrier base, but in terms of social application: the diffusion of a variety of audio–visual messages from a single point (the studio) to a large number of receivers (domestic television sets).

It follows from this definition that the studio *is* a prerequisite of television. Broadcasting was born within a studio and continues to be inconceivable without one. This being the case, there are two necessary aspects of television production that separate it from film production. The first is multi-camera shooting – necessary to provide, at any moment, two or more images from which the director can choose. A single camera would preclude a smooth transition from one shot to the next or from the presenter to the presented material. The second consequence is a control gallery of some kind, in which this choice can be effected and from which the output can be either transmitted direct or recorded for later screening (neither of these functions is normally carried out by the studio camera itself).

Usually the camera area and the control area are located in a single fixed physical space – the television studio complex – and this forms the hub of the broadcasting operation. But since live material is required from outside this complex, mobile mini-studios – outside broadcast (OB) units – have been developed. These allow the transmission of events which could not conceivably be restaged in the studio (such as football matches) and give the enhancing eye-witness quality so vital to the credibility of television reporting (the reporter is *at that moment* at the scene of the event and mediates it immediately for the viewer). But like the main studio, OB units are multi-camera set-ups directed from a control suite and operate, indeed, in exactly the same way as studios.

The same system is common to all studio production, whether it is drama, entertainment, current affairs programming, news, discussions, or announcements. The existence of two, three, or more cameras, relaying simultaneously and continuously (for direct transmission or recording) the whole progression of an ongoing event, contrasts sharply with film practice. With film, the single camera records successively the various individual stages of an event. It is common practice for these to be shot out of sequence and restaged several times, since a choice and a reordering can be made at the editing phase. By contrast, the multi-camera approach of television prolongs the basically parasitic attitude which, as we have seen, was contained in the initial vision of broadcasting. The event is created (lit, organized, enacted) in the studio as an actual event which has a tangible, coherent existence in time and space. It is then shot in ways that respect this temporal and spatial continuity. This approach is most obviously apparent in studio work, but it applies also to multi-camera location work. The positioning of the cameras of an OB unit obeys the same principles, and the operation is identical, whether the event is shot for live transmission or is – in the revealing phrase – 'recorded live' for later transmission.

Film has no equivalent to the procedures for choosing – simultaneously with the shooting – between the images from the various television studio cameras and other inputs as offered on the viewing monitors in the television control room. The effect is again to emphasize the extreme limitation of the extent to which television reshapes its material as far as shooting is concerned. The successive images of a sequence shot live by television cameras may look superficially like an edited film sequence. But in fact they have a unique and intimate link, being the *record* of real time continuity, not – as is the case with film – the construction of an apparent continuity. There is no possibility of repacing the event – lengthening or shortening aspects of it for dramatic effect – in the way customary with film. Again the same is true of location work shot by an OB unit. A recorded event may be shortened for television transmission, but the 'highlights' shown will comprise large real time blocks, sewn almost invisibly together, not a radical restructuring of the event.

In television, the time of the depicted event, the time of its fragmentation and synthesis in the control room, and the time of its transmission or recording are identical: all have exactly the same real time-span. Even when the real time consecutiveness of an event is broken visually (as when the action is interrupted for an 'action replay' of a goal in a live transmission of a soccer match), the effect of seeing the event from the viewpoint of another camera (or of the same camera but this time in slow motion) in no way approximates to the experience of seeing the successive shots which constitute the strictly imaginary time-span of a film sequence. In television, the primacy of the fleeting moment (the goal) is enhanced, but the integrity of the real time is preserved through the continuity of the commentator's voice. When normal transmission is resumed, it is evident that time has passed for the participants as well as for us: the event has continued unseen (the players have lined up for the restart after the goal) while we have been watching the replay.

The nature and extent of the reconstruction of reality by television is very different from that of film in other respects too. As is so often the case, industrial and institutional practice can be seen to offer invaluable evidence in support of what might seem to be abstract theoretical distinctions. If we need confirmation that in television the depicted event before the camera retains a primacy lost when identical events are reshaped by the film-making process, we need only consider the institutional relationship of writer and director. The subordination of the script-writer to the director in cinema is as much a part of the film industry's organization of production as it is of the critic or theoretician's appraisal of the medium: a film is *by* its director. A television play, on the other hand, is invariably credited to the author of the script.

This argument should not be taken as accepting that television is in truth a 'window on the world' or any such analogy favoured by broadcasters. The images and sounds we obtain from a television set are constructed ones and can in no way be confused with a real view of the depicted event. We can see this work of construction clearly at two distinct levels, that of the technology and that of the institutional practice.

In television the camera image is not privileged as it is in film. The studio camera is not normally its own recorder, but merely one end of a chain which of necessity goes through studio control – and possibly via a video recorder – before it reaches the point of transmission. Whether or not it is recorded, it can be manipulated within the chain before transmission. Even in the early days of purely live television, there were various possibilities of image manipulation. In the 1950s, for example, producers had access to both 'inlay' – masking part of the output of one camera and substituting the output of another, so that two people in different studios miles apart would appear to be talking to each other, and 'overlay' – superimposing a character shot against a blank background on to a separately shot location scene (Morgan 1961: 105–6). Now, in the 1980s, the possibilities of manipulation are enormous and the particular patterns of electronic impulses from a selected camera can be processed, repeated, reframed, recoloured, combined, or synthesized with material from other sources, either consecutively (by intercutting) or concurrently (by a whole range of split-screen and super-imposition techniques), whether or not a video recorder forms part of the chain.

The manipulation habitually suffered by the image in television (as when a variety of configurations of still images, moving pictures, split-screen effects, and graphic designs are produced around the image of the news presenter at his or her desk) has no parallel in film imagery. In film, such transformations of the camera image would be marked off as 'special effects' and reserved for special genres (such as the science-fiction film) or for isolated moments of transition or climax (as in the montage sequences of many 1930s movies). Where a parallel to this television practice does occur is in the treatment of film sound which, as we have seen, is always mixed and filtered in conventional production. But the crucial point is that all this manipulation of sounds and images does not in any way lessen – from the perspective of the technology – the television medium's live potential.

Television does indeed consistently attempt to present itself as live and unmediated, but any examination of actual broadcast output shows how this potential is tamed and muted by the institutional practices of television. We have here a key instance of the way in which, when technological potential and social control come into conflict, the social pressures become dominant. Broadcasting was felt from the first to have a potentially enormous political and social impact, and universally the state has intervened to control the birth and organization of broadcast institutions. Truly live television is by definition uncontrollable – it cannot be precensored, or edited, or shaped by careful committee decision. The basic institutional and representational practices of television are therefore best understood as a set of strategies designed to defuse the potentially explosive quality of our direct access to live happenings. Many chat shows, football matches and theatrical variety shows proudly proclaim themselves to be live, and the format of the ostensibly live show is very common (from *The Muppet Show* to situation comedies with dubbed-on laughter tracks). However, there are always strong elements of control: the totally ritualized formats for chat shows, the positioning of a mediating reporter between us and the subject matter in most documentary forms, the use of presenters chosen for their well-spoken innocuousness introducing pre-recorded material which merely masquerades as live, the avoidance of unscripted, improvized drama, and so on. These are issues to which we shall need to return when we consider television's way of addressing its audience.

Video production

If a film is an artefact which aspires to (and indeed on occasion becomes) art, and original television strives to become an event, video is perhaps best defined as a recording material in search of a mode of production. Both film and television had very secure identities from the start. Although film was a development of still photography, the addition of movement and projection gave it a completely new identity, so that it could immediately find an independent role and a social application quite distinct from that of its predecessor. Television's social application echoed that of radio, but its possession of images to complement its sounds made it totally distinctive. It has been able to maintain this new identity despite making use of pre-existing films and eventually employing video tape as a recording material (just as radio has been able to utilize records and sound tape).

As we have seen, video did not have, in origin, a secure and distinctive identity of this kind, since in its first decade of application – until the mid-1960s – it was no more than an adjunct to television, a neutral recording substance, simply giving added flexibility to broadcast output. Moreover, the domestic video recorders marketed to allow viewers to control broadcast output (through the time-shifting which still accounts for an estimated 80 per cent of their use) did not – of themselves – give rise to new forms of purely video production. Instead the second major domestic application to develop alongside time-shifting has been the family viewing of bought or hired video copies of feature films originally produced for cinema release.

Video could only come into its own as a medium when provision of portable video camera and recorder units freed it from subservience to broadcasting and the domestic video cassette system. But even here a confusion over definitions arises because of the extremely primitive form of the first of these units to be marketed. The Sony Portapak – first introduced in the west in 1965 – comprised no more than a camera and a recorder. Its half-inch reel-to-reel system gave black-and-white images and a single synchronous sound track. These images were extremely difficult to edit and the sound was virtually impossible to dub or overlay. The Sony portapak's incompatibility with broadcasting – that is its inability to meet basic broadcast engineering standards and the impossibility of transferring its images and sounds adequately to the professional video recording formats – clearly marked this system as 'substandard video'. In contemporary terms it was a rival of the home-movie Super 8

128

film system – introduced the same year, 1965 – while the exciting revolution in *professional* sound-image shooting centred on the new flexible light-weight 16 mm synch-sound systems which had come into being after the invention of the Nagra tape recorder in 1958.

Despite these evident limitations, there was an initial vogue for seeing portapaks as examples of 'access to the media', which was a catchphrase in the late 1960s (Berrigan 1977). The new video system was perfectly suited to certain social applications, such as surveillance work, serving as a tool for community action and for some forms of basic teaching aid. At the same time, some artists made use of the portapak, especially in interactive or performance situations and as gallery installations. There are still important applications of video which remain on this basic level of production with its concentration on simple reporting or documentation. Firstly there is the increasing use of ENG (Electronic News Gathering) cameras by broadcast teams for on-the-spot reports. Secondly, the spread of home video recorders has eventually encouraged the domestic use of video cameras to supplement conventional still photography with moving pictures of such family events as weddings, funerals, baby's first steps, etc. All of these varied uses colour our perceptions of video's potential, just as amateur snapshots help shape our view of still photography.

It is no disrespect to this twenty-year tradition, and the body of estimable work that it has produced, to point out that in the 1980s video production can mean something far more complex and creative. With the advent of the Sony three-quarter-inch U-matic colour cassette system in the early 1970s, video production away from the broadcast studio began to have access to the possibilities of editing and processing its sounds and images. Subsequent systems have increased the range, flexibility, and sophistication of sound and image manipulation. This is more than a simple addition of new facilities: it redefines the whole nature of video production to take in post-production as well as shooting. In the process, the economics of the medium are transformed. Whereas with U-matic – and subsequent systems like Betacam – video remains a low-cost *recording* medium, costs rise enormously when the full cycle of production *and* post-production has to be gone through, because of the expense of computerized post-production hardware.

The effect of this is to lift video production out of the domestic, 'snapshot' sphere, offering a leap equivalent to that from Super 8 to 16 mm filming, a shift (potentially at least) to fully professional production. The discussion of video which follows concentrates on this level of production – extending, say, from the resources likely to be found in a well-equipped university or polytechnic media course to those available for a professional production such as a Channel Four independently produced drama-documentary, shooting on the Betacam format and using a Soho facilities house for post-production work. In short, it implies access to recording, editing, mixing, and processing facilities for both sound and image.

Video production follows the pattern of film in being a single-camera production system, which has no need of either a studio or a control room and which separates out the stages of shooting and editing which are fused in multi-camera television production. Indeed, the equipment required for video shooting has marked similarities to the 16 mm Arriflex or Eclair camera plus Nagra sound recorder used for *cinéma vérité*: camera, recorder, microphones, lights, tripod, etc. The individual takes of a video shot can be watched by the director and members of the crew as they are recorded (a television monitor is a uniquely video addition to the equipment). But since the choice and arrangement of these shots needs to be made subsequently through editing, a finished video lacks the live characteristics of the television system and has no need of broadcasting's elaborate direct address methods.

As a shooting system video fragments the action, but tends to respect the unity of the event staged for the camera far more than the classic film style does. There are a number of factors which favour a long-take style with comparatively few cuts. The video system of recording everything on a single tape, so that sound and image are locked together synchronously, encourages the video-maker to adopt a naturalistic approach in which 'truth to life' can all too easily be equated with reducing fragmentation to a minimum. Technical developments – in particular the zoom lens used almost universally for video (and increasingly for film)

130

– make long takes relatively easy to acquire. The video-maker in particular is incited to use this technical capability by the small-size screens on which most tapes are shown. For example, the long-held close-up of a single talking head which would be intolerable blown up on a big cinema screen can be quite acceptable to the viewer when seen on the screen of a domestic-style television receiver.

In professional production there are also financial incentives for a long-take style, which derive directly from the high cost of operating the machines used for editing the master tapes. There are two widely practised methods of editing. The first, 'on-line' editing, involves making an immediate assembly of the material from the master tapes, and this can be very expensive if numerous intricate cuts need to be made. The second method, 'off-line' editing, involves the transfer of material to low-band U-matic or VHS format, so that editing decisions can be worked out in a low-cost situation. But since this method needs more time (stretching video post-production to the time-span customary for film) and the decisions have to be reproduced using the master material in high-cost facilities, there is still every incentive to keep the number of cuts low. None of these considerations applies to film, where the editing equipment is relatively low-cost, and where the cutting of the master negative to match the assembled work print is charged at a standard figure per 100 foot of film, regardless of the number of edits (unless, of course, the shots are so short that edits have to be matched by eye and not, in accordance with standard practice, by the edge numbers common to the negative and the work print).

Although video production tends to preserve the unity of the event in this way, it does not similarly maintain the integrity of the image. It is common for video cameras to make their own automatic adjustment to variations in light levels, with a constant tendency to embellish reality (to brighten a dull, rainy day, for example). Video methods of recording and reproduction also cause considerable variations of colour and tone when the images are viewed on different replay machines. In addition to these technical modifications of the image, there are also possibilities for conscious manipulation by the video-maker – by adding or subtracting colour, for example – either in the chain from camera to recorder, or when preparing a final assembly of the edited master material. This latter possibility is vital to the definition of video adopted here. Although video still benefits from the credibility achieved by black-and-white photographic prints as early as the nineteenth century, it is more appropriate to see its images as always being as artificial as, say, the hues of a technicolour film print.

Video editing involves the same processes of selecting takes and finding the rhythm of a sequence as film editing, and separately recorded sound can similarly be added at the dubbing stage. But the working procedures of video editing are very different. The video tape is not assembled by physical cuts and joins, but by each shot being transferred in turn to a new master tape. These shots have to be assembled sequentially since – with present technology and until video editing is fully computerized – sequences cannot simply be put in a new order, as happens all the time in film editing. If, for example, the video-maker wants to remove shots two and forty-eight and reverse the order of shots eighteen and nineteen, then the whole tape has to be remade again from start to finish. Video editing lacks all the direct handling and the craft skills inherent in film editing. It is much more of a conceptual activity, with the video editor needing to be able to pre-plan a whole assembly, from first shot to last, before realizing it in the editing suite. Trying out a variety of patterns for a sequence means making the sequence in its entirety several times over.

In film-making, the director's immediate involvement with his or her own work normally ends with the completion of the fine cut of the picture and with the mixing, in the dubbing studio, of the various sound tracks which have been prepared. With video, however, the involvement of the maker does not end here. At U-matic level video-makers can personally produce the master copy; at professional level it will be produced in their presence. If there is special effects work, the maker will be closely involved in all the procedures by which both sounds and images are processed and synthesized. This is a crucial aspect of video production, which is ideal for bringing together material from a variety of sources, modifying, adjusting, and fusing images in ways impossible (or extremely expensive) with film.

132

In the case of video, it is the maker who personally communicates with the engineers and technicians who will realize, in his or her presence, the various special effects (wipes, dissolves, freeze-frames, split-screen effects, colourizations, superimpositions, titling, etc.) for which, in film-making, directors would simply provide coded instructions on the work print.

Even though video tape is often used in broadcasting merely to facilitate the flow of material which characterizes television, video as a medium in its own right consists of discrete works, just as the cinema does. But at present the independent video-maker lacks a real market enabling costs to be recouped outside broadcast television. One can anticipate that the latter system will in future be receptive to specifically video-style production, simply because it is so indiscriminately parasitic a medium. Already the advent of computerized graphics and the showing of increasing numbers of pop videos have widened the range of acceptable or expected television imagery, and there seems no reason why video-makers should be inhibited from making specifically video-style works, while at the same time seeking finance from broadcast sources. The constant extension of network broadcast times and the expansion of cable and satellite transmission can only offer additional outlets for video in the long run.

Nevertheless, just as films have traditionally had a second, 'non-commercial' market outside the movie theatres (in film clubs, educational establishments, etc.), so too video-makers can expect to find showings outside the broadcast institutions. One area at which they can aim is constituted by the millions of home video recorders, but the audience need not necessarily be exclusively domestic. Multichannel radio and the record industry already show clearly that the same domestic equipment can be used, at different times, to serve a number of quite distinct audiences: at some times whole families, at others special groups such as home-bound mothers or teenagers. Already various distribution circuits for video exist, and video has shown that it has the potential to become the communal mode which television never gave us, with tapes shown to an intimate (but non-family) audience which has gathered specifically to see them and can therefore be expected to accord them the kind of attention given to films. Such presentations need not, moreover, be restricted by the limitations of the domestic television set. There are numerous examples of video work designed to use big-screen video or a battery of different video monitors and sound-amplification sources.

Further reading

A useful preliminary to any consideration of the huge array of currently available technical manuals and handbooks is Pateman (1974). This deals specifically with Davis (1966), but the issues it raises are relevant to the whole range of technical writing on film, television, and video. The role of the script is well analysed by Staiger (1979a, 1979b), and clear insights into the traditional Hollywood approach can be derived from the once popular books on 'how to write for the movies', such as Bertsch (1917), Lane (1936), and Marion (1937). A good introduction to conventional film technique is Arijon (1976), and Happé (1975, 1983) gives clear accounts of the basic technology. For film editing see Reisz and Millar (1968), Burder (1968), Crittenden (1981), and Walter (1982), and for the whole range of sound techniques see Nisbett (1979, 1983). Ellis (1982) offers the best basic comparison of film and television, although he admits that he confronts television 'as a member of the cinema audience'. The various manuals by Millerson (1982a, 1982b, 1985) are standard introductions to television production. A good example of the initial approach to video production is Murray (1975) which is subtitled 'A basic guide to portable TV production for families, friends, schools and neighbourhoods'. Most video handbooks ignore totally the real potentials of post-production work; see, for example, Moore (1984): 'Today to make an accomplished film you need only have a video camera and two video-cassette recorders (the second one is for editing, and can be borrowed from a friend)'. Among the various handbooks for the amateur see Dean (1982), Owen and Dunton (1982), Watts (1984), Jackson (1985), Brookes (1985), Graham (1986), Elliott (1987), and Winston and Keydel (1987) from the UK, and Fuller, Kanaba, and Brisch-Kanaba (1980), Rosen (1984), and Bishop (1986) from the USA. For a more professional approach see Millerson (1983, 1987) and, especially, Mathias and Patterson (1985).

134

6 MODES OF ADDRESS

> It is clear that the manner in which the viewer is
> addressed, the precise way in which the desire to know
> is invoked and gratified by the exposition, is a matter of
> political importance.
>
> (Bill Nichols 1981: 206)

As we have seen, each of the new sound and image media has
found a particular space for itself in society, a specific orientation
that has come to dominate how we regard the medium in
question, despite a possibly wide array of other applications.
Furthermore, each of the three differing production systems
makes a specific contribution to the orientation of the various
audio-visual media. The production methods of film help lead
that medium towards an art of visual narration, just as those of
television help towards the creation of the 'events' to which live
presentation aspires. As heir to these production systems, video
is able to reproduce the various ways of addressing the audience
characteristic of its predecessors. But just as it has its own
distinctive production methods, so too video has its own specific
ways of addressing its audience. The present chapter is concerned
to define both the various inherited modes of address and those
specific to video. Its starting–point is of necessity the audience
itself: how we perceive images and sounds and how the viewing
context shapes our involvement.

Audience perception

Film theory offers many accounts of the interaction between
spectator and film, but most of these assume a passive audience.
The spectator is 'positioned' by the text, 'pinned down' by its

135

stylistic strategies, or even 'duped' by its narrative illusion. The general view of the television viewer is even more extreme: he or she is depicted slumped in front of the set with barely enough life or energy even to switch channels. This chapter sets out to question this approach to how we, as members of an audience, deal with the sounds and images offered to us by the media. Its concern with the *active* audience is perhaps best made apparent if we begin with a consideration of how we respond to the methods of story-telling common to film, television, and video. A useful guide is David Bordwell's *Narration in the Fiction Film* (1985), the underlying approach of which has relevance to documentary as well as fiction, and to television and video as well as film.

Bordwell roots his approach in the experimental study of perception which derives from Herman von Helmholz and traces the close connections between our preconscious and our conscious perceptions (Gregory 1966). At the first level, we are able – without conscious effort – to turn a chaos of swirling, pulsating sensations into a stable world. This act of construction on our part occurs despite such potentially disruptive phenomena as eye flicker and head movement. In a similar way, it is at this preconscious level that we construct a universe of colour out of the stimulus of light at different wavelengths and intensities. At a more conscious level, we similarly probe our environment, seeking to interpret and make sense of it, to give it stability and coherence. We do not deal consciously with masses of raw, unprocessed data, instead we submit all incoming stimuli to an immediate, active analysis which draws on our prior knowledge in order to estimate likelihood and to weigh expectations.

In our interaction with the world, we bring to bear framing schemes of knowledge, sets of anticipations (Bordwell 1985: 31). It is this process which allows us quickly to recognize the face of a friend at a crowded airport, or to pick out the voice of an acquaintance above the hubbub of a noisy bar. We do not sit back to gather all the evidence and to weigh it dispassionately. We take an active role, placing a bet, as it were, on a likely outcome. If we are correct, we are rewarded with a proper recognition. If we are wrong, we simply revise our judgement on the basis of the new information and promptly wager again.

In this approach, perception is seen as an active, ongoing process which can improve with experience. As our framing expectations, our criteria, become better defined with practice, so the probability of a successful perception increases.

Since there is no great gulf between how we perceive the natural world and how we perceive media sounds and images (Bordwell 1985: 32), an awareness of the active role of human perception is crucial to successful media production. Media sounds and images are credible to an audience only in so far as they meet some of the normal conditions of perception, that is to say, offer us material in a form that approximates to some extent to the ways in which we perceive the world. To tell a convincing story or to offer a documentary report, the maker must therefore structure a pattern of sounds and images which will encourage active receptivity. In other words, systems invented to record the world become systems of *representation* when used to create fictional or documentary works.

In so far as we act as members of an audience, we construct the story or argument out of the inevitably partial information which a film, television programme, or video tape offers us. Perhaps the least significant aspects of media perception are the illusory ones (Gombrich 1960; Gregory and Gombrich 1973). The very mechanisms of perception which enable us to experience a stable world, inevitably lead us to turn the flicker of light coming to us from the cinema or television screen into a steady flow. Similarly, the small differences between successive film or video images are perceived as evidence of motion, even when we are intellectually aware that we are seeing a flow of still images, and synchronous speech is 'heard' from the lips of the performers, when we know we are hearing sound from a loudspeaker situated alongside the screen.

At a more conscious level, when viewing a narrative film or tape, we make the same constant assumptions as in ordinary life (Bordwell 1985: 38–9). We construct hypotheses, which are confirmed or denied as the work unfolds before us. Using the information provided by the film or tape, we work to put the events into a coherent and meaningful sequence and to understand the actions and motivations of the characters. The frames of reference which we bring to bear derive from our knowledge of what a story is, our viewing of other films and tapes, and our general experience of the world. But because we first encounter stories at a very early age, we tend to be unaware of the fact that we are constantly involved in this act of putting the story together. In fact, viewing a film or tape is as learned an activity as, say, riding a bicycle.

Our various frames of reference all give us slightly different perceptions of the unfolding story. A lifetime's experience of listening to – and telling – stories means that we know that a particular sort of questioning is required (Prince 1973: 9–10). We rearrange the plot events into a chronological order and, in particular, we sort out from the sequencing (first this happens *and then* that) the key causal connections (that happens *because of* this) (Bordwell 1985: 49–50). From our knowledge of other films we bring expectations of a certain type of character and a certain type of story. We assume, for example, that a Hollywood movie will offer well-defined settings and characters and that the central figure will engage actively in some task or quest, the accomplishment of which will bring the film to an end. We tend to test the credibility – the 'realism' – of a film partly against such genre expectations ('This is how a western movie hero is expected to act') and partly against our experience of real life ('That's how people do behave in such a situation').

Viewing a narrative film or video, we construct the story (the chronological sequence of events with the cause-and-effect chain clarified and the motivations of the characters made plain) from the information which is given us. This information comes in two forms: firstly, the plot (the actual arrangement of the events within the fiction, with all the necessary build-up, blocks, retarding devices, and suspense involved in telling a gripping tale); secondly, the style (the patterning of the actual shots, sounds, staging, and performance that make up the film or tape) (Bordwell 1985: 51–2). While the audience's active involvement in the unfolding of the work in time is perhaps clearest in fictional narratives, the same principles are at work in other forms such as the documentary and the live television show. If we wish to distinguish between such forms in terms of the way in which they address their audiences, a prior consideration must be the differing physical situations of these audiences.

The situation of the audience

While the fundamental characteristics of the perception of sounds and images are identical whatever the medium, our interpretation of – and involvement in – the material offered to us varies widely according to the viewing context. In this connection, we can distinguish clearly between the film spectator, the television viewer, and the audience for video.

Our response to, and participation in, film stories derives both from the context in which we see them and from the particularity of projected motion pictures. Film history is usually dated from 28 December 1895, the day on which spectators first *paid* to see films. This is very important in helping us to define how we look at films. We have paid to see a particular showing of a particular film, and we expect comfort, darkness, and a lack of intrusion from our fellow spectators. Thus, although film viewing is a collective phenomenon, it is an individual experience for each spectator. Nothing is allowed to come between the individual and the action on the screen. We bring an uninterrupted attention to a film because we have paid to see it, knowing the performance will occupy only two or three hours of our time, after which we shall be able to drink a coffee or a beer, comment on the performances, report on our day's activities, etc. meanwhile all we have to do is to suspend our disbelief and untangle the plot offered to us (Metz 1974: 4).

From the start, cinema adopted a theatrical mode of presentation, and the key relationship is that between the spectator and the screen, which is normally much larger than a domestic interior would allow. This screen is an ambiguous space. On the one hand, it is a real space, having certain dimensions and a specific degree of luminosity. On the other hand, it loses this reality when it is filled with projected images and becomes the site for an imaginary action. Christian Metz, in his book *Film Language*, stresses that it is because the spectators inhabit a physical space quite separate from this imaginary sphere that, paradoxically, the cinema possesses an enormous impression of reality (Metz 1974: 10). There is nothing to prevent the spectators from submitting to the unceasing flow of images and projecting their imaginations into the fictional world of the film.

The successive viewpoints give us, as spectators, a particularly privileged view of the action (Browne 1975–6). This view is much richer than that obtained by looking through a window or a keyhole. It is not limited to the perceptions of any one of the characters, nor is it a totally omniscient, god-like view. Certain information can be held back by the film-maker in order to maintain suspense. Nevertheless, we are allowed a unique position, both inside and outside the action simultaneously. We are magically absent to the screen characters, who behave as if we could not see them, but at the same time they are present to us (Cavell 1971: 25–6). As a result, we can see these characters in their most private moments. The darkness which envelops us as spectators allows us to feel totally secure in this privileged position: the pleasure which cinema offers us, its paying customers, is that of seeing intimately but without any personal threat, a voyeurism of a quite unique kind.

The situation of the television viewer is very different. Early studies of television tended to ignore the implications of the fact that television is customarily watched in a family situation. The key questions originally confronted by sociologists – the size of audiences and the effects of programming – tacitly assumed that watching television was an activity akin to seeing a film. In fact television viewing, though occurring in the home, is not a private, individual activity: it is a social experience. Even the element of personal choice is muted. For many people an evening's viewing represents a series of 'deals' and compromises with other members of the family ('You can watch *Crossroads* if I can look at the snooker later') (Morley 1986: 19). In his analysis, which summarizes recent debates as well as offering his own research findings, David Morley points out the amazing range of other activities which can accompany watching television: eating, knitting, arguing, listening to music, reading, letter-writing, vacuum cleaning, etc. (1986: 22). While early analysis was often concerned with the possible confusion of television fiction with the viewer's reality, Morley's work shows that in fact the connection is more complex. Viewers have a full awareness of how *Crossroads*, for example, is different from real life, but at the same time they are able to use the situations which occur within its dramatic narrative actively, as a way of focusing and illustrating issues relevant to their own lives (1986: 31).

Whereas seeing a film (like reading thrillers or romance fiction) lifts the audience out of their immediate situations and problems, watching television is intimately caught up with these latter. As a result, the individual programming is in some respects less significant than the viewing context. What is watched is, for example, closely linked to the power situation in the family, with possession of the remote control device serving as a mark of authority. The way members of the audience respond depends very much on how they see their own identities as men or women (Morley 1986: 146–72). The women Morley interviewed tended to enjoy soap operas only guiltily (feeling that there were other things they ought to be doing around the house), while the men often stated a preference for factual programming (as if watching fiction were somehow 'unmasculine', and hence a waste of time).

The range of response to – and use of – television is astonishing, but very little of it approximates to film viewing (1986: 22). For some individuals and families, watching television is a pretext for conversation (rehearsing the views which will later be put forward at work, in school, or while shopping). For others, it is a sign of opting out, concentration on a television programme being used as a way of refusing conversation. Television provides a constant companion for the lonely, but for family groups living in cramped situations it can mark out domestic space, allowing whatever separation or physical contact is required. It helps define the day's schedules (the times for meals, for putting the children to bed, and so on), but it can also serve as a reward or punishment for the young. The very fact of switching off the set can have a wider significance, indicating the importance attached to visitors, or marking the seriousness of a family event (such as a bereavement). Morley argues convincingly that far from being passively consumed, television is used very actively in the domestic situation. Meaning is deciphered and debated, enjoyed communally, or rowed over. Programming is appreciated for its predictable qualities or used as a unique form of stimulus – a point emphasized by Stuart Hood in his introduction (1986: 8–9).

The audience for video may of course be no more than a

simple combination of these two modes of viewing: a family gathered to watch in a domestic setting a hired tape of a film originally made for cinema release. Yet even the most banal use of the domestic video cassette recorder for time-shifting implies a control by the spectator absent from conventional television viewing. The flow of television sounds and images has been stopped, choices have been made, and viewing can conform to the family's other priorities and their own leisure-time schedules rather than having to obey the vagaries of broadcast institutional decision-making. As soon as we move away from this domestic setting, moreover, and consider work made specifically by video production methods, radically new possibilities immediately become apparent.

Video is not tied to the limitations of the movie theatre or domestic interior: a video tape may run as an endless loop in a gallery installation, be part of a performance situation, or require a battery of monitors and speakers for its variety of images and multiple sound sources. Video can be seen to bring a new vitality to a spread of viewing situations extending from institutional or educational contexts to gatherings of avant-garde artists and their public. While 16 mm films used in audio-visual aids contexts have tended to suffer from being seen as inferior to 'real' cinema, and avant-garde practice has habitually been marginalized in film culture, video has the potential to be a positive *communal* form, bringing together small but involved audiences, breaking down old barriers and fusing previously separate forms and genres.

With its unique flexibility and power to synthesize sounds and images, video can animate a space which has hitherto been only tentatively occupied. It can bring together the home movie and the fictional narrative, the historical factual record and the visual experiment, the audio-visual instructional loop and the avant-garde exploration of space and duration. Video has the ability to rediscover the immediacy and excitement of the Victorian lantern lecture show, which has been lost through the growth of cinema as a mass medium of dramatic story-telling and through the institutionalization of television. Video, in short, can bring back the personal style of presentation to match the personal quality of expression which its production methods allow.

142

On the basis of these clarifications of how sounds and images are perceived and the distinctions between the various audience contexts, we can now move on to consider how the various forms of media output are structured to address their audiences.

Mode of address

The initial question of how a film or tape addresses us – directly or indirectly – is quite easy to answer. At one extreme, in the conventional Hollywood movie, the actors never address us directly or even acknowledge our presence, while at the other extreme, as exemplified by live television programming such as the news, we encounter presenters who apparently look directly at us and seem to address their words to us individually. Other forms of film, television, and video lie somewhere in between. The 'fly-on-the-wall' observational stance of *cinéma vérité* lies closer to the Hollywood end of the spectrum, whereas the conventional documentary, in which an unseen narrator's voice explains the images to us, is self-evidently a direct address form, and so closer to live television presentation. The distinction is so basic that it might seem pointless to make it. But in fact – as Bill Nichols has shown – this drawing of attention to the necessary connection between text and spectator does have important consequences (Nichols 1981). The notion of a mode of address allows us to go beyond an inert formal analysis of the differing stylistic features of a work, so as to examine the ways in which the spectator interacts with it. As with David Bordwell's theory of narrative, Nichols's work allows us to envisage an active audience which is guided by the underlying strategies of the film or tape's construction, but is engaged in the work of fleshing out the text from the inevitably fragmentary material that is offered.

It has already been argued that in order to address us in any significant way – to convey meaning and emotion – sounds and images need to be shaped at all levels. Just as the key distinction when we are considering story-telling is that betwen plot (which the film or tape supplies) and story (which we piece together out of the plot elements), so too, when we are considering questions of address, the crucial division is that between the aspects of reality recorded on film or tape ('what happens in front of the camera or recorder') and the fictional or non-fictional 'world' which they prompt us to construct. All the audio-visual media continue to draw on the credibility which attached itself quite early to the photographic image, and many forms claim to offer us, if not reality, then at the very least 'a window on the world'. But as soon as we begin to examine the elements of their construction in so far as they relate to the audience, it quickly becomes apparent that we are given, not a direct view, but a shaped and mediated facsimile, not a reproduction, but a representation.

What is filmed or taped may be material of many kinds – recorded specifically for this production or taken from an archive, staged or unstaged, overtly fictional or fiction masquerading as reality. Often the boundaries between these categories will be deliberately blurred. Many seemingly unstaged, observational shots in a documentary will in fact have been rehearsed and repeated. Often authentic visual footage (of the First World War, for example) is overlaid with sound effects recorded much later. It is important, in analysing the audio-visual media, to clarify the precise distinctions between these varying degrees of reality. But the key element remains the manner in which this material is shaped and assembled, so as to lead us to construct a particular world. At this level a whole range of crucial questions concerning the mode of address present themselves. Is there a narrator? If so, where does he or she stand in relation to the text? What is the balance of image and sound? Does the unity and coherence of the text lie in the image track or in the verbal exposition? What are the significant omissions from the world which the audience is invited to build up?

All formal choices are statements about the world, about the nature of communication and about the particular relation of maker and audience. Any media analysis therefore needs to probe what the structure of the work implies as well as to examine its overt content. Since such a mode of analysis may seem abstract when set out as a set of general questions, it is perhaps appropriate at this point to look briefly at the various types of media structure – the varieties of film from the Hollywood movie to *cinéma vérité*, the modes of documentary and live television production, the forms of avant-garde work in sound and image – to which video is heir.

It is cinema, with its theatrical mode of distribution and its production system based on a separation of the stages of shooting, editing, and exhibition, which has developed the most elaborate forms of indirect address. In production terms, the conventional fictional feature film offers a series of staged, totally contrived events, filmed out of order and rearranged during the editing, which present themselves as credible but not true. There is no ambiguity in our response: we are entertained without being fully taken in, happy to accept a fiction which gives us excitement, pleasure, and suspense without requiring from us more than a willing suspension of disbelief. But the fictional world created in such a film has several distinctive features. The images with their reinforcing, supportive sounds allow the events to unfold with a temporal and spatial logic within a closed, self-contained universe which is harmonious within its own bounds. The players act to the camera (and hence through it to us), while showing no awareness that they are being watched, either by the camera at the shooting or by us when the film is projected. Although we may be consciously aware of the actors – whether stars or character players – the boundary between actor and role is never in doubt. For example, we never confuse Cary Grant as he is in real life with the parts he plays, even though his ambiguous screen persona draws much from his tormented personality.

Both the closed unity of the filmic world and the fact that although the players are present to us, we are absent to them, help create a seemingly natural world. This sense is enhanced by the situation whereby the events have no apparent narrator but seem to tell themselves. Even when we are given an ostensible narrator – as in *Double Indemnity*, for example, where the leading actor emerges out of the night to record his story on the office dictaphone – this figure never talks directly to us. Even recurrent shots of him dictating or passages of voice-over commentary do not allow him to dictate the visual pattern of the narration. As the film unfolds, he is swallowed up in the narrative, a character on a par with all the others. This basic pattern is common to virtually all Hollywood movies except the bizarre Raymond

Chandler adaptation, *Lady in the Lake*, which attempts a true first-person narration. There the actor-director Robert Montgomery – in the persona of Philip Marlowe – talks directly to camera to introduce the story which is then largely told through a camera which constantly shows what purports to be his literal point of view (so that we see the hero-narrator only when he stands in front of a mirror).

Crucial to the credibility of the conventional Hollywood movie is the economy of the narration: twenty or thirty short sequences, each pared down to a minimum of dialogue and a maximum of evocative action. The rhythm of the cutting, with its constant shift between general observation and specific (often matched) character viewpoints and its dramatic compression of action, gives us no time for reflection. The effect is enhanced by the various continuity devices, among them the set of rules designed to ensure the basic stability of the characters in successive shots, and the use of cuts on action and the employment of sound continuity to disguise the fragmentation of the action. The effect is to create a seamless, unified world, totally acceptable as a facsimile, since we are not asked to believe it, but simply to go along with it for the duration of the film.

Advances in 16 mm film technology and the new market offered by television led in the 1960s to the development of one of the most paradoxical of all documentary forms, *cinéma vérité* or direct cinema (Issari and Paul 1979). Here, using minimal crews, light-weight cameras and highly portable tape recorders, the film-makers set out to allow us direct access to other people's lives. Real events are filmed in synch and presented – without music or a visible narrator – in ways designed to minimize our awareness of the contrivance. But although the characters are seemingly indifferent to the film crew, we know logically that the intrusion of the film-makers must affect their behaviour. As a result, the contradictions of this form are immense. The fact that the characters never address the film-makers directly nor show any awareness of being observed, does not mean that they are being themselves. It is surely truer to say that they are *acting* themselves, but the gap which should exist between being and acting is constantly blurred.

Oddly enough, although the film-makers are customarily

never seen in a *cinéma vérité* work, the marks of their presence (indicated by, say, camera wobble or microphone shadow) serve in some way to authenticate the view given us: the sense that this is not fiction but real life, filmed newsreel-style as it happens. Conversely, all the evidence of the editing process is usually concealed, although up to twenty hours of material may have been shot to give a half-hour finished work. *Cinéma vérité* films hide the fact that they are shaped and edited by keeping ostensibly to a real chronology – often that of a real-life crisis situation, such as a trial or the opening night of a Broadway play. Despite the contradictions of the form, such films offer us as spectators the unique voyeuristic situation common to fictional films, but this time it is real lives – not wholly fictional events – that we are watching. Again, as with fictional films, seeing is believing and we watch from a position of security. Since the characters never acknowledge our existence, we enjoy our unique insights untroubled by any personal complicity in the dramas acted out before us. *Cinéma vérité* has traditionally been a film form, but it is one which is eminently suited to video, as a kind of extension of video's surveillance role.

The technological developments which gave rise to *cinéma vérité* also prompted a great upsurge of independent or underground film-making, particularly in Britain and the United States. Although experimental film-making has a long history – going back to the early years after the First World War in Europe – there was no precedent for the explosion of independent 16 mm film-making in the late 1950s and early 1960s, when avant-garde films of every conceivable kind began to be made in large numbers. These low-budget films had a very different economic base from that of the mainstream commercial movie and expressed the film-makers' personal concerns with a directness impossible in the context of a film industry mass producing high-cost works for immediate, transient consumption. All of these new films question to some extent the established codes of film narrative and – thanks to unusual stylistic methods and unconventional subject matter – create a new relationship with the viewer. Because early portable video systems were often used most inventively within a fine art/independent film-making context, this new direction taken by film is extremely important in defining an initial aesthetics of video and the immediate audience response to the new medium.

It is impossible to generalize about the vast array of diverse styles embraced by the term 'experimental cinema', but in Britain there emerged a tendency which was to have a key influence on the development of video as a medium for artistic expression. This was the so-called 'structural-materialist film', made by a loose grouping of film-makers centred on the London Film Makers' Co-op, set up (on the New York model) in 1966. Here – in the work of film-makers like Peter Gidal and Malcolm Legrice – a quite new relationship with the spectator was sought, since the makers largely rejected all thought of content as such and turned their backs on all the illusion-creating techniques and processes of the conventional film (Gidal 1976; Legrice 1977). Instead of offering realistic representations of fictional events and seeking to shape and manipulate the spectator's emotions, these film-makers sought to make their audiences consciously aware of the material aspects of film.

This led to a concern with the 'actuality' of the film-maker's materials and processes. This form of cinema focused firstly on the camera and took as its content the characteristics of the film material itself: celluloid and emulsion, but also scratches, sprocket holes, splicing tape, edge numbering, dirt particles, process stains, and so on. Secondly, it involved the use in production of an optical developer and printer. This allowed the film-maker to transform short sequences, to build them up through the use of loops, repetitions, and superimpositions, and to derive fresh content from printing 'errors', such as image slip. The third key element was the projector and, along with this, the screen. The structural-materialist film-maker used double and multiple projection, mixed film with slides, explored the space between projector and screen (using alternative light sources in the auditorium and performance in the stream of light from the projector) and emphasized the duration of the performance through sequences of blank spaces, use of loops, flicker effects, and so on. In this way, the normally hidden elements of the conventional film experience were separated out and problematized, as the spectator was incited to reflect consciously and attentively on the whole nature of film-making and viewing. These ideas, along with those of other avant-garde film forms, found their echo in the work of subsequent video-makers, particularly those concerned with 'scratch video', who similarly used a range of video techniques to lay bare the conventions of the television process.

It is the genre of film most neglected by film theorists – the documentary – which brings us closest to television modes of address. Documentary extends across a variety of media (Corner 1986) and has a history which can be traced back to 1895, when Louis Lumière filmed a number of actual events, such as workers leaving his factory or a train entering the station near his summer home of La Ciotat, for inclusion in his earliest programmes (Barsam 1974; Barnouw 1974). But because the growth of the film industry was largely the result of the application of film to the telling of stories, the factual strand of film-making has received far less attention. When it is investigated, documentary shows clearly that the fictional feature film draws on only a part of the potential of film as a medium of expression. Whereas the conventional fictional film derives its power to fascinate from the mode of indirect address, which allows us to watch while remaining unseen and unchallenged, documentary shows that films can also address us directly.

The titles of silent documentaries and the commentary ubiquitous since the early 1930s give us information, comment, and argument directly. In this way the customary balance of sound and image is reversed, since with documentary it is the sound track which, by logically ordering the exposition, points out the issues being raised. Just as the caption of a news photo is crucial in removing the ambiguity of the photographic image (naming the person depicted or locating the scene in time and space), so too the commentator's voice in a documentary shapes our involvement and brings together the various types of images (film clips, still photographs, graphics, maps, diagrams, etc.) which are used as illustrative support. This voice has authority, whether the speaker is seen or – as is usual in traditional film documentaries – remains an unseen presence. In the first instance the commentator benefits from the effect of synchronous sound (which gives weight and conviction to the images), in the second instance he – or very occasionally she – derives a god-like authority from being both invisible and seemingly omniscient. While many accounts of documentary, particularly those by practitioners of the form, assume that the commentator can be neutral and the depicted material can comprise 'facts', it is clear on reflection that the tone, accent, gender, and stance of the commentator is crucial in establishing a connection with the viewers and in shaping the way they look at the visual material.

However, just as we do not need to believe that a fictional film is true in order to enjoy it, so too we can appreciate a documentary even if we know it cannot be wholly neutral. We do, however, need to accept the reasonableness of the commentator, since documentary is a form which above all addresses us rationally. Even the most powerful documentaries on harrowing subjects strive to hold our emotions in check and to obtain our lucid acceptance. In the case of documentary, the dreamlike aspects of film projection so important to fictional film-making are underplayed and stress is placed instead on the *evidence* which the camera obtains at the moment of shooting. In this way documentary can claim to offer us knowledge and a fresh insight, but the shaping of its material is crucial. However dispassionate the presentation may be, a whole series of rhetorical and retarding devices is inevitably employed to hold back the full knowledge promised to us at the outset, thereby maintaining our attention until the final revelation allows the work to come to a satisfying conclusion. Similarly the format itself carries implications of all kinds: notions of order and rationality, the idea that the world is knowable and that seeing is believing. At the same time, the unseen commentator allows documentary in its traditional form to open up a gap between images and sounds, which allows scope for powerful effects of counterpoint and ironic interplay. In this respect, documentary offers valuable lessons for video-makers who wish to have full control over the shaping of their material. One way to do this is to be willing at times to break the automatic (and ultimately banal) synchronization of sound and image which video recording offers.

Television presentation brings a fresh immediacy to the direct mode of address typical of documentary but, by showing the presenter or reporter, closes down this potentially creative split. In the various forms of live or 'recorded-live' television presentation the address is as direct as possible, with the presenter looking straight into the camera (and hence directly at us) and conducting an apparent dialogue with us. There is no mystery about this presenter: he or she co-exists or – in the case of a recorded programme – appears to co-exist in our real space and time. The same mode of address has also been developed in specifically television styles of documentary, although these are very clearly recorded and edited forms. The conventional arrangement is for the celebrity personality to be shown standing physically between the camera and the subject of the programme (to which his or her back is characteristically turned), offering us a flow of words which continues without pause across image cuts and changes of location.

The television mode of direct address is as complex as the indirect system of film, but its components are essentially verbal. It is by their words – backed up by relevant looks – that the presenters pass authority to each other, introduce the topics for discussion to us, draw in subsidiary figures (reporters, experts, witnesses), and pull together the threads of the argument to provide a satisfying conclusion (Brunsden and Morley 1978: 58–60). As in the feature film, certain key aspects of the address system are concealed. In particular the whole technological complexity of a television studio employing dozens of people or the hierarchy of personnel involved in a film crew are hidden. As a result, the presenter stands out and gains authority as the apparent source of all the material (live and pre-recorded, studio-based, or obtained by satellite transmission) that makes up a news programme, or of all the images (which may have taken a devoted team a year to shoot) in a nature documentary. Separated off in this way from the real context of production and carried by the force of the direct mode of address, the presenter seems to be shifted directly to the television set in our own sitting-room and to be talking to us personally. In this way, the realm of the imaginary is transferred from the screen (which is its location in the fictional film) to the relationship, the apparent dialogue, between the presenter and us. The remarkable fusion within television's mode of address of the direct and the imaginary is one reason for its difficulty in marking off an authentically fictional world – as is shown by the constant rebuke that realistic television drama is not 'true' and by the mass of mixed forms of documentary-drama and drama-documentary to which the medium has given rise (Goodwin, Kerr, and Macdonald 1983).

It will be apparent from the preceding discussion of mode of address that although video is a new medium, the video-maker is by no means working in a void. Video is, by definition, an eclectic medium and obviously it can be used simply to reproduce and – if necessary – synthesize the forms of its various predecessors. All of these, as we have seen, strive to present themselves as natural and unproblematic forms and their practitioners claim to reproduce the world 'as it is', when in fact they offer representations of it. A realization of this is the first step towards the critical awareness necessary for full use of video's potential.

The various types of mode of address have been described here as forming parts of a spectrum extending from the Hollywood movie to live television presentation (as exemplified by news presentation). It should be apparent that these two extremes are the result of high-cost production methods, crews of hierarchically organized specialist technicians, and particular possibilities of distribution, none of which are available to the individual video-maker. But they do offer invaluable insights into the range of possible modes of audio-visual address to which video may aspire. The conventional narrative film offers the clearest insight into the way in which a mode of indirect address can allow a particularly compelling form of fiction to be created. The rules for manipulating time and space worked out in the film industry offer useful guides for the video-maker, even if video lacks the particular magic which film derives from its usual context of a darkened auditorium and big screen projection. At the other extreme, television programming shows ways of structuring a direct address approach which, thanks to a recognition of the importance of a live (or apparently live) verbal presentation, is able to overcome the limitations of the small screen size of the home television set and the intrusions of the domestic interior.

In addition, video-makers can examine the various hybrid forms (of which the examples chosen here were *cinéma vérité*, avant-garde film, and documentary) which were developed or modified when technological developments in the decade preceding the advent of video offered the combination of accessible and flexible 16 mm film production systems and new distribution outlets through broadcast television. Consideration of these forms is particularly important, since there is a clear analogy here with the situation of video, which has developed so as to become a versatile and creative medium at a point of fresh technological innovation in both production (computer-aided systems) and distribution (cassette, cable, and satellite).

Further reading

Useful general studies of narrative are Prince (1973) and Scholes and Kellogg (1966); Bordwell (1985) offers a complex but rewarding study of film narrative. Metz (1974) and Cavell (1971) give helpful introductory insights into the relation of the spectator and the feature film, while Browne (1975–6) is an invaluable piece of detailed analysis. The general 1970s film theorization of the spectator is typified by Heath (1981); this view is contested (from a standpoint somewhat different from that adopted here) by Wilson (1986). Nichols (1981) contains a pioneering study of mode of address in documentary which has wide implications. Barsam (1974) and Barnouw (1974) are largely untheorized histories of documentary; Corner (1986) is an excellent and wide-ranging collection of articles. For *cinéma vérité* and its implications see Issari and Paul (1979) and Wyver (1982). The British avant-garde of the 1970s finds its views well reflected in Dwoskin (1975), Gidal (1976), and Legrice (1977). The best accounts of the television audience are Brunsden and Morley (1978) and Morley (1986), while Goodwin, Kerr, and Macdonald (1983) reflect the debate around mixed modes of television, such as 'drama–documentary'.

PART THREE
VIDEO AS VIDEO

Videotape is something else. One reason for this is that the industry has developed in a quirky way, not always following the predictions and prescriptions of the manufacturers and publicists; people are surprised at what it does because they haven't been warned. In addition, people often get an immediate sense of the startling potential of video – it doesn't take long to see that its development may literally change the world.

(Michael Murray 1975: 8–9)

Although it is comparatively easy to develop a technological history of video, it is virtually impossible – at this time – to write a meaningful history of video as a creative medium. In the case of film, there is a great diversity in the films which make up the significant landmarks in 'the history of cinema', but collectively they all form part of an economically extremely important sector of sound and image reproduction: a multimillion dollar industry with a world-wide system of production, distribution, and exhibition. This entertainment industry has a central importance however we look at 'film': from the point of view of the manufacture of celluloid, the production and sale of equipment, or the place of cinema in the spectrum of contemporary mass communication.

This is no longer true when we turn to video, where its application to broadcast television passes virtually unnoticed and creative work seeking to exploit its full potential is largely confined to the margins: extremely low-budget production which does not reach a mass audience but is – at best – confined to, say, the Bracknell Video Festival, Arts Council Tours, and very occasional screenings, late at night, on Channel Four. In this sense the situation of video is very like that of contemporary photographic art. As Ian Jeffrey observes, there has never been 'a mainstream in photography, only strong currents evident here and there for brief periods' (Jeffrey 1981: 8). This point is backed up by John Berger, who notes that:

> Within a mere thirty years of its invention as a gadget for an elite, photography was being used for police filing, war reporting, military reconnaissance, pornography, encyclopedic documentation, family albums, postcards, anthropological records (often, as with the Indians in the United States, accompanied by genocide), sentimental moralising, inquisitive probing (the wrongly named 'candid camera'): aesthetic effects, news reporting and formal portraiture.
>
> (Berger 1980: 48)

While it is still possible for historians to construct a meaningful thread through the early developments of photography (particularly the period during which it was reaching its full technical potential and accessibility), the present-day scene since the photographic industry became a major multinational organization can no longer be described in traditional ways. Helmut and Alison Gernsheim's otherwise excellent volume, *A Concise History of Photography* (1971), for example, disintegrates into non-historical categories in its summary of the post-Second World War scene: 'contemporary portraiture', 'fotofilm', 'reportage' and 'colour photography'. Faced with the same problem, Ian Jeffrey, whose *Photography: A Concise History* shows his keen awareness of the extent to which the history of photography discriminates against whole sectors of photographic practice, is able to maintain a coherent picture only by asserting that the recent history of photography is 'in large part' an American history, thereby ignoring huge areas of achievement (Jeffrey, 1981: 204).

The basis of video's economic development is the explosion of demand for the domestic video cassette recorder, which had found a place in half the nation's homes in the UK within seven years of its introduction in 1979 – a progression unmatched by any other example of domestic communication technology.

Graham Wade estimates that by the mid-1980s the UK video market alone was worth in the region of £1.3 billion a year, of which about £1 billion was made up of video hardware (Wade 1985: 26). He also estimates that by 1985 about 130 million blank cassettes had been sold and that, despite the problems caused by piracy and the public campaigns against pornographic material (the so-called 'video nasties'), sales of pre-recorded cassettes had passed 2.5 million a year. In this industrial and marketing context, the area of independent video production is economically insignificant.

The difficulties of defining a specific video history are compounded by the contradictions of the first creative form to which the domestic video recorder has given rise: the pop-music video (Laing 1985: 78–83). In general terms this can be seen as an expected response to the opportunities offered by the creation of a new audio-visual channel and yet another example of the bringing together of the originally diverse areas of sound and image recording which must inevitably result from the current multimedia transnational industrial organization. With the pop video, music recording unequivocally enters the mainstream of the mass media (from which it has been too long – and wrongly – excluded by some sociologists). The fact that the impetus for the new form originates in the wider social and economic forces rather than in some simple technological determinant (such as the specific potential of video tape) is shown by the way in which pop videos, though edited and distributed in video format, are usually shot – like television adverts – on film. They constitute a flourishing form, with some 800 individual videos made in Britain in 1984 and perhaps double that number in the United States (Laing 1985: 78). But in origin the pop video is an advertising form, a new type of publicity for the pop group or performer in question. For this reason the broadcast organizations have in the past usually refused to pay for screenings – thereby denying the form an autonomous existence – although the US twenty-four-hour video channel, NTV, did begin paying royalties in the mid-1980s.

The pop video is also a form in which the standard assumptions of visual predominance in an audio-visual medium no longer apply. The key commercial element is clearly the music. Moreover, since this music is itself a studio product which probably cannot be reproduced by live performers in concert, there can often be no question of the use of the normal techniques for subordinating sound through synchronization (so that the image seems to *produce* the sound). The result is a form which is both fascinating and self-contradictory: distributed in video format but shot on film, free-wheeling yet constrained by its advertising function, visually innovative yet subordinated to its sound track, an individual artefact which is parasitic on a separate and commercially more important object (the record or cassette), a part of the distinctive youth culture that needs to be played through the equipment forming the focus of family life. Despite – or perhaps because of – these contradictions, the pop video points to the new potential of video as a medium in its own right.

Portapak video equipment was first introduced in the west at a turbulent time of social upheaval and optimism at the end of the 1960s. It was widely welcomed, since it was assumed that, just as the new 16 mm film equipment developed at the beginning of the decade had made filming simpler and more accessible for documentarists and avant-garde film-makers alike, so the new video technology would allow 'access' to broadcasting (Berrigan 1977). This belief was unfulfilled, since the gap between what the new equipment could offer in technical terms and what was demanded by accepted broadcast standards was unbridgeable. Video did, however, form a significant part of the post-1968 'counter-culture' in both the USA and Britain, and often found a focus in co-operative ventures like the New York and London Film Makers' Co-ops.

In Britain one significant strand of video work took its place alongside the new avant-garde film movement in the art colleges, which had been a focal point of the May 1968 euphoria and confrontation. As a result video was seized upon by artists engaged with modernist styles of painting and sculpture, performance and conceptual art. As Stuart Marshall has pointed out, artists concerned with education (and often working part-time in art colleges) founded the first specifically video organizations – such as London Video Arts – and created the first substantial body of video art, giving the medium the respectability that allowed it to be seen as a fundable activity by institutions such as the Arts Council (Marshall 1985: 68). There was, of course, a huge diversity of work undertaken, but Marshall picks out two contrasting preoccupations: a concern with the specific – non-filmic – aspects of video technology and a critique of illusionism, leading to a confrontation with conventional television forms (Marshall 1985: 69). Subsequent work has been influenced by a number of developments – shifts in the emphasis of film theory, feminist study of representation, socially committed community activity – so that although this area of video creativity remains a minority culture, it has considerable vitality in the late 1980s.

Current video activity takes many forms: documentation as well as discovery, social application as well as artistic endeavour, personal self-expression as well as extensive big-business use. Here we are concerned less with individual achievements than with the overall potential of an incredibly versatile medium, and the following chapters set out to examine the aesthetics of video sound and image in the light of recent contributions by film theorists. The work undertaken in film theory on narration, on point of view and the look, and on sound in relation to the image has often been accompanied by detailed and probing analysis of particular instances. The result is a number of remarkable insights which have great relevance for video, although of course they need to be rethought so as to take into account the different situation of the spectator and the new balance of sound and image characteristic of video.

7 AESTHETICS OF VIDEO SOUND

> More than colours and forms, it is sounds and their
> arrangements that fashion societies. With noise is born
> disorder and its opposite: the world. With music is born
> power and its opposite: subversion. In noise can be read
> the codes of life, the relations among men. Clamour,
> Melody, Dissonance, Harmony; when it is fashioned by
> man with specific tools, when it invades man's time,
> when it becomes sound, noise is the source of power
> and purpose, of the dream – Music. It is at the heart of
> the progressive rationalization of aesthetics, and it is a
> refuge for residual irrationality; it is a means of power
> and a form of entertainment.
>
> (Jacques Attali 1985: 6)

In our consideration of video aesthetics, we can draw valuable
lessons from film theory, but – as has been constantly stressed
throughout this study – the imbalance caused by over-emphasis
on the image in film theorization becomes a positive falsification
if we apply its insights without modification to video. As the
historical sections of Part One demonstrated, the story of sound
and image reproduction offers a pattern of constant interaction
in which sound is by no means always the lesser partner. The
establishment of the synchronous sound film in the late 1920s,
for example, was an instance of the colonization of the film
industry by powerful companies grown rich on the profits from
radio (that is to say, sound transmission). Video traces its
parentage in terms of its modes of address and aesthetics,
through television and the sound film, to two ancestors: radio
and silent cinema. For this reason, the two-part discussion of

video which follows reverses the conventional order and pays attention first to video sound.

Varieties of sound-image relations

From the very start in the 1890s, the grey soundless spectres moving on the cinema screen seem to have demanded a musical accompaniment. The various explanations usually advanced to justify the employment of cinema musicians (whose salaries, by the 1920s, had come to have a considerable impact on the economics of film exhibition) are that the music was needed to hide the clatter of the projector and to protect the individual spectator from the various noises (shuffling, coughing, whispering) emanating from his or her neighbours. But a further explanation is surely the ghostlike nature of the figures in these projected images, inhumanly cut off from their inherent and inevitable sounds. Music was required to remove the aura of death from the insubstantial wraiths on the screen and to give them body and weight.

Another – often forgotten – sound element in early cinema was the verbal presentation by the compère or fairground operator. Just as the structure of the more developed narrative films of the decade up to 1906 was largely modelled on existing forms like the lantern slide series or the stereograph sequence (Fell 1974: 122–63), so too the mode of presentation involved an equivalent to the magic lantern lecturer. The Lumières set the pattern when they chose a family friend, the conjurer Félicien Trewey, to present the first London showings of the cinematograph in 1896. The words of the presenter standing alongside the screen guided the audience in their reception of the images by locating the scenes, identifying the characters, and telling the story, thereby forming a verbal context within which the images were seen and appreciated. From the early 1900s, however, western film-makers were concerned to internalize the narrative – to make the images tell the story unaided – and gradually the presenter was displaced. It is usually assumed that he had disappeared from Europe before the First World War, but documentation on this point is scarce, and Norman King reports having encountered a travelling projectionist who presented his collection of silent films personally in a Provençal country town as late as 1981 (King 1984: 2–15). In a scheme of presentation such as this, the images do not dominate, instead they are reduced to little more than illustrations in a performance shaped by the physical and audible presence of both presenter and musicians.

What is clear from historical studies of eastern cinema is that this initial mode of presentation remained customary in India (Baskaran 1981: 81) and especially in Japan (Anderson and Richie 1959: 23–6) long after it had largely disappeared in Europe, indeed until the coming of sound-on-film in the early 1930s. In Japan the presenter or *benshi* came to be the key figure in film exhibition throughout the silent period, placing his own interpretation on the film and using the opportunity to instruct the audience. In a system such as this, the meaning of the film lay wholly in the interpretation placed on its inevitably ambiguous images by the presenter, and to see the same images commentated by two different *benshi* was to have two entirely different film experiences. The importance of the *benshi* was reflected both in the payments they received and in their billing in the cinema advertising: in both cases they ranked as equals to the best-known players and directors. This instance of variation to what can all too easily be assumed to be a universal and inescapable pattern of film narrative shows the potential transformation of a new medium like video which has yet to find its particular equation of creativity and economic viability.

As film-makers in the west developed the complex codes of temporal and spatial organization which allowed them to discard the presenter and yet build very substantial film narratives, music continued to play a key role in the film experience, now serving to bind together into a single flow the photographic images and the explanatory or dialogue intertitles. Music supported the images, but was not swallowed up by them. The musicians maintained an independent status, since they were located unambiguously in the auditorium along with the audience, and the sounds produced were not subjected to mechanical reproduction. Film-makers aspired to create realistic forms of story-telling, but film viewing involved bringing together three quite separate strands, all bearing part of the meaning: the photographically reproduced and projected images, the written intertitles needing to be read, and the real music coming from the spectator's own physical space and environment.

The coming of synchronous sound had an enormous impact on the cinema, changing its means of expression as well as its economics (Gomery 1980b). The photographic images now became a continuous, seamless flow, of the kind aspired to by the many silent film-makers who had sought to reduce their intertitles to a minimum. As the titles vanished, their place was taken by a new element, the voice of the performer, and the music now became reproduced sound (recorded and then optically transferred, so as to run parallel to the images on the celluloid strip). Radio could produce the capital needed for the transformation of cinema, and it could strengthen the ranks of the film stars with many of its own popular performers, but its own techniques of recording and balancing sound were of little help to film-makers. Radio speech was characterized first and foremost by the direct address system which it subsequently bequeathed to television, but which was largely irrelevant to a film medium which remained wedded to fictional narratives in which the spectator is addressed only indirectly. Similarly radio drama, with its intimate link with the listener and its preservation of aural clarity within a purely imaginary dramatic scene, could offer few pointers to film-makers concerned to preserve and enhance a realistic dramatic space combining image and sound.

Early sound cinema is particularly fascinating in retrospect (Wood 1984: 16–24). The efforts of the early 1930s film-makers to achieve an integration of sound and images with equipment (cameras, sound recorders, editing benches, and mixers) which was not capable of achieving this with any predictable degree of fluency, give invaluable pointers for the practice of contemporary video-makers. The difficulties experienced then by film-makers struggling to achieve a creative fusion serve to underline the complexity of sound-image relations. An awareness of this is particularly important for video-makers whose situation is quite the opposite: able to achieve effortless synchronization of sounds and images, they need to strive consciously to break out of the prison which synchrony creates.

As we have seen, the advent of the sound film led to a whole range of expedients: multi-camera shooting (but the use of a range of cameras with different focal lengths did not equate with the successive positionings of a single camera and multiple takes), the playback system (but the intrusion of the pre-recorded music track at the moment of shooting did little to help create an on-screen dramatic tension), the back-projection system (which split the unity of the image track, as actors performed in front of projected locations). All these production strategies from the early 1930s, before perfect synchronized shooting and recording of image and sound was achieved, can be seen as indicators for a potentially creative interplay of sound and image in a video system which is often cramped by its effortless synchrony, but for which sound-image divisions of this kind are technically perfectly feasible (Altman 1980a: 3–15).

In traditional cinema sound and image on the release print run side-by-side but twenty frames out of alignment, the separation being required because, at projection, the sound track must move continuously, while the images are exposed intermittently – as a series of stills – at the gate. The key development of the early 1930s was the ability to mix and re-record sound tracks without too much loss of quality. This allowed the addition of separately recorded music and effects to a studio recording which would normally comprise no more than a clean, clear recording of the dialogue. The use at editing of a number of separate sound tracks running side-by-side and synchronized, but each carrying different sound information, led inevitably to the hierarchization of sound to which we shall need to return later (Doane 1980b: 47–56).

Since both images and sound recording used optical methods until 1951, improvements in film stock emulsions were crucial to sound as well as to image quality. The change to magnetic recording in the early 1950s improved sound quality at the recording and re-recording stage, but did not revolutionize the sound heard by cinema patrons, since for economic reasons release prints continued to have optical tracks. Magnetic sound offered a new freedom of manipulation and better sound quality, but perhaps in retrospect its key effect is its symbolic dethroning of photography. Whereas skilled editors in the 1930s and 1940s had been able to 'read' optical sound tracks visually, sound now became legible only through the use of magnetic playback facilities. The same happens, of course, to the images with video recording. Indeed it is indicative of the new balance of sound and image in video that the images, too, are now recorded by, and accessible only through, the magnetic recording system originally devised for sound.

The same shift away from photochemical means is to be found, as we have seen, in television. The discarding of mechanical image-making in favour of electronic systems – as in the BBC decision to discontinue the Baird transmissions in February 1937 – meant a move away from film, since the great drawback of Zworykin's process (and hence of EMI's emitron camera) was its difficulty in scanning film images. Although film material now forms a major part of television output, telecine devices did not come into operation until well after television had established its organizational structures, and the cinema – with its pronounced visual emphasis – could play little part in the original definition of television as a broadcast medium. As a result of being 'live' – imprisoned within a studio and lacking an adequate recording system – television drew strongly on radio, inevitably adopting its mode of direct verbal address. In many ways it was literally 'radio with pictures': BBC news, for example, owed nothing to the well-established film newsreels, but was from the start run by recruits from radio, who conceived the news as an essentially spoken report, supplemented with pictures as far as these were available. It was not simply the small screen size and the black–and–white images that made television a sound–dominated medium: in origin its finance, its technology, and its organization echoed sound radio. Subsequent technical developments – perfected telecine systems, higher picture definition, colour – have strengthened the visual quality of television, while its sound reproduction has remained generally static, still lacking the hi-fi stereo quality available now from records and compact discs. But the effect is to create a balance of sound and vision, not a medium in which sound can be seen to have a wholly subordinate role.

It will be seen from this brief survey that video can be defined as the culminating point in a development which goes back to the beginning of the century. Its position is far more central than that of film. Indeed the complex system of visual organization perfected in the cinema between the disappearance of the lecturer or presenter and the arrival of sound-on-film can even appear in this light as something of an aberration. The fact that this 'aberration' has produced so many works of striking artistic quality does nothing to reduce its singularity within the overall growth of sound and image reproduction. Certainly film is far from being the fundamental mode for the organization of all audio-visual communication (against which video and television must be measured) that much film theory assumes it to be.

It is important to place video sound within this complex history of sound-image relationships simply because of its technical perfection. Synchronous sound shooting comes effortless to video – without the clapper-boards, the synchronized locking of camera and recorder, and the arduous assembly of sound and picture material in synch at the editing bench necessary for film production. As a result, a naturalistic aesthetic seems implicit in video, limiting the medium to the production of blocks of sound and image locked immutably together. At the same time, video's editing methods – internalized within a system of linked replay and recording machines – lack all the manual effort and skill demanded by film editing. The video cassette, with sound and picture packed neatly away in synchronous harmony, provokes a very different initial response at the editing stage from that stimulated by the twin tracks of picture and sound running side-by-side, but clearly differentiated by their carrier bases (celluloid in the one case, tape in the other), characteristic of film editing. The latter inevitably allows an awareness of the construction and artificiality of the eventual married print and incites an urge to play sound *against* picture.

The argument of this chapter and the concluding discussion of the video image is that the art of video begins when this naturalism is confronted, and synchronization is reduced to its proper place within a varied overall pattern of sound and image relationships. As Tom Levin has pointed out, much film theory – from Bela Balasz to Christian Metz, from Stanley Cavell to Jean-Louis Baudry – assumes that there is no possibility of separating real from recorded sound, that the two are ontologically identical (Levin 1984: 56). In fact nothing could be further from the truth. Recorded sound is inherently artificial and is organized in ways as complex as the visual perspective system with which we are all so familiar in painting and photography. It is to this issue that we must now turn our attention.

The construction of video sound

There are clear differences in how we, as spectators, perceive and respond to pictures and sounds, and these are factors to which we shall need to return. But if we begin at the point of video production, when the sounds and images are recorded, the similarities between the two operations are extremely close. To adopt Alan Williams's definition of sound as 'audible disturbances of air in the form of wave motion in a particular configuration of space' (Williams 1980: 52) is to emphasize an often neglected aspect – the context of hearing. If the context of hearing changes – from a huge concert hall to a small bedsit, from outdoors to indoors – then 'identical' sounds (those of a solo violin, say, or a gunshot) must sound different.

The fact that in normal circumstances we are not aware of this difference and hear the 'same' violin or gunshot on each occasion is not a basis for assuming that the two sounds *are* identical. We have already seen that our visual perception is organized so as to maintain the sense of a coherent, stable world despite the existence of such potentially disruptive and obtrusive phenomena as eye flicker and head movement. Our aural perception works to carry out a similar operation, telling us that a single violin or a gunshot sounds the same in two different acoustic environments and thereby satisfying the common-sense assumption, needed for an ordered existence, that a violin sounds like a violin and a gunshot like a gunshot. We can be quite reasonably certain that an adjustment of this kind is being made in our aural perception, simply because there are so many other everyday instances of such adjustments. All of us have been in the situation of trying to conduct a conversation in a noisy environment. In such instances we hear the voice of our companion much more clearly than can actually be the case. The sound is not focused (like a visual close-up) so as to amplify the sound: we do not hear our companion's voice louder, we simply hear it more distinctly, with the background hubbub reduced – and this can only be the effect of the workings of our human perception, since objectively the voice is still enmeshed in its ambient sound.

It is clear then that the transfer of a sound from one environment to another – which happens inevitably when a sound is recorded and replayed – must change that sound, even if we are able to perceive of a record-replay system which does not offer any distortion whatsoever. In fact, of course, this can never be the case. Indeed, John Belton's comments on the Dolby noise-reduction system, which produces a clear sound by effectively cutting out surface noise, point to some of the paradoxes of the situation. Firstly, the quest for 'natural' sound involves a total manipulation (artificially enhancing the amplitude during recording and reducing it – together with the tape hiss – on playback). Secondly, Dolby's near total elimination of noise results in a sound that is 'too perfect, that is ideal to a fault'. As Belton observes, in cinema (and the argument applies also to video),

> a certain amount of noise has become necessary to signify realism; its absence betokens a sound that has returned to an ideal state of existence, to a point just before it enters into the world and acquires the imperfections inherent in its own realisation. The sound track has become artificially quiet, pushing beyond the realism of the outside world into an inner, psychological realism.
>
> (Belton 1985: 67)

Even if the amount of distortion in the record-replay system is so small as to be inaudible in normal circumstances, while still offering an aural 'presence', there must still be a change when we consider that the microphone records the sound from one particular perspective and the loudspeaker replays it from a different point in a new environment. We are not dealing here with a transfer of 'reality' from one point to another, but with a system of recording (and hence of representation) akin to that of the film camera/projector or the video camera/monitor systems of visual representation. Alan Williams is correct to argue that sound recording is best understood not as offering us reality but as giving 'one perspective on it, a *sample*, a *reading* of it' (Williams 1980: 53).

Talk of recorded sound being real is in any case misplaced, since all that we demand of those media which give us a sense of realism is that they fulfil some (not all) of the conditions of perception and do not obtrusively call attention to their status as reproductions. Here the crucial problem of sound arises since, of course, any recording system creates its own distortions to add to those inherent in the transfer of sound from one environment to another (the Dolby system, for example, cuts the very tops and bottoms off the sounds) (Belton 1985: 67). Indeed, as anyone who has ever used a tape recorder is aware, the microphone is a particularly inefficient way of obtaining a single, clear perspective on the all-embracing, three-dimensional phenomenon which is sound. It is certainly far less efficient than a camera, and to offer an acceptable recording of any complex sound event a whole battery of microphones with different specific directional characteristics is required. The fact that perhaps half-a-dozen microphones placed or suspended at various points have been used for the recording of a symphony orchestra does not mean that the resultant sound, balanced by means of a mixer and fed to us through the monaural speaker system of a conventional television set, offers us any sort of actual equivalent to the real experience. It merely fulfils – as a representation – enough of the conditions of perception to be acceptable, even satisfying, to us as an audience.

Video sound is a construct not simply in terms of the microphones and mixers used at the moment of recording, but also in the subsequent processes of sound assembly and editing which video shares with film. Again the parallels with the editing of the images are striking. There are a number of standard procedures to give a better sound quality, to avoid audible distortion and to improve the signal-to-noise ratio. These include the hierarchization of sound tracks, the use of sound dissolves, the overlaying of sound-over-picture cuts and the creation of a sound perspective which involves matching microphone placing to shot type by close miking for close-ups and keeping the microphone at a distance when recording sound to accompany long shots (Doane 1980b). This latter procedure gives significant results, since a microphone placed at a distance from a person speaking picks up not only the direct sound of the voice, but also the reflected sound as this bounces off the walls, floor and ceiling, thereby producing a perceptibly different quality of sound. These sound procedures are very much akin to the better-known 'rules' for avoiding visual disorientation (listed in all the technical handbooks) whereby the creation of dramatic space in conventional film and video narrative involves such procedures as the prohibition of crossing the imaginary 180-degree line drawn through the scene (since otherwise the characters may appear to shift bizarrely from one side of the screen to the other) and the maintenance of the same axis or a move through at least 30 degrees between successive shots (so as to avoid a jump cut).

Conventional sound practice in video, as in film, has its own specific hierarchy (which can, of course, be disturbed for artistic effect), ranking speech above music, and music above general sound effects. Where a number of tracks are laid for subsequent dubbing, these will reflect this hierarchy, and in professional practice it is often only the first – speech – which is recorded at the moment of shooting. Again these procedures have their parallel in the foregrounding of character and action in the image track by the framing and centring of figures within a shot.

In a real sense, the art of sound recording and editing is to control those elements of sound of which we become consciously aware only at moments of rupture (the whirr of the refrigerator which is only noticed when the door is opened, the ticking of a clock which is 'heard' only when it stops). The filtering and balancing of sound and the avoidance of 'holes' in the sound track (which will be perceived by a listener not as silence but as evidence of mechanical breakdown) through the use of a continuous 'atmos track' of ambient sound are operations very similar in function to the variety of image procedures, ranging from match cutting and cutting on movement to the grading of prints, by which shot changes are concealed. Another important parallel involves the use of a voice-off to bring in a character visually absent from a scene and a sound-off to indicate a threat or surprise. These work in much the same way as the look off-screen, which triggers a cut to what is seen and so brings into play a space which was hitherto unseen (for an elaboration of this point see pp. 193–4 ff.).

Underlying all these sound procedures is a principle inherited from classic Hollywood continuity cinema, namely that just as 'good picture editing' involves making the transition from shot to shot invisible, so too 'good sound editing' is inaudible, that is to say, nothing draws attention to the artifice of the recorded sound or makes us stop to think what it is that we are hearing. Conventional practice in video, film, and television assumes that sound must be subordinated to the image. The principal means for ensuring this is the synchronization of sound and image, the means by which the illusion is created that the sound does not come from a loudspeaker but is *produced* by the image, and that the words are indeed uttered by the player in shot. Of course none of these so-called rules has any prescriptive force, and even within conventional narrative and documentary production video- and film-makers will break them on occasion. But they do provide the basis for audience expectation of sound-image relationships.

The conventional sound system inherited by video from film is subtle but effective. Based on contrivance at every level, its aim is clearly not to give the real sound assumed by some theorists, but to shape the given elements of the sound material in ways that approximate to – but are not identical with – human perception. Again the parallel of sound and image is close. Although the human eye can pick out an element of an overall scene to which our attention is particularly drawn, it does not give us visual close-ups. But the film and video system of shots from varying distances and angles can offer an acceptable and easily understandable visual pattern to connote increased attention. In a similar way, the conventions of sound balance and perspective do not reproduce what we actually hear, but they do give us the necessary cues to read the scene's intended meaning.

By the time that video was invented, however, cinema also offered a whole series of sustained assaults on these conventions, particularly in the wake of such European directors of the 1960s as Jean-Luc Godard and Alain Resnais. Several of Godard's films of this period allow us aural experiences of a kind totally denied us by Hollywood. *Vivre sa vie* (1962), for example, has scenes permitting us to judge the alienating effect of recording with a single omnidirectional microphone in a real cafe interior and the impact of removing all trace of sound from a portion of a sequence. The importance of innovations such as these is twofold. They offer new patterns of sound–image combination which can be emulated or developed futher, and at the same time they emphasize the extent to which the procedures described in all the standard production handbooks are no more than conventions, to be varied when new responses are sought from an audience. Both these lessons are helpful to video-makers whose work is inevitably coloured by their prior experience – as spectators – of film and television, but who are working in a medium with distinctively new potentials for sound–image combination.

Sound, space, and screen

The relationship between images and sound is complex and shifting, even within the confines of a single work. It is also difficult to discuss here, since there is no body of video tapes which the readers of this book can be assumed to have seen. I have chosen therefore to take my examples of particular effects from well-known feature films (most of them available on video tape), taking care to discuss them in terms which do not distort the different balance of sound and image in video. This is not too difficult and constraining, since there is a broad area of general sound–image relations common to both video and film, particularly since film sound recording has used electro-magnetic tape for the past thirty-five years. Where this is not the case I have made specific references to the differences in the discussion that follows.

Clearly we need ways of treating the sound–image relationship which do not automatically assume the predominance of the images and so operate by first describing these images and then asking how the sound 'helps' in the communication of the meaning which they have established. The argument here will be that the images themselves are far from being clear and unequivocal carriers of meaning. Just as news photos need captions and silent cinema needed intertitles, so too the images of a video tape need sound to remove their basic ambiguity. The best way to understand the role of sound in video is to consider the various spaces which the sound track occupies and constitutes in conjunction with the image track which accompanies it on the video tape (Doane 1980a).

We can define three such spaces in any video (or any film) and in crude terms we can say that if the images dominate the first space and hold their own in the second, the third space is wholly the sphere of sound. The first of these spaces is the most obvious: screen space. This is a space which can be plotted and measured unambiguously. We can tabulate the shots and transcribe in columns alongside them the dialogue, the music, and the effects. This least problematic of spaces is unequivocally that of the images.

The second space requires a more careful definition. It is the imaginary space of the fictional or non-fictional world which the work creates. The term used by film theory to distinguish it is the 'diegesis', and this is a useful term since the Shorter Oxford English Dictionary defines diegesis as both 'a narrative' and 'a statement of the case', allowing us to apply the term to both fictional and documentary works. We are concerned here not merely with the space which is actually seen and heard, but also with the absent space *implied* by the sound and images at any particular point. Diegetic space is the space which exists in our minds as we put the video together, including the elements which have not yet been explicitly seen and heard.

An excellent filmic example of this occurs at the very beginning of Michael Curtiz's 1940s film, *Mildred Pierce*. A man is shot down, looks off-screen, murmurs the world 'Mildred' and dies. We are not shown the person who shoots him and at whom he looks until the very end of the film, but this absent image haunts the whole film. Since we naturally assume that Mildred is the killer, this shapes our whole response to the film – until we eventually discover that the killer was her daughter, whom she has been trying to protect. The whole of *Mildred Pierce* plays, in almost textbook fashion, on the ambiguity of the unseen and unheard that can form part of the diegetic space, while being absent from the literal screen space. Obviously a thriller of this kind is an extreme example, but any video-maker has the opportunity to play in small ways with the audience's desire to hear and see, and to create involvement through a delayed gratification of this desire.

The third space which we need to consider is unambiguously the realm of sound, comprising the space occupied by those elements which are not part of either screen or diegetic space (they are unseen and unheard by the participants, but play a large role in determining our response, as members of an audience, to the sound and images). This is the space occupied principally by the commentary or voice-over and by the accompanying background music.

Screen space

At the level of screen space – the level with which the technical handbooks are most concerned – the images inevitably have primacy, since we are, in effect, defining sounds solely in terms of their relationship to the images. If we take the screen as our starting-point, there are just two initial categories: on-screen sound, for which the source of the sound is present on the screen, and off-screen sound, where the source is absent. The first function of on-screen sound is to fill one of the roles occupied by music in silent cinema: to reinforce the combined realism of the photographic reproduction and the movement by giving weight and substance to the images. The action becomes more solid, more convincing, when we hear the door slam shut or the gun go off. All that is required here is that the two aspects of the event coincide in time: that the sound occurs at the very moment the door slams or the shot is fired.

However, sound was not introduced into film – and does not continue to be employed in television and video – simply in order to provide sound effects. It is there primarily to give us speech. Although *Don Juan*, released a year earlier, had contained synchronized music and effects, we normally consider *The Jazz Singer* to be the first real sound film, since it was the first to contain synchronized dialogue. The sound film is therefore felt to have been born on 6 October 1927, when the first audience heard Al Jolson proclaim, 'Wait a minute, wait a minute, you ain't heard nothing yet'. The importance of speech in video, film, and television would be hard to exaggerate. A powerful two-way tension operates between speech and image: a character who is shown needs to speak to confirm his or her identity and existence; at the same time a character who is heard needs to be seen.

This tension is a major element in conventional narrative, where it can be used to portray the emotional connections and power relations between characters. Taking 'the simplest narrative fact imaginable – two characters talking in a car', Raymond Bellour has shown how the relationship of the characters played by Humphrey Bogart and Lauren Bacall in Howard Hawkes's version of *The Big Sleep* (1946) can be defined through the ways in which their mutual confessions of love are depicted as they drive towards the film's final shoot-out (Bellour 1974–5: 7–17). When Vivian (Bacall) says 'I guess I'm in love with you' in close-up, Hawks cuts immediately to a two-shot in which both speak and Marlowe (Bogart) keeps part of his attention on his driving, taking the car round a bend. When, three shots later, Marlowe echoes Vivian's words with his own admission of love, there is an immediate cut to Vivian in close-up. She does not speak, just looks lovingly off-screen at Marlowe. In this simple exchange the whole Hollywood system of representing stereotyped gender relations can be seen in miniature: the man talking and externally active even in moments of tenderness, the woman mute and adoring.

Speech/silence patterns are used equally effectively in Elia Kazan's *On the Waterfront* (1954), as exemplified by the conversation between the ex-boxer Terry (Marlon Brando) and his corrupt older brother Charlie (Rod Steiger), who is trying to stop him from testifying against the gang boss. This is the scene containing Brando's memorable assertion: 'You don't understand. I could have had class. I could have been a contender. I could have been somebody. Instead of a bum, which is what I am, let's face it.' The twenty-one-shot scene begins with Terry saying, as they get into the car, 'Nobody every stopped you talking, Charlie,' and culminates in three big close-ups during which Charlie is totally silent. The shifting patterns of speech and silence capture perfectly Charlie's realization of defeat (he is promptly executed by the gang boss) and Terry's growth to articulate awareness, which will lead him first to testify and then to break the corrupt union boss's power by leading the men back to work.

The manipulation of images and sound to exploit to the full the sense of completion which comes from their fusion in synchronized speech has a role to play in documentary, too, where highly effective alternations of synchronous interview material and voice-over comment can be constructed. The technique of synchronization is generally seen as the principal means whereby sound is subordinated to picture. Certainly one key to understanding how sound–image relations operate is to see how sound is deprived of an independent existence when, with lip synch, the image appears to produce the sound. In a fascinating speculative article, Rick Altman has argued that the situation is in fact quite the opposite, and that the sound track is 'a ventriloquist who, by moving his dummy (the image) in time with the words he secretly speaks, creates the illusion that the words are produced by the dummy/image whereas in fact the dummy/image is actually created in order to disguise the source of the sound' (Altman 1980b: 67). Altman's argument involves all three types of space with which we are concerned here and we shall need to return to its contentions later. Whatever the case, it is clear that synchronization gives independence to the person or the fictional character who is seen and heard to speak. Through synchronous speech he or she is able to become an active agent in narrative cinema or a living witness to the truth in documentary.

In addition to the synchronized speech and effects which are unequivocally on-screen, there is also a neglected category of sound which every video-maker soon discovers to be crucial. This is the background sound which is neither fully on-screen nor off-screen: the tiny sounds making up the atmosphere of a room, the noisy bustle of the street, the rippling of the stream, or the noise of the wind in the trees. Although it relates closely to what we see on the screen, there is no point at which it is attached synchronously (in practice it is often added as a recurring loop at the dubbing stage). Conventional video, film, and television are all systems which refuse silence and in which 'dead sound' or 'a hole in the sound track' would imply mechanical breakdown. The category of on-screen/off-screen sound forms a bridge between screen space and diegetic space in two ways. Firstly, the seamless flow of background sound within a scene implies the unity of a space that is made up of a number of individual shots. Secondly, the flow of images from one scene to another is enhanced by a slight overlap when the cut occurs: the continuation of the sound disguises the abruptness of the transition.

Diegetic space

The diegetic space is physically unmeasureable, since it combines the space on the screen with what is *implied* when a character looks out of shot or a sound occurs off-screen. In general terms, diegetic space in narrative cinema can be defined as what the characters see and hear, and the progression of the story is very much concerned with bringing what is temporarily unseen and/or heard off-screen into focus and into the screen space. Diegetic space in documentary is more complicated to define: a paradoxical imaginary space which contains and shapes the real (photographed and recorded) material which is the ostensible subject matter. It may be created simply out of the fusion of the successive images and natural sounds offered to us without comment. But if a documentary contains interviews, the diegetic space must include the space (to the left or right of the camera) at which the interviewees look as they speak. It is implied that this off-screen space is occupied by the narrator, although in fact some other questioner (whose existence is now elided) may well have been located there at the actual time of shooting. In so far as the narrator appears in shot and talks directly to us synchronously (as is normal in conventional television), the diegetic space differs radically from Hollywood's narrative space in being open-ended (Morse 1985: 4).

In considering diegetic space, we are concerned particularly with off-screen sound. The patterning of on-screen and off-screen dialogue can be used to great effect, as the car conversation scenes referred to above show clearly. One role of off-screen sound is to imply a three-dimensional space of which the two-dimensional image on the screen is only one perspective. The overlapping of dialogue also serves to fuse the pattern of shot/reverse-angle shot by means of which the visible screen space is constantly enlarged, into a seamless unity. At this level, too, certain specific characteristics of sound come into play, in particular the fact that, although we can only see in terms of light travelling in straight lines, we customarily hear round corners. In our everyday life sounds often come to us from sources which we cannot immediately identify, and in narrative systems like video and film, off-screen sound can function as something mysterious which needs to be located. Off-screen sound is a creator of tension, anxiety, and unease in the spectator, hence it is crucial to the task of maintaining narrative flow and sustaining our involvement, until the mystery can be resolved and the tension eased.

In fact the source of an off-screen sound need never be specified, and an ambiguity can remain which is never fully resolved. A striking example of the power of this effect comes in Ingmar Bergman's *Persona* (1966), most of which deals with the time spent by the sea by two young women. Elisabeth (Liv Ullmann) is an actress recuperating from some kind of breakdown on stage, who now refuses to speak. Alma (Bibi Andersson) is the nurse hired to care for her, who chatters incessantly to fill the void created by Elisabeth's silence. On one occasion Alma talks till late into the night about her early sexual experiences and then lets her head drop onto her arms at the table. While the camera remains directed at her, we hear Elisabeth's voice saying, 'Now you must go to bed, Alma, otherwise you'll fall asleep at the table'. Since Elisabeth's back is turned towards the camera and she is subsequently silent and inscrutable, we have no way of knowing whether the words were actually spoken or whether they were merely imagined (or dreamed) by Alma. If they were spoken, the words have an immense significance, as the only unforced words Elisabeth utters in the whole film. The fundamental ambiguity prepares the audience perfectly for the magical following scene in which the two women mysteriously come together and merge appearances. This scene, bathed in a strange luminosity and accompanied by other off-screen sounds (the ghostly sounds of an unseen ship's foghorn), is an unfathomable mixture of reality and dream.

Extra-diegetic space

When we come to consider extra-diegetic space – the particular realm occupied by the voice-over, the commentary, and the music – we reach an area which is still ill-defined. Perhaps because it so unequivocally belongs to sound, it has received comparatively little attention from film theorists. Yet it is evident that even if the words and music are ignored, unheard, by the characters in the video or film, they play a key role in shaping the way in which we, as members of the audience, respond. Just as atmos tracks and sound overlays provide a bridge from screen to diegetic space, so too a voice-over which gives simply the thoughts of the character in shot (an equivalent of the theatrical inner monologue) can serve as a lead-in to the discussion of the area of extra-diegetic sound. If such spoken thoughts are totally internalized (that is, not heard by any other character) and represent no more than the character could know and think at that precise moment, they cause no especial problem, operating simply as aural equivalents in terms of interiority to flashbacks which are firmly located in a single individual character's consciousness. But it has often been remarked that flashbacks are complex, since they frequently contain information that the character cannot know and are customarily shot in ways which do not privilege the character's own point of view. Voice-overs function in a similar way, and difficulties of definition and analysis arise as soon as a separation occurs between the voice and the diegetic sound and images.

An immediate example occurs in Billy Wilder's *Double Indemnity*, the story of a doomed romance which ends in murder and mutual hatred. The thread through the film is provided by the confession recorded on an office dictaphone by the insurance agent-cum-killer Walter Neff (Fred MacMurray). The film is illustrated by a succession of sequences depicting the development of his relationship with Phyllis Dietrichson (Barbara Stanwyk). But from the very beginning of the film a gap opens up between Neff's words and what we actually see on the screen. Immediately after he has met Phyllis for the first time, Neff is left alone for a brief while in the sitting-room, which he describes in terms echoing James M. Cain's original novel. This voice-over breaks the unity of the text: it describes dust particles which are totally absent from John F. Seitz's crystal-clear images and gives names Neff cannot possibly know at this moment to the family members depicted in the photographs on display.

This simple example points to the tendency of the voice-over to assert its independence of the images. It has a firm basis for independence since, although film images unfold in the present tense and in a third person narration, a voice-over is generally in the first person (acknowledging an 'I' if not a 'you') and using the past tense to tell of events which, from its point of view, are already complete, even if they are still unfolding on the screen. The voice-over commentaries common in European art cinema tend also to have a decidedly literary tone. They may set up direct links with the original novel, as in Robert Bresson's adaptation of Bernanos's *Journal d'un curé de campagne/Diary of a Country Priest* (1950), which includes images of the diary/commentary being written (Browne 1980). On other occasions the voice-over may be the opportunity for the author to enter the film in person, as when Jean Cocteau and Jean-Luc Godard use their own voices to pass comment on the unfolding images. In this area of cinema the autonomy of the sound track has been asserted most forcefully by the French novelist and film-maker Marguerite Duras, who took the sound track of one film, *India Song* (1975), and used it, virtually unaltered, for a second film with quite unrelated images, *Son nom de Venise dans Calcutta désert* (1976) (Ropars-Wuilleumier 1980). In all such cases the effect is to make intertextual connections – with the source, with the author, or with some other work – of a kind forbidden in conventional (Hollywood-style) narrative procedure. This practice, like so many aspects of film, has useful lessons for videomakers concerned to find new ways of defining their personal relationship with their work and their audiences.

One of the key innovators who, in the late 1950s and early 1960s, made feature films conceived as an equal interplay of music, voice, and image was Alain Resnais. Films like *Hiroshima mon amour* (1959) and *L'Année dernière à Marienbad/Last Year at Marienbad* (1961) reflected Resnais' experience in documentary film-making, where the commentary has enormous importance (Armes 1968: 36–65). It is fair to see the spoken word as playing as key a role – through the commentary – in documentary as it does – through the spoken dialogue – in conventional fictional film-making. Indeed, if we adopt the Oxford English Dictionary definition of diegesis as 'a statement of the case', it becomes reasonable to see the sound track, not the images, as constituting the essential core of the video or film documentary, the conceptual universe, where the exposition is logically set out and the verbal arguments are put. In television forms of documentary the narrator customarily appears on the image track, but the core remains the narrator's words, not his or her appearance.

If we wish to take this line of reasoning to its extreme, it is even possible to assert that with documentary the diegetic lies in the words and that here it is the images which are the outsiders. Certainly it is self-evident that, as in the days when fictional films had live presenters, to change the commentary is, in a very real sense, to change the whole work completely. Chris Marker illustrates this wittily in *Lettre de Sibérie/Letter from Siberia* (1958), when he shows the same set of images three times, each with a different commentary:

> Yakutsk, capital of the Yakutsk Autonomous Soviet Socialist Republic, is a modern city in which comfortable buses made available to the population share the streets with powerful Zyms, the pride of the Soviet automobile industry. In the spirit of socialist emulation, happy Soviet workers, among them this picturesque denizen of the Arctic reaches, apply themselves to making Yakutsk a better place to live.

> Yakutsk is a dark city with an evil reputation. The population is crammed into blood-coloured buses while the members of the privileged caste brazenly display the luxury of their Zyms, a costly and uncomfortable car at best. Bending to the task like slaves, the miserable Soviet workers, among them this sinister-looking Asiatic, apply themselves to the primitive labour of grading with a drag beam.

> In Yakutsk, where modern houses are gradually replacing the dark older sections, a bus, less crowded than its London or New York equivalent at rush hour, passes a Zym, an excellent car reserved for public utilities departments on account of its

scarcity. With courage and tenacity under extremely difficult conditions, Soviet workers, among them this Yakut afflicted with an eye disorder, apply themselves to improving the appearance of their city, which could certainly use it.

(Bordwell and Thompson 1979: 190)

The third component of the extra-diegetic space is the most difficult of all to pin down adequately, comprising the music which has not found its place in the screen space through the inclusion of a live performer, a radio, or a gramophone in the images (which would imply that the characters could hear it). The problems of dealing with music in relation to video or film are encapsulated in the anecdote with which Tony Thomas begins his *Music for the Movies* (1973). A keen enthusiast of film music, Thomas was constantly asking his friends what they thought of the musical score of the film they had just seen together. The answer was invariably 'What music?' (Thomas 1973: 11–12). There is no fully adequate explanation for the survival of conventionally used music in cinema after the arrival of sound-on-film, even in ostensibly realistic films. Certainly the role which has been posited here as the most likely purpose behind the inclusion of music in silent film performances – what has been termed 'to breathe into the pictures some of the life that photography has taken away from them' (Eisler 1951: 59) – would seem to have been filled by synchronous speech and sound. Yet music persists.

Music continues to fill the variety of roles which Thomas lists: filling the empty spaces in the action or dialogue, building a sense of continuity, underlining the drama, pinpointing emotions and actions, and creating an atmosphere. Above all it is 'able to shade emotion, to lighten or darken moods, to heighten sensitivities, to imply, to suggest, to define character and refine personality, to help generate momentum or create tension, to warm the picture or cool it, and – most subtle of all – to allude to thoughts that are unspoken and situations that remain unseen' (Thomas 1973: 17). The need fulfilled by music clearly goes far beyond anything covered by the producers' dictum that if the movies were better, they would not need music. The persistence of music would seem to point to an inherent lack in the images which runs quite contrary to the assumptions of most film theory, particularly that dealing with the visual strategies by means of which the spectator is positioned. Certainly the continued importance of music points to the need to query the applicability of much theoretical study of film to video, where the sound–image balance is so different.

It also underlines the importance of music to a medium like video which is less able than film to rely on a purely visual means of making an impact. The simple equivalence sometimes proposed of video imagery and synthesized music seems a particularly inadequate response to a sound–image relationship full of creative potential. Perhaps what needs most to be stressed is the separateness of music. There are clear differences in how we perceive sound and images, in that our ability to absorb fast-cut, intricately patterned, successive images is not matched by our ability to distinguish and 'place' sounds. The analogy with the frame of a painting is one which points to a creative use of music in video, implying both a set of correspondences in tone and proportion and at the same time the possibility of off-setting the image and creating some form of counterpoint to it.

Conclusions

It is difficult to offer clear–cut conclusions to the discussion of an area as complex as sound in relation to video and film images. What the existing literature on the subject seems to show is that a conventional film approach which takes the images as paramount offers little help in the elucidation and definition of film and video sound. On the other hand, the proposal by Rick Altman that we should see cinema as ventriloquism, seems to veer too far in the opposite direction. Instead of addressing a lack in the efficacy of silent projected motion pictures, which would account for the introduction of sound-on-film and make the notion of silent video or silent television virtually inconceivable, Altman puts forward the suggestion that 'we are so disconcerted by a sourceless sound that we would rather attribute the sound to a dummy or a shadow than face the mystery of its source-lessness or the scandal of its production by a non-vocal (technological or "ventral") apparatus' (Altman 1980b: 76–7).

Altman's approach is stimulating in the manner in which it avoids the customary pitfalls and blind alleys of earlier sound theorization. But it raises as many questions as it answers, and attributes a curiously unconvincing role to the audience. Surely the true pleasure of ventriloquism is not to be found in a desperate search for a sound source, but rather in the sheer playful delight in being fooled by a wholly human skill, as with a conjurer (or a film projector). Although we know intellectually that video and film images do not speak, the illusory power is sufficient for us to go along with the proposition that they do, since as a result we are able to enjoy a pleasing narrative or an informative report. Despite these limitations, Altman's reversal of the image/sound hierarchy offers the basis for a new way of writing media history which gives a proper place to sound.

Cinema was invented to record movement and succeeded in doing so remarkably well: the result was the establishment of a convincing screen space which allowed cinema to be marketed for a while as a scientific novelty. But in order to be turned into a really profitable entertainment commodity, it needed not simply to record movement but to represent life (or some aspect of it). From the first, film images alone were felt to be unable to do this. Music was added, and a presenter was engaged to introduce and explain the images. The efforts of the narrative film-makers who invented the chase film – exemplified by D. W. Griffith – turned this screen space into a diegetic space which could function without a presenter. They created this more complex, imaginary space (that of a compelling fiction) by developing the techniques of cross-cutting, whereby we, as the audience, are incited to put together into a single flow the two halves of the action which the film plot offers us successively and alternately: the pursuer and the pursued. The chase film, silent film comedy, and melodrama all benefit from a musical accompaniment and can have a balletic perfection, but the diegetic space they occupy could still potentially be enriched by the addition of sound.

When sound-on-film came, however, the emphasis on synchronous dialogue reasserted the importance of screen space, redefining film as recording once more, although this time the recording of a pre-existing stage play. Gradually image, speech, and effects came to be handled with greater subtlety so as to create a rich audio-visual diegetic space, but a cinema limited to these means would have remained an affair of purely external action. To achieve interiority the resonances of the extra-diegetic (voice-over and/or music) – and hence the freeing of sound from synchrony – were required. They are still indispensable today. Even a tentative sketch of this kind which, like Altman's concept, leaves many questions unanswered, allows us to see the three types of space (screen, diegetic, extra-diegetic) as successive enrichments of the film medium (visual record, action drama, interiorized drama) on which video can draw. Such an approach also allows us to be confident in asserting the crucial importance of an awareness of the history and aesthetics of reproduced sound for the full creative development of video's potential.

Further reading

While sound was largely ignored or misunderstood by early film theorists, a considerable amount of valuable work on film sound – which is highly relevant to an aesthetics of video – has been published in the 1980s. For brief histories of the evolution of sound technology see Altman (1980a) and Belton (1985), while Fielding (1967) has several useful pieces. Doane (1980b) offers a helpful introduction to the ideology of sound-track construction. For music see Thomas (1973) for a popular introduction, Gorbman (1980), and especially Eisler (1951); Adorno's uncredited contribution to the latter book is discussed by Rosen (1980). Stimulating accounts of various aspects of the sound/image relation are Levin (1984), Williams (1980), Altman (1980b), King (1984), and Wood (1984). Television talk is dealt with by Morse (1985) and Tolson (1985). Useful pieces of specific detailed analysis are Bellour (1974–5), Browne (1980), and Ropars-Wuilleumier (1980). My own approach to sound and space owes much to Doane (1980a), Percheron (1980), and especially two books unfortunately not translated from the French, Chion (1982, 1985).

8 AESTHETICS OF VIDEO IMAGE

> Finally, there was a wholesome lesson in the discovery
> that vision is not a mechanical recording of elements but
> rather the apprehension of significant structural patterns.
> If this was true for the simple act of perceiving an
> object, it was all the more likely to hold true also for the
> artistic approach to reality. Obviously the artist was no
> more a mechanical recording device than his instrument
> of sight. The artistic representation of an object could
> no longer be thought of as a tedious transcription of its
> accidental appearance, detail by detail.
>
> (Rudolf Arnheim 1974: 6)

The previous chapter discovered a considerable area of overlap
between video and film in their shared aesthetics of sound. This
is hardly surprising, since feature films had universally used tape
for the recording of sound for well over a decade before the first
portable video recorders were introduced in the west. The
situation is very different when we turn to the video image,
which has qualities and potentials very different from those of
the film image. There are again some areas of overlap, but what
is taken over – whether it is the filmic system of the look or the
television direct address pattern – is radically transformed.
Video is such a new and untried medium that it is perhaps
presumptuous to attempt to define its aesthetics at this stage.
But on the basis of the preceding discussions of video's historical
and social contexts, a few – admittedly tentative – comments can
be offered.

Video is perhaps best seen in terms of a polarity. On the one
hand, it is immediate, literal, actual, and naturalistic; on the

other, it is simultaneously contrived, distanced, synthetic, and analytic. This divergence is reflected in its costing structure: low for recording, high for processing and synthesizing the resultant images. The immediacy stems from the ease of shooting and the instant replay, which make it usable as an increasingly popular variant on (and supplement to) the still camera for domestic use: the home video as a medium to follow the home movie and the family snapshot. In a discussion on the uses of still photography, John Berger makes a distinction between 'photographs which belong to the private experience' and 'those which are used publicly'. This distinction is very relevant to video, which echoes photographic practice in its personal, private dimension:

> The private photograph – the portrait of a mother, a picture of a daughter, a group photo of one's team – is appreciated and read in a context *which is continuous with that from which the camera removed it.* . . . Such a photograph remains surrounded by the meaning from which it was severed. A mechanical device, the camera, has been used as an instrument to contribute to a living memory. The photograph is a memento from a life being lived.
>
> (Berger 1980: 51–2)

The contrivance and distance of video stem from the contrasting potential which always exists because of the nature of electronic recording for transforming the image. Post-production work involves equipment with a high capital cost and the services of a well-paid engineer, but it must form part of any consideration of video because, at the level of either personal exploration or independent production for Channel Four, it remains within the immediate control and direct concern of the video-maker. Even at its most sophisticated technical level, video remains a personal medium throughout the whole production cycle. This is an immediate difference between video and film, since, as Peter Wollen notes, at least since the coming of sound, the film laboratory

> became completely divorced from the work of the director and cinematographer; it became an automated, industrial process with its own standard operating procedures. Anyone

who has made a film will be familiar with the opacity of the laboratory.

(Wollen 1982: 172)

The video image

There is a whole mythology of the video image which stems from Marshall McLuhan's celebrated definition of television in *Understanding Media*, which was published in 1967 on the eve of the appearance in the west of the Sony portapak:

> The mode of the TV image has nothing in common with film or photo, except that it offers also a nonverbal *gestalt* or posture of forms. With TV, the viewer is the screen. . . . The TV image is visually low in data. The TV image is not a *still* shot. It is not photo in any sense, but a ceaselessly forming contour of things limned by the scanning-finger. The resulting plastic contour appears by light *through*, not light *on*, and the image so formed has the quality of sculpture and icon, rather than of picture.

(McLuhan 1967: 334)

This kind of reasoning confuses rather than clarifies the true differences between video and film images. The unsubstantiated assertion that 'with TV, the viewer is the screen' is no substitute for an examination of the significant differences between, on the one hand, sitting in the dark in a public place in front of a huge cinema screen and, on the other, watching a small domestic television screen in one's own sitting-room. Although they enjoyed an immense vogue at the period during which video first became widely used, the particular distinctions which McLuhan proposes are largely spurious. The television image is no lower in data than 16 mm film, the notion of a 'scanning-finger' is no more than a metaphor (it does not make the medium 'audio-tactile'), the formation of the image occurs at too great a speed for the viewer to be aware of how it is assembled, and the distinction between 'light through' and 'light on' is meaningless, since there is no difference in the way in which film and video picture information reaches the eye (Miller 1971: 121–6; Winston 1985: 258–63).

There is of course a valid distinction between the ways in which video and film colour images are *produced*, although both operate on the principle that a full range of colour can be produced from just three primaries: blue, green, and red (Curtis 1985: 22). A colour video image is formed by a system of *additive* colour mixing, whereby the sensation of white is produced as a result of combining the outputs of the blue, green, and red sources, and the complementary colours are formed by combining (in their correct proportions) just two primaries: green and red to give yellow, green and blue to give cyan, and red and blue to give magenta. For the past thirty-five years, film has used exclusively *subtractive* colour systems, whereby the original blue, green, and red records are printed as yellow, magenta, and cyan respectively. In the resultant projected image, blue is formed by the absence of yellow, green by the absence of magenta, and red by the absence of cyan. Black results from the concentration of all three complementaries, while white stems from the absence of all dyes.

This additive/subtractive division between video and film is not the reflection of some mystical hot/cool distinction between the media. Early film colour systems which preceded the introduction of the now dominant Eastman Color (subtractive) system in 1952 explored both additive and subtractive methods (just like early colour processes for still photography). The advantage of the subtractive process for film is simply that the filters needed for an additive process reduce the available light by a third, whereas the subtractive process gives a projected image of great transparency. This distinction in the production of colour images is, in any case, irrelevant to how the resultant images are received by the eye. At the point of reception, what is crucial is not how the colour was produced (the eye does not differentiate between additive and subtractive methods), but what the characteristics of the colour are in terms of such factors as brightness, saturation, or hue.

In fact many of the key technical aspects of the formation of the video or television image are clearly and understandably based on film precedents. As we have seen, 'high-definition' television involves at least 400 lines, because this allows it approximately to match the resolving power of the 16 mm film image (even in a 625-line system only 575 are needed for the picture information) (Winston 1986: 58). The choice of 25 frames per second stems partly from the desire to synchronize the television receiver with UK mains frequency (50 Hz or cycles per second): being half the mains frequency means that hum-related picture interference is stationary and hence less annoying. But it also approximates closely enough to the 24-frame-per-second speed of projected sound film for the difference to be ignored in telecine transfer.

The interlacing of the two 312½-line fields to form the single 625-line television frame gives a field frequency of 50 cycles per second (which exactly matches mains frequency), just as the double-bladed shutter of the modern movie projector gives a doubled frequency of 48 frames per second (and hence a total lack of flicker) without the film speed needing to be increased beyond 24 frames per second. Another crucial area of comparability between video and film lies in the shared optical system. The target image size on a typical video camera tube is similar to that of a single 16 mm film frame, so that (with correct adaptors) 16 mm movie lenses can be used with video cameras. Even lenses specifically designed for video give an image quality close to that of 16 mm film. Similarly, the aspect ratio of a video camera and television studio monitor is the same as that of 16 mm film (4:3), although domestic receivers are normally set for a ratio of 5:3 (Curtis 1985: 21).

Fundamental to the shaping of the image in video – as in film and photography – is the concept of perspective. The media do not offer us some brute, untouched reality, but a shaped and ordered representation or illusion of reality. As we saw in chapter 1, perspective is a fifteenth-century construct, a system designed to allow us to render a three-dimensional reality accurately on a two-dimensional surface. It is perhaps easiest to understand as the image drawn on a sheet of glass held up between us and reality. It is not – and does not pretend to be – reality. It is not a system of *trompe-l'oeil* deceit: we are aware of the surface (in this it is unlike both reality and a mirror image). Moreover it is a static, monocular rendering. As we also saw in chapter 1, perspective – like the nineteenth- and twentieth-century visual and audio-visual media that employ it –

is not neutral. It makes its first appearance at the very beginning of the European move towards world domination and finds its technological application at the height of European imperialism.

Perspective in painting is a system that allows 'corrections'. A much quoted example is the conventional perspective rendering of a column of pillars seen head–on, which makes no attempt to reproduce the optical truth that the pillars at both extremes will appear wider to the human eye (Gombrich 1960: 215–16). In a similar way, cameras and lenses have to be seen not as objective instruments, but as human artefacts designed to 'correct' anomalies in the same way, so as to render an acceptable perspectival image, not reality itself. It is also worth noting that the application of perspective to the film image at the end of the nineteenth century is parallel to the reassertion of linearity in film narrative. At the very moment when all traditional forms of representation (including perspective) were under particular threat as avant-garde art moved away from conventionality and towards the various new forms of artistic modernism, film re-asserted all the old rules, thereby setting the pattern subsequently to be followed by television.

Perspective is best seen as a construct which satisfies our need to find order and coherence in the world. As Aaron Scharf has observed, the greatness of the discovery of perspective was not that it conformed literally to optical truth, but that it 'embodied something more fundamental: the need to see the world that way'. As we consider the video image, we need to bear in mind the extent to which human beings have invested credibility in their visual media. The various technical and personal factors involved in any act of shooting mean that we cannot define the photographic or video image as a completely true rendering of nature. Yet – as has been pointed out – 'we have *learned* to see the world as the camera "sees" it' (Scharf 1965: 31).

Immediacy

If we want to establish initial differences between video and film images we can, of course, begin with the question of dimension. Although, with the creation of ever smaller audience spaces in multiscreen cinema complexes and the simultaneous development of video projection systems, the two media are coming steadily closer together (and there are already instances of overlap) (Wischmeyer 1986: 26), films have traditionally been shot for big-screen projection, while the video-maker customarily has to be satisfied with domestic-sized monitors. Whereas films have therefore dealt with literally larger-than-life figures, video's aesthetics are conditioned by a scale which, in general, moves down from the human proportion. The importance of dimension when one is dealing with reproduced images is very clear from photographic exhibitions. While painted miniatures stand up well to gallery exhibition, normal-sized photographs often seem totally dwarfed by the gallery walls, although they may look very impressive if reproduced exactly the same size in the exhibition catalogue. It is this discrepancy – rather than any spurious McLuhanesque division between 'light on' and 'light through' – which gives film stars their mythical dimension, whereas television players are consistently confused with the roles they play (there are even reports of television performers being sued by the organizers for turning up to open, say, a fête in their own appearance rather than that of their television series persona).

Other technical factors also contribute to the naturalistic literalness of the video image. The almost universal use of the zoom lens with video cameras implies an optical system which is capable of keeping the image in focus while the focal length is adjusted from wide-angle to telephoto close-up. To this extent it inevitably respects the real time continuity of a scene, even if there is some distortion of the space. This latter distortion, which allows foreground and background to be held together as the field of view changes with the operation of the zoom, is itself less disruptive of spatial continuity than the traditional film system based on the editing together of successive shots from different distances and angles. As we have seen, this tendency is supported too by the economics of video post-production, which offer significant savings (because of the operating cost of sophisticated editing equipment) in the assembly of a work out of a limited number of long takes.

The sense of a literal, unmanipulated video image extends far beyond the operation of a surveillance camera. A whole range of factors contribute to this impact: the flexibility with which a light-weight video camera can be manoeuvred; the instant replay facility; the synchronous bounding of sound and image (with, on occasion, the impression created in the audience that any imperfections of the sound track are marks of how 'real' the image is); the ability of video cameras to operate at very low lighting levels (rendering unnecessary the skills of the film industry's highly paid directors of photography who not only lit a scene but sculpted it in exquisite relief); and the maintenance, thanks to the zoom lens and the limitations of editing, of real time and (to some extent) real space relations. It is worth noting that these technical factors are best described as contributing to a sense of non-manipulation, rather than as serving as features of a positive realist style: video is literal and actual, but it is not necessarily realistic and never real.

The fact that video can effectively reproduce the systems of signification, styles, and modes of address of its two predecessors, film and television, does give it a certain freedom. As far as the film system is concerned, the intricate pattern of the look developed in feature film drama is obviously relevant (Mulvey 1975; Willemen 1976). Video, too, has the opportunity to create dramatic space and involvement through a patterning of the various looks. Like film, it can deny the camera's role in 'looking' at the action and the spectator's look at the screen, concentrating instead on the looks exchanged between the characters on screen. The effect, as in film, is to privilege the characters, who emerge as the apparent creators of the dramatic action, independent entities who 'tell their own story', without the need of an external narrator (Browne 1975–6: 26–38). Discussing, in the previous chapter, the continuing role of music in film drama, I have already questioned the extent to which, even at the height of Hollywood, the system of looks alone can be said to actually *position* the spectator. The ambiguity of the Hollywood visual system is, I would argue, far greater than most film theory allows (otherwise there would be no need of music), and in any case this (potential) ambiguity is undoubtedly enhanced when the system of looks is taken over by video, which lacks the advantages of both the big screen and the theatrical presentation.

The diminished power of the look in video is matched by video's relation to the 'web of words' characteristic of television discourse. Of course any television programme can be recorded on video tape, and the transmitted output and the video recording are superficially identical. But as Jorge Luis Borges's masterly story, 'Pierre Menard, Author of Don Quixote', makes dazzlingly clear, two literary texts may be verbally identical and yet it is possible to construct an argument proving that the second is 'almost infinitely richer' (Borges 1962: 45–55). The same can be argued of the live programme and its video recording. If credence is given to the proposition advanced earlier that broadcasting does not consist of a series of discrete works but of an (ideally endless) succession of abstract time-slots, then to stop the flow by means of video recording and replay is to make a crucial intervention. On the one hand, since the continual flow is vital to any definition of television, our ability to stop the flow transforms our relationship to that institution: recording gives us a new power and autonomy. On the other hand, the programming which occupies the time-slot is itself transformed. This is most evident when the programming is live: there is no comparison between watching, say, a football match as it happens and viewing the same material in subsequent recorded transmission. It is also arguable that any programming which is recorded, and so wrenched from its position in the flow, undergoes a change comparable in extent to that undergone by a film made for cinema release when it is transmitted on television. Certainly the whole system of television direct address is totally transformed when it ceases to be live and is made part of a video production.

The disadvantages of video as a medium relying on small-screen presentation are of course identical with those of any work shot for broadcast transmission, whether on film or tape. Often broadcast institutional practice demands that two video cameras are used simultaneously (television outside-broadcast unit style), but if the output of each camera is recorded separately for subsequent editing, video retains much of the freedom traditional to film. Indeed the small-screen domestic viewing situation renders the recording substance (film or tape) virtually indistinguishable to the general viewer, unless the

194

colour balance is distorted by the kind of standards change needed to show US video recordings on the UK broadcast system. A confirmation of this is offered by *Boys from the Blackstuff*, one of the BBC's most successful drama series, which was shown on BBC2 late in 1982 and repeated almost immediately, in January and February 1983, on BBC1. Few if any of the millions of viewers of the five-part, basically video-shot series will have noticed that Episode five, *Josser's Story*, was actually shot on film. At this level of professional broadcast production, the decision to shoot four episodes on video tape and one on film was essentially a costing one: the BBC's particular ways of budgeting meant that four video episodes could be shot for the cost of three film ones. But the indistinguishability of video from film for the general public in the resulting work – which is a triumphant expression by director Philip Saville of Alan Bleasdale's vision – shows the enormous potential power of video as a production medium for broadcast transmission (Millington and Nelson 1986). Video cannot rival film in respect of the powerful impact unique to projected big-screen theatrical film presentation, but it can match it perfectly if the outlet is television broadcasting and the domestic receiver.

Video, like film, has an advantage over still photography in that its images unfold in time. Discussing the limitations of photographic knowledge of the world, Susan Sontag notes that

> photography implies that we know about the world if we accept it as the camera records it. But this is the opposite of understanding, which starts from *not* accepting the world as it looks.
>
> (Sontag 1978: 23)

Although video, like photography, deals with 'how the world looks', its images are moving, not still, hence they are essentially narrative images and this is a potential source of real understanding:

> In contrast to the amorous relation, which is based on how something looks, understanding is based on how it functions. Any functioning takes place in time, and must be explained in time. Only that which narrates can make us understand.
>
> (Sontag 1978: 23)

Video combines narrative images containing precisely this potential for understanding with a unique ease of handling. The result is a powerful instrument which is particularly useful in situations where the intended outcome is not a product but a process. Just as no definition of video can ignore the 'home-movie' dimension, so no aesthetics of video can omit totally those applications in which the nature and quality of the work produced is secondary. One such area is community video practice where, to quote a committed practitioner, the main concern is

> not to develop a finished product. Tapes do get made and [in] almost every session there is a product; but the intended audience is usually the group itself, and the emphasis is not on the product but on the whole process of making the tape. It is impossible to understand the product without reference to the process and the two are inseparable.

> (Shaw 1986)

Here we have a social variant of Berger's definition (see p. 187) of the private photograph or video which must be appreciated in a context continuous with that from which the camera has removed it. The role of video in community work, especially in work with the disadvantaged, is to act as a catalyst for co-operative interation, giving people the confidence to take control of their own lives and encouraging them to see themselves as having ideas worth expressing. Co-operation on a video production of this kind can give an awareness of both how fruitful communal action can be and how it functions in terms of roles and responsibilities. To some extent it demystifies technology and leads to a better understanding of the media, but its main purpose is not to offer a training which produces video-makers (few will in fact work on a tape again). Instead its clear aim is to create the awareness which allows people to conduct their lives better. Concerns such as these are evidently peripheral to the aesthetics of video production which is being sketched here. But this particular dimension of video application is important as perhaps the ultimate expression of video's immediacy: the power of simply shot and lit images when backed up with recognizable synchronous sound and made immediately available on replay to those engaged in recording them and appearing in front of the cameras.

Contrivance

Footage showing forceful (particularly violent) images – combat scenes, plane crashes, urban confrontations between police and protesters – can have a direct and powerful impact on us. Whether shot on video or film, by professional reporters or amateurs using 'home–movie' formats, such images are experienced as immediate and 'real'. But in general the electronic image, however accurate in detail, does not quite possess the almost magical power of the still photograph. Looking at a video image, one does not have the feeling that provokes Susan Sontag to write that

> a photograph is not just an image (as a painting is an image), an interpretation of the real; it is also a trace, something directly stencilled off the real, like a footprint or a death mask.
> (Sontag 1978: 154)

A video image is actual, not real, and we remain aware that it is a rendering of reality, even when it gives us undigested segments of real time sounds and images. In this respect, video recording resembles sound recording more than photography: however precise it may be, it carries with it an awareness of possible contrivance, of artifice. In the case of the video camera this attitude is surely totally justified, since video is a technology symptomatic of the public role given to images in a capitalist society: it records aspects of the surface of life, but it embellishes, prettifies, as it records. There has been a lengthy debate within film theory about the ideological role of the movie camera and of the western system of perspective (Comolli 1977, 1986), but there can be none about the video camera. It is openly, transparently, both an instrument for celebrating what *is*, rather than what could be achieved by social change, and, at the same time, a machine for making life seem more pleasurable than it is.

We have already seen that recorded sound which appears natural – whether in video, film, or television – is in fact a shaped and highly contrived phenomenon. The edited video

197

image, similarly recorded on electro-magnetic tape, is best understood in the same terms, rather than through any analogies with photography. Just as the sound track is customarily constructed in a dubbing studio from a variety of sources – synchronously recorded speech, separately recorded effects and voice-overs, looped atmos tracks, and music produced in a quite different acoustic environment – so too the video image track when handled in the editing suite ideally accommodates material from virtually any camera source: stills, film in any format, studio-produced multi-camera television, video tape shot with a single portable camera, computer-generated imagery. All this material is synthesized and homogenized, and the result is a system in which mixed formats (such as 'drama-documentary', dramatized documentary, and documentary drama) are common, and essential differences become blurred. In addition, because at the point of consumption all this publicly produced material is reduced to the same basic domestic format, the distinction established by Berger between public and private imagery also becomes blurred. Part of the hysteria about video 'nasties' is explicable in terms of an external invasion of essentially private space: the fact that the family video recorder and television set make up a system ideally suited for showing pornography is particularly troubling for moralists.

The ability to rework and recontextualize given images is at the source of the political claims made for video in general and for one important strand of independent work in particular – what is usually known as 'scratch video'. This is the attempt to turn the tables on television and consciously to manipulate and distort images from a medium whose output is so often felt to be insidiously shaping our lives. In one sense scratch video can be seen as a subversive extension of the attitude behind such prime-time television compilation programmes as *It'll Be Alright on the Night*, in which a collection of production out-takes featuring various disasters (actors fluffing their lines, scenery falling over, props failing to work, passers-by intruding into the shot) is used to mock gently the pretensions of the media industries and their stars. The significant difference is that the best scratch video operates on the finished, transmitted product (whether film or television programme). The first act is one of piracy: breaking the law of copyright by appropriating the example of media output for a new public purpose. The second is the inversion of the intended meaning by a variety of simple editing methods, such as transposing parts of a speech so as to upset its political message, or using repeat edits to ridicule the gestures of a political leader.

The status of scratch video is open to considerable debate. For an advocate like Andy Lipman,

> scratch takes the broadcast media as its paintbox, the video recorder as its palette, and the TV screen as its canvas. Producing counter-definitions of reality, if only to say 'it's not like this', has always been the political meaning of art.
>
> (Lipman 1985)

The actual political usefulness of such a 'guerilla' approach is questionable. Scratch methods can deflate pomposity and expose the political rhetoric of a media event, but this falls some way short of taking a positive stance or offering the basis for a genuine critical analysis. Often its methods produce a slick surface rather than a profound statement, and the eagerness with which scratch methods have been taken over by the makers of advertising and pop promo videos points to the essentially pleasurable innocuousness of its procedures.

Equally important to a definition of video contrivance are the ways in which video equipment and procedures are liable to distort the image at every stage from production to screening. The flexibility offered by computerized control systems is in theory designed to help the video-maker. In fact such systems often intrude between the video-maker and reality in far more significant ways than is customary in either still photography or the feature film. In so doing, they deny the video medium its claim to be a simple rendering of the real world or an uncomplicated 'mirror image' of it. At shooting, the automatic gain and light controls can give a distorted image, since they shape the signal according to a reading of the average light level for most of the screen, often distorting the relationship of foreground figure and background. Bright lights moving across the image can leave a blurred after-image, like the trail of a high-flying plane. Colour can be added to the video image or subtracted from it at either recording or editing stages. And when the work is finally viewed, there are likely to be significant differences in aspect ratio, colour balance, and luminosity between the monitors attached to the editing suite and the ordinary domestic television receivers used outside.

These inherent distortion factors, which can of course be used selectively for artistic effect but which generally need to be combated by the video-maker, are usually given less consideration in discussions of video than the almost limitless extent to which video images can be effortlessly processed – by design – in a conventional video editing suite. Current comparatively low-cost equipment can wipe and fade, dissolve and superimpose, stop-frame and colourize, overlay or key-in images, split the screen into a variety of shapes, patterns and configurations, or transform the naturalistic image into a mosaic pattern. When video is linked to specialist computer devices the range of manipulation is almost infinitely expandable.

To take just two examples, the Fairlight CVI (Computer Video Instrument), designed specifically for pop promos, has a wide range of live digital video effects: overlay of processed image on direct image; inbuilt stencil (key or matte) and chroma-key; digital cascading of units, providing multiplane and more complex combinations of effects; trigger and control of visual parameters by music/audio source; real time pan, zoom, stretch of still images; mosaic/pixelation; extensive colourizing capability; strobe or freeze function; variable trailing; multiplane effects (three apparent planes using one unit); mirrors – horizontal, vertical, and overlapped; smooth pans and continuous glides; double exposure, and so on. In a similar way, the Quantel Paintbox, designed specifically for designers, can carry out a whole range of graphic design functions: it can instantaneously resize and crop pictures to specific dimensions or grid references; convert colours; create original artwork in a variety of textures (paint, chalk, airbrush, wash); offer a range of graphic aids including lines, rectangles, circles, elipses, in any brush size; provide a stencil facility for easy masking, painting, or airbrush work, hard or soft edged; assemble pictures using cut and paste facilities where images can be masked, cut, rotated and pasted in full detail, and so on.

Obviously not all of these effects have been available to (or demanded by) independent video artists, but such effects as are employed are within the total control of the artist: video special effects are not separated off behind laboratory doors, as is the case with film. Moreover, since many video artists have a second identity as makers of pop promos, an awareness of the full range of technical potential for image manipulation is a factor in their approach to independent work. One of the problems of evaluating video art is the extent to which it is dominated by the technology available at a given moment. In broadcast television we are all familiar with the way the designers of the credit sequence for virtually every new or revamped television series will turn to a particular video facilities house so as to have access to some new video processing device costing hundreds of thousands of pounds (such as a Bosch FGS 4000) and so employ its novel way of hurtling letters and objects through an apparently three-dimensional space. Similarly independent video work of a particular year often shows clearly which new manipulative devices have just become cheaply available, with the result that an initial novelty soon becomes a stale convention in a way that owes more to fashion than to artistic development.

Video art and its technology

This brings us to one of the most complex of questions concerning video as a means of creative expression: the relationship between video art and its technology. The 'entanglement of early British video with late modernism' has been excellently explored by Stuart Marshall. He notes that by the late 1970s,

> modernism had reached its zenith in painting and sculpture.
> . . . Painting had achieved almost total reflexivity; it spoke only the conditions of its own material existence. Conceptual artists working within the commercial gallery system began to focus attention on the processes of art production rather than the art object itself.
>
> (Marshall 1985: 67)

This was bound to influence video-makers, who came from

201

very similar educational and artistic backgrounds, as they sought a specific video art practice. Their efforts could also not fail to be shaped by the current commercial art scene, in which artists 'claimed a political significance for this work by arguing that it challenged both the art historical and gallery definition of the work as a cultural and marketable commodity', while at the same time the gallery owners 'adapted their marketing strategies to recuperate these works as saleable commodities' by offering 'documentation of performance, site-dependent and conceptual art in place of the work itself' (Marshall 1985: 67–8).

In their attempts to match the reflexivity of contemporary modernist (and post-modernist) painting, video innovators also had a valuable model – as we have seen – in the efforts of the film avant-gardists working in such contexts as the New York and London Film Makers Co-ops. It has been stressed that video is a flexible medium which can be endlessly processed and modified. But it cannot be manipulated in the literal sense – that is, handled or treated by manual means – and the consequences of this become clear when we consider it in relation to the three areas of avant-garde activity set out above (pp. 148–9). If we look first at equivalents to the manipulation of celluloid and emulsion, we see immediately that all interventions on the tape have to be made electronically and that any transformations must be carried out during playback. Since video editing is not fully computerized and there is no random access to material, video-makers can only work sequentially with material available to them in a purely linear fashion. Therefore they need to bring outside ideas to a medium which, until set in motion at playback, is inert as well as inaccessible and has none of the concrete materiality with which the image track confronts the film-maker (or the block of stone confronts the sculptor). This makes video creativity a conceptual activity, but work with images has none of the tradition of abstract analysis to be found in music. Since connections between music and mathematics have traditionally been close, composers have often found it easier than image-makers to adapt to the abstract conceptual thinking required by an electronic system.

A discrepancy of a somewhat different kind is to be found when we consider video equivalents to the Co-op movement members' development and printing of their own images. For the film-makers this was perhaps the key stage in their work, a very distinctive second opportunity to exercise control over the materiality of film. Peter Gidal captures very well the sensation of 'having access into and thereby through and thereby onto the possible processes of representation':

> You sit there with a machine and you are process, no more or less than the machine, because the handling is necessary yet does not cause an effect – quite a different matter from painting, for example. . . . When you loop a strip of master film material (threading) onto a printer and attempt to pull it through in order to 'see' how the reproduction will appear if the original is *not* led through automatically on the sprocket-wheel, you are attempting to set up a difference between image and its reproduction.
>
> (Gidal 1980: 152–3)

The sense of liberation felt by film-makers at this moment has, of course, to be measured against the technological history of the film medium: the fact that for fifty years or more such operations had always been carried on behind closed laboratory doors. The situation of video-makers could hardly be more different. While physical intervention is denied them, there is every opportunity to change and process the images and no inaccessible laboratory to confront. Their problem is rather to find reasons (aesthetic, social, political) for the use of any or all of the types of image transformation which are at hand and virtually effortless to achieve.

The third avant-garde concern – with performance space – looks at first sight more promising, since video can cope well with multiscreen projection and a variety of performance situations. But exploration of duration is difficult, since video lacks film's hypnotic power, and any video performance is in a very real sense peripheral, since it is impossible for the video-maker to intervene between the video recorder and monitor. Once more the video-maker is forced to interact from the outside. This comparison of divergent avant-garde possibilities indicates clearly the limitations of the video-maker's powers of intervention on the (elusive) materiality of video. In so far as video can be expected to develop an independent practice this is likely to focus less on the specificity of video – a medium whose materiality 'consists of a complex pattern of invisible electromagnetic charges on a reel of magnetic tape' (Marshall 1985: 69) – than on aspects of representation: image, sound, and performance intermixed.

One area of likely development is the growing connection of video and popular music, although at present this is a somewhat murky area, using mixed media and combining inputs from advertising, avant-garde practice, and fashion within a blatantly commercial context. In a fascinating study of the 'conditions of music', Alan Durant sees video as working as an important catalyst in the changing audio-visual style of rock music on three separate levels. The first is the emergence of new music video genres 'stylistically based in gestures of performance at present recorded in rock documentary and musical, but gradually projected into more elaborate mime and scenario'. These are likely to lead to a marginalization of records and performance and a shift from the aural emphasis of early rock 'towards a new dominance of the visual, elsewhere promoted by the increasing cultural centrality of television'. But this new emphasis will in turn lead to the new techniques of relating and juxtaposing sounds and images becoming part of the general vocabulary and style of film, advertising, and television itself (Durant 1984: 232–3).

If the pop video is one pointer to the future another is the development of increasingly complex mixed forms of drama and documentary in television. Video with its unique range from actuality to contrivance has a clear role to play here. But it also has the potential to create quite new forms of dramatic and narrative organization. To take a tiny example, it has been argued above that video's narrative image, unfolding in real time, is one source of its power, its actuality. But equally importantly the flow of time can be arrested: video can deal with still images and freeze-frames. Also, since the tape containing the original camera material is not 'used up' in making the master copy (as a film's negative is used up when it is physically cut and cemented to provide the source of the master print), an image, a gesture, a movement can be repeated in absolutely identical form.

These aspects of control of time – combined with its analytic potential – are currently limited largely to sporting events (to repeat goals, stumpings, and knock-outs) but they could serve as the basis for one aspect of video's untried narrative potential. The question immediately arises as to why this is not currently being realized, why in the late-1980s we still have to deal with essentially marginal forms when we consider the aesthetics of video. We need to explore why a medium which fits television's requirements so well and is now so firmly established as a domestic entertainment facility has still to find its individual position in the mainstream of commercial audio-visual production.

The future of video

I have remarked elsewhere on the fact that in writing any history of cinema the very vocabulary of development and progress is all-pervading, giving

> the almost inevitable creation of a fake but persuasive pattern based on some unarticulated biological model: the infant cinema . . . its first tentative steps . . . growth to maturity . . . decline in face of television.

> (Armes 1985: 1)

Equally all-pervading is the urge to end any study of media developments with a look into the future. I find myself drawn in this direction with the present consideration of video aesthetics, fortified (in my own eyes at least) by the need to justify the tentativeness of the preceding observations and by the view – to which I have continually returned – that video needs to be seen not in a void but in the whole spectrum of audio-visual media and, at the same time, must be defined not in terms of its past achievements but its actual potentialities.

Jeanne Thomas Allen has noted that the history of the invention of cinema needs to be seen in relation to wider aspects of nineteenth-century industrialization: the institutionalization of invention (for which the Edison laboratories at Menlo Park, New Jersey, were the prototype); the principle of standardization (originating in the armaments industry and leading to the establishment of a machine-tool industry independent of any particular manufacturing interest); and the role of patents (dominant in a divisive way in the nineteenth-century media, but pooled by giant corporations to allow the growth of broadcasting and given free to the world by Philips in its drive to establish the audio cassette). Ignoring parallel developments in *sound* reproduction and replication, Allen observes that:

> mechanical production of visual images accomplished in the sphere of mass culture what was also occurring elsewhere in the economy. Photography, mechanical reproduction and industrial standardisation are related through the realisation of a mass market for less expensive and seemingly infinitely replicable products.
>
> (J. T. Allen 1980: 30)

Certainly one key to a (non-biological) understanding of media history is to pick out those pointers which allow the usually concealed substratum to be glimpsed. Two particularly revealing examples can be cited here. Firstly, Ben Brewster's observation that Etienne Marey's 'photographic gun' used the principles of the Gattling gun to obtain the succession of pictures needed for the study of animal locomotion (symbolically anticipating the links between communications developments and the US military–industrial complex) (cit. J. T. Allen 1980: 31–2). Secondly, Brian Winston's apt if surprising chapter title, 'Bing Crosby invents video tape, 11th November 1951', which underlines the extent to which media developments are driven by the needs of entertainment – the electronics division of the singer's company, Bing Crosby Enterprises, which had pioneered sound tape in the 1940s, commissioned from Ampex the prototype video recorder demonstrated publicly in 1951 (Winston 1986: 83). On a more personal note, Winston, who is unequivocal in his estimate of video cassette recorders as '*the* crucial device to expand entertainment television', which will have 'the most significant effect on all current and proposed systems for the mass distribution of audio–visual signals, including cable' (1986: 2), describes his own undisrupted career in a high-tech industry at the cutting edge of technological development:

Twenty-three years ago when I joined the broadcasting industry, video tape was already nearly a decade old, yet here I am in the mid-1980s still happily working with film and teaching others to do the same.

(1986: ix)

Just as the key factor to consider in attempting to understand the invention of cinema – as was pointed out at the beginning of the 1970s in a series of articles (Comolli 1977: 132) – is the *delay* (since the principles had long been known and the practicalities were easy to solve), so too the key question with regard to the future of video is to account for its continuing marginalization as a *production* medium. This situation is all the more surprising in view of the centrality of video to such processes as bringing together sound and image industries (the pop video), recycling existing material for resale (video versions of old films), and recording media events (so as to turn them into marketable commodities). Clues are to be found in Winston's work which is without doubt the most rigorously worked-out investigation into the technological development of the communication and information media.

He points out that invention is not the starting-point, but involves both prior scientific competence – leading to 'ideation' (the formulation of the technological idea) and the creation of prototypes – and an external 'supervening necessity' (particularly one which will make the invention seem commercially worth-while). Winston also includes between invention and what he calls 'technological performance' (production, spin-offs, redundancies) a fourth factor which he terms the 'law' of the suppression of radical potential:

Constraints operate firstly to preserve essential formations such as business entities and other institutions and secondly to slow down the rate of diffusion so that the social fabric can absorb the new machine. . . . Whatever the general perception, there has been no speed-up in the measurable rate of change. If anything, there has been a significant diminution in the cut-throat nature of the market place because the desire for stable trading circumstances, coupled with external restrictions and

monopolistic tendencies, works to contain the crudest mani-
festations of the profit motive.

(Winston 1986: 24)

This model, although it offers a complex look at the nature of
invention and development, takes us only as far as the
emergence of the eventual product into the social sphere. There,
as we have seen, the media undergo further transformations in
their specific application and every subsequent technological
change is also a site for a clash between the supervening necessity
of transformation and the forces of the status quo harnessed
under the banner of the suppression of radical change. The
outcome is often stalemate, particularly as change throws up
contradictions. To take the example of domestic video, the
needs of the consumer in terms of an ideal system are coherent
but wide-ranging: a spread of functions including the replay and
duplication of purchased or hired material, the transfer of
material available in other formats, off-air recording, and
domestic production. These are comparatively easy to supply in
a single machine from the point of view of equipment
manufacture, and in their turn they create a profitable market for
the sale of blank tapes. But for producers of broadcast or pre-
recorded material the facility which allows personal recording
(and hence duplication) raises all kinds of problems of ownership,
copyright, and piracy (thereby threatening profitability).

Despite this fundamental clash the domestic video market has
been exploited with exemplary thoroughness and offers a
striking example of ways in which certain technological developments can overcome Winston's 'law'. In this case the contradiction is resolvable because the suppliers of blank and pre-recorded
tapes are the same companies, and if they choose to make tapes
available to the pirates they can still make profits and only their
recording artists will suffer financially. However, the barriers to
universal video production are more intractable and derive
mainly from problems of standardization. There is at present a
lack of compatibility between the UK 625-line system and the
US 525-line format, and between the three colour systems
(United States NTSC, British PAL, and French SECAM). At
the crucial juncture when the systems emerged, there was no

single multinational force in video with the power (in terms of resources for equipment and materials manufacture, advertising, and world-wide distribution) to take on the role adopted with regard to film by Eastman Kodak, which first established the 35 mm format internationally for all feature film production at the turn of the century and then, in 1923, imposed 16 mm as the definitive gauge for all non-professional production (J. T. Allen 1980: 31).

The lack of standardization of video means that film remains, in the late 1980s, the more convenient medium for international production and marketing. To overcome its shortcomings video would ideally need to adopt, world-wide, a single standard, perhaps the 1,000-line high-definition system with stereo hi-fi sound for which prototypes already exist (Winston 1985: 259). But what is lacking is Winston's supervening social necessity, and again film offers an example of what is required. Although the 16 mm format was universally established in the 1920s, it was not until the 1960s that adequate, flexible synch-sound systems were introduced. The external necessity here was clearly the demand for location filming by television broadcast institutions. The 16 mm image was, in technical terms, perfectly adequate for their needs, and they could afford to buy the new system since they had no extensive existing investment in 35 mm film equipment. As a by-product of their decision the new system also became available to documentary and avant-garde film-makers, transforming the definition and scope of independent cinema.

From the point of view of video, however, the timing of this decision was disastrous. Had video been available then in its current form, it would in all probability have taken the place usurped by film. In fact the 1960s development of 16 mm film pre-empted the development of video which ought logically to have occurred in the 1970s. As it is, while there is no doubt that all broadcast production will *eventually* be made on video, there is certainly no immediate financial incentive for broadcast companies to undertake a revolutionary transformation. The cost differences between video and 16 mm are not sufficient to justify the upheaval involved in discarding film (and hence disrupting existing work practices and union agreements, writing off expensive capital equipment, retraining staff or making them redundant, and so on). A more likely pattern for the adoption of video is an initial impetus in reporting (where coverage of special events like a general election increasingly demands a vast array of simple filming units), followed by a gradual introduction of video – in face of institutional and union opposition – into drama and documentary. It is only when this has occurred – and experience shows that such transitions take far longer than can be reasonably imagined – that video technology will begin to create its own independent and fully distinctive aesthetic and the full potential of the medium will become apparent in mainstream production.

Further reading

Much of the technical data here is taken from Curtis (1985). Winston (1986) is by far the most thorough chronicler of the invention and introduction of communication and information technology. Bolter (1986) is excellent on the computer and its relationship to our society. The views of McLuhan (1967) are contested by Miller (1971) and Winston (1985). Key articles on recent developments in film theory, including Mulvey (1975), Browne (1975–6), Willemen (1976), Bellour (1974–5), Doane (1980a), and Comolli (1986) are contained in the anthology by Rosen (1986). Original articles by Wollen, J. T. Allen, Doane, and Gidal feature in Lauretis and Heath (1980). For earlier material see Nichols (1976). Millington and Nelson (1986) is an excellent account of the production of a television series shot on video. There is comparatively little material of value on video itself, but see Marshall (1979, 1985) and Lipman (1985). For music videos see especially Durant (1984) and Laing (1985).

CONCLUSION
Video in
the computer age

> Computer thought is wholly a matter of convention, of formal rules acting upon contentless symbols. Whether numbers or letters are represented as bit strings in the machine, the representation is one of pure denotation. . . . Bits within a computer are logical symbols that mean nothing more than they are deemed to mean in the context of a particular program.
>
> (J. David Bolter 1986: 76)

This study began with a plea for a new perspective on the study of video. Its three main sections have looked at video in its historical and social contexts and as a medium in its own right. It remains now to consider the potential role of video in the computer age which we are now entering. First the transistor and then the microchip transformed the sound and image media during the period since the Second World War. Transistor radios, electronically equipped still cameras, solid-state video recorders, and so on have been developed and become part of our lives. The link between these new forms of media and computer technology is evidently close. But do the twentieth-century media – and particularly video – have something distinctive to offer in return?

In what is, to date, our most informative and illuminating study of the cultural role of the computer, J. David Bolter chooses it as the 'defining technology' of our age (1986: 8–12), drawing comparisons with the potter's wheel in the ancient world, the mechanical clock in the seventeenth century, and the steam engine in the nineteenth (1986: 41). Bolter does not argue that such technologies *create* societies, rather he points to their role in shaping human thought, creating a focus for philosophical and mathematical speculation, and thereby defining a certain world–view which can be seen as characteristic of the era in question.

Bolter is keen to stress aspects of the computer's handling of space, time, language, and memory which echo earlier periods, even the ancient world. But the computer also brings many things which are new. In particular, Bolter stresses the turning away from nineteenth–century Romantic aspirations and ambitions and the new concentration on the finite, the immediate, the close–to–hand. In handling these aspects of our life, the computer works by abstraction. It remains on the level of purely symbolic logic, mass producing information not material products, and retaining, for the computer programmer, many characteristics of a game: allowing an enormous (though finite) number of permutations, but only within extremely well–defined logical rules.

Bolter's 'archetypal picture' of our age is that of the isolated, asexually dressed scientist at a computer terminal in a sparsely lit, sparsely furnished room, cut off from the turmoil of life and drawing all the information needed, not from books, but from the memory banks of the computer itself (Bolter 1986: 166). This image points perhaps more clearly than any other to the need for an alternative image of human beings in relation to the world and themselves. What is surely needed is a complementary system of communication which will put men and women in touch with each other and with the world around them. It will need to feed their desire for art, entertainment, and information, bring their immediate present into contact with the historical past, and cater for their senses and emotions as well as their intellect. Video, it seems to me, is ideally placed to occupy this role.

As we have seen in the present study, the systems of sound and image reproduction and transmission span the transformation of western society from mechanical to electronic technology and reflect a profound modification of our relation to external reality. The nineteenth-century systems are exemplified by the film camera and projector: precise mechanical engineering combined with an immediately perceptible direct link to reality. The computer stands at the other extreme: able to operate at a billionth of a second because it lacks moving parts, but dealing only with abstract information. The importance of video in this context is that it has a foot in both camps. The video recorder is both a precisely engineered machine (designed to ensure, for example, the steady passing of the tape past the heads) and an electronic sound and image processor. Similarly, electro-magnetic tape has a sensitivity to light akin to that of photographic emulsion, while being as inherently manipulable and transformable as a pure computer-style information system.

From this perspective the key aspect of video is not what it shares with those tapes which serve as external memory sources for a computer, or even the fascinating area of overlap constituted by computer-generated graphics, but rather those live action elements which make it *complementary* to the computer. While the latter deals only with its abstract symbols arranged neatly in binary code, video can act immediately on the objects and people around us. Video editing and post-production work are, as we have seen, in many ways conceptual activities, akin to operating a computer terminal (though with the drawback at present of linear, not random, access to sounds and images). But shooting remains an activity of direct intervention in life, and one which is increasingly open to all. Video's scope of application – like that of still photography – ranges from the professional to the casual. Whatever the approach, video, by reproducing objects and drawing them from their contexts, gives them a new life. As Walter Benjamin observes, in permitting the copy to meet the viewer or listener in his or her own situation, the technique of reproduction 'reactivates the object reproduced' (Benjamim 1973: 223). Thus video – again like photography – offers more than just an inert facsimile of the object.

In video we have, then, a form of recording which is both a compatible part of the electronic information-processing systems of the computer age and a medium able to contribute something in its own right. At the end of his book, Bolter argues strongly that we need to 'find ways to bring history into the computer world' (Bolter 1986: 229), so as to make the riches of the past accessible to new generations whose sources of information and knowledge will be electronic storage devices. Video, as both a twentieth-century medium with its roots in an earlier age and a recording device of unrivalled flexibility, is well-placed to fill the need which Bolter defines. But at the same time, video is an independent creative medium which, as well as echoing or repeating past achievements, can be looked to for new fusions of sound, image, and performance, new ways of representing time and space. It has the potential to be truly the art of the twenty-first century.

BIBLIOGRAPHY

Aitken, H. G. J. (1985a) *Syntony and Spark: The Origins of Radio*, Princeton: Princeton University Press.
—— (1985b) *The Continuous Wave: Technology and American Radio, 1900–1932*, Princeton: Princeton University Press.
Alberti, L. B. (1956) *On Painting*, New Haven: Yale University Press.
Allen, J. T. (1980) 'The industrial context of film technology: standardisation and patents', in T. de Lauretis and S. Heath (eds) *The Cinematic Apparatus*, London: Macmillan, 26–36.
Allen, R. C. (1979) 'Vitascope/-Cinématographe: initial patterns of American film industrial practice', *Journal of the University Film Association* 31, no. 2, 13–18.
Altman, R. (1980a) 'Introduction', *Yale French Studies* 60, special issue, 'Cinema/Sound', 13–18.
—— (1980b) 'Moving lips: cinema as ventriloquism', *Yale French Studies* 60, special issue, 'Cinema/Sound', 67–79.
Anderson, J. L. and Richie, D. (1959) *The Japanese Film: Art and Industry*, Rutland, Vermont, and Tokyo: Charles E. Tuttle.
Andrew, D. (1984) *Concepts in Film Theory*, New York: Oxford University Press.
Arijon, D. (1976) *Grammar of the Film Language*, London: Focal Press.
Armes, R. (1968) *The Cinema of Alain Resnais*, London: Tantivy Press.
—— (1985) *French Cinema*, London: Secker & Warburg.
—— (1987) *Third World Film Making and the West*, Berkeley: University of California Press.
Arnheim, R. (1974) *Art and Visual Perception*, Berkeley: University of California Press, revised edn.
Attali, J. (1985) *Noise: The Political Economy of Music*, Manchester: Manchester University Press.
Bagdikian, B. H. (1983) *The Media Monopoly*, Boston: Beacon Press.

Balio, T. (1976) *The American Film Industry*, Madison: University of Wisconsin Press.

Barnouw, E. (1966) *A History of Broadcasting in the United States: Volume I – A Tower in Babel*, New York: Oxford University Press.

—— (1968) *A History of Broadcasting in the United States: Volume II – The Golden Webb*, New York: Oxford University Press.

—— (1970) *A History of Broadcasting in the United States: Volume III – The Image Empire*, New York: Oxford University Press.

—— (1974) *Documentary: A History of the Non-Fiction Film*, New York: Oxford University Press.

—— (1982) *Tube of Plenty: The Evolution of American Television*, New York: Oxford University Press, revised edn.

Barsam, R. M. (1974) *Nonfiction Film*, London: George Allen & Unwin.

Barthes, R. (1977) *Image–Music–Text*, London: Fontana.

Baskaran, S. T. (1981) *The Message Bearers: The Nationalist Politics and the Entertainment Media in South India, 1880–1945*, Madras: Cre-A.

Bates, A. W. (1984) *Broadcasting in Education: An Evaluation*, London: Constable.

Bellour, R. (1974–5) 'The obvious and the code', *Screen* 15, no. 4, 7–17.

Beloff, H. (1985) *Camera Culture*, Oxford: Basil Blackwell.

Belton, J. (1985) 'Technology and aesthetics of film sound', in E. Weis and J. Belton (eds) *Film Sound: Theory and Practice*, New York: Columbia University Press, 63–72.

Belz, C. (1972) *The Story of Rock*, New York: Harper & Row, second edn.

Benjamin, W. (1973) *Illuminations*, London: Fontana.

Berger, J. (1972) *Ways of Seeing*, Harmondsworth and London: Penguin and BBC.

—— (1980) *About Looking*, London: Writers and Readers Publishing Cooperative.

Berrigan, F. J. (1977) *Access: Some Western Models of Community Media*, Paris: Unesco.

Bertsch, M. (1917) *How to Write for Moving Pictures*, New York: George H. Doran.

Bishop, J. (1986) *Home Video Production*, New York: McGraw-Hill.

Black, P. (1972) *The Mirror in the Corner: People's Television*, London: Hutchinson.

Bolter, J. D. (1986) *Turing's Man: Western Culture in the Computer Age*, Harmondsworth: Penguin.

Bordwell, D. (1985) *Narration in the Fiction Film*, London: Methuen.

—— and Thompson, K. (1979) *Film Art: An Introduction*, Reading, Mass.: Addison-Wesley.

—— Staiger, J., and Thompson, K. (1985) *The Classical Hollywood Cinema: Film Style and Mode of Production to 1960*, London: Routledge & Kegan Paul.

Borges, J. L. (1962) *Ficciones*, London: Weidenfeld & Nicolson.

Boyle, A. (1972) *Only the Wind Will Listen: Reith of the BBC*, London: Hutchinson.

Braverman, H. (1974) *Labor and Monopoly Capital*, New York: Monthly Review Press.

Briggs, A. (1961) *The History of Broadcasting in the United Kingdom: Volume I – The Birth of Broadcasting*, London: Oxford University Press.

—— (1965) *The History of Broadcasting in the United Kingdom: Volume II – The Golden Age of Wireless*, London: Oxford University Press.

—— (1970) *The History of Broadcasting in the United Kingdom: Volume III – The War of Words*, London: Oxford University Press.

—— (1979) *The History of Broadcasting in the United Kingdom: Volume IV – Sound and Vision*, Oxford: Oxford University Press.

—— (1985) *The BBC: The First Fifty Years*, Oxford: Oxford University Press.

Brookes, K. (1985) *Video Film Making*, Hemel Hempstead: Argos.

Browne, N. (1975–6) 'The spectator-in-the-text: the rhetoric of *Stagecoach*', *Film Quarterly* 29, no. 2, 26–38.

—— (1980) 'Film form/voice-over: Bresson's *The Diary of a Country Priest*', *Yale French Studies* 60, special issue. 'Cinema/Sound'.

Brunsden, C. and Morley, D. (1978) *Everyday Television: 'Nationwide'*, London: British Film Institute.

Burder, J. (1968) *Editing 16 mm Films*, London: Focal Press.

Caughie, J. (1984) 'Television criticism: "a discourse in search of an object"', *Screen* 25, no. 4–5, 109–20.

Cavell, S. (1971) *The World Viewed*, New York: Viking Press.

Chion, M. (1982) *La Voix au Cinéma*, Paris: Cahiers du Cinéma.

—— (1985) *Le Son au Cinéma*, Paris: Cahiers du Cinéma/Editions de l'Etoile.

Cipolla, C. (1970) *European Culture and Overseas Expansion*, Harmondsworth: Penguin.

Coe, B. (1981) *The History of Movie Photography*, London: Ash & Grant.

Comolli, J-L. (1977) 'Technique and ideology: camera perspective, depth of field', part one, *Film Reader* 2, 128–40.

—— (1986) 'Technique and ideology: camera perspective, depth of field', parts three and four, in P. Rosen (ed.) *Narrative, Apparatus, Ideology*, New York: Columbia University Press, 421–43.

Compaigne, B. M. (ed.) (1979) *Who Owns the Media?*, New York: Knowledge Industry Publications.

Corner, J. (ed.) (1986) *Documentary and the Mass Media*, London: Edward Arnold.

Crisell, A. (1986) *Understanding Radio*, London: Methuen.

Crittenden, R. (1981) *Manual of Film Editing*, London: Thames & Hudson.

Cultural Statistics and Cultural Development (1982), Paris: Unesco.

Curtis, B. (1985), *Video Production Technology: Notes on the Theory and*

Practice of Low-Band U-matic Equipment, London: V.E.T.

Davis, D. (1966) *The Grammar of Television Production*, London: Barrie & Rockliff, revised edn.

Dean, R. (1982) *Home Video*, London: Butterworth.

Dearling, R. and Dearling, C. (1984) *The Guinness Book of Recorded Sound*, London: Guinness Books.

Deming, R. H. (1985) 'Discourse/talk/television', *Screen* 26, no. 6, 88–92.

Deslandes, J. (1966) *Histoire Comparée du Cinéma: Volume Two*, Paris: Castermann.

Doane, M. A. (1980a) 'The voice in cinema: the articulation of body and space', *Yale French Studies* 60, special issue, 'Cinema/Sound', 33–50.

—— (1980b) 'Ideology and the practice of sound editing and mixing', in T. de Lauretis and S. Heath (eds) *The Cinematic Apparatus*, London: Macmillan, 47–56.

Docherty, D., Morrison, D., and Tracey M. (1986) 'Who goes to the cinema?', *Sight and Sound*, 55, no. 2, 81–5.

Durant, A. (1984) *Conditions of Music*, London: Macmillan.

Dwoskin, S. (1975) *Film Is*, London: Peter Owen.

Eisler, H. (1951) *Composing for the Films*, London: Dennis Dobson.

Elliott, G. (1987) *Video Active*, London: BBC.

Ellis, J. (1977) 'The institution of cinema', *Edinburgh '77 Magazine* 2, 56–66.

—— (1982) *Visible Fictions*, London: Routledge & Kegan Paul.

Enzensberger, H. M. (1972) 'Constituents of a theory of the media', in D. McQuail (ed.) *Sociology of Mass Communications*, Harmondsworth: Penguin, 99–116.

Escarpit, R. (1966) *The Book Revolution*, London: George G. Harrap, and Paris: Unesco.

Febvre, L. and Martin, H-J. (1976) *The Coming of the Book*, London: New Left Books.

Fell, J. (1974) *Film and the Narrative Tradition*, Norman: University of Oklahoma Press.

—— (ed.) (1983) *Film Before Griffith*, Berkeley: University of California Press.

Fielding, R. (ed.) (1967) *A Technological History of Motion Pictures and Television*, Berkeley: University of California Press.

Fox Talbot, H. (1969) *The Pencil of Nature*, New York: Da Capo Press. Original edn – London: Brown, Green, and Longmans.

Freund, G. (1980) *Photography and Society*, London: Gordon Fraser.

Frith, S. (1983) *Sound Effects: Youth, Leisure and the Politics of Rock*, London: Constable, revised edn.

Fuller, B. J., Kanaba, S., and Brisch-Kanaba, J. (1980) *Single-Camera Video Production*, New York: Prentice Hall.

Garnham, N. (1973) *Structures of Television*, London: British Film Institute.

Gelatt, R. (1977) *The Fabulous Phonograph, 1877–1977*, London: Cassell, revised edn.

Gernsheim, H. and Gernsheim, A. (1971) *A Concise History of Photography*, London: Thames & Hudson, revised edn.

Gidal, P. (ed.) (1976) *Structural Film Anthology*, London: British Film Institute.

—— (1980) 'Technology and ideology in/through/and avant-garde film: an instance', in T. de Lauretis and S. Heath (eds) *The Cinematic Apparatus*, London: Macmillan, 151–65.

Goldsmith, A. (1979) *The Camera and its Images*, New York: Ridge Press and Newsweek.

Gombrich, E. H. (1960) *Art and Illusion*, London: Phaidon.

Gomery, D. (1976a) 'The coming of the talkies: invention, innovation and diffusion', in T. Balio (ed.) *The American Film Industry*, Madison: University of Wisconsin Press, 196–211.

—— (1976b) 'Writing the history of the American film industry: Warner Bros and sound', *Screen* 17, no. 1, 40–53.

—— (1976c) 'Problems in film history: how Fox innovated sound', *Quarterly Review of Film Studies* 1, no. 3, 315–30.

—— (1976d) 'The "Warner Vitaphone Peril": the American film industry reacts to the innovation of sound', *Journal of the University Film Association*, 28, no. 1, 11–19.

—— (1977) 'Failure and success: Vocafilm and RCA innovate sound', *Film Reader* 2, 213–21.

—— (1979) 'The movies become big business: Publix Theatres and the chain-store strategy', *Cinema Journal* 18, no. 2, 26–40.

—— (1980a) 'Economic struggle and Hollywood imperialism: Europe converts to sound', *Yale French Studies* 60, special issue, 'Cinema/Sound', 80–93.

—— (1980b) 'Towards an economic history of the cinema: the coming of sound to Hollywood', in T. de Lauretis and S. Heath (eds) *The Cinematic Apparatus*, London: Macmillan, 38–46.

—— (1986) *The Hollywood Studio System*, London: British Film Institute and Macmillan.

Goodwin, A., Kerr, P., and Macdonald, I. (eds) (1983) *Drama-Documentary*, London: British Film Institute.

Gorbman, C. (1980) 'Narrative film music', *Yale French Studies* 60, special issue, 'Cinema/Sound', 183–203.

Graham, I. (1986) *The Videomaker's Handbook*, London: Octopus.

Gregory, R. L. (1966) *Eye and Brain: The Psychology of Seeing*, London: Weidenfeld & Nicolson.

—— and Gombrich, E. H. (eds) (1973) *Illusion in Nature and Art*, London: George Duckworth.

Guback, T. and Varis, T. (1982) *Transnational Communication and Cultural Industries*, Paris: Unesco.

Hall, S. (1976) 'Television and culture', *Sight and Sound* 45, no. 4, 245–9.

Halloran, J. (1970) *The Effects of Television*, London: Panther.

Happé, B. (1975) *Basic Motion Picture Technology*, London: Focal Press, second edn.

—— (1983) *Your Film and the Lab*, London: Focal Press, second edn.

Heath, S. (1981) *Questions of Cinema*, London: Macmillan.

Hood, S. (1980) *On Television*, London: Pluto Press.

Issari, M. A. and Paul, D. M. (1979) *What is Cinéma-Vérité?*, Metuchen· Scarecrow Press.

Jackson, K. (1985) *Newnes Book of Creative Video*, London: Newnes.

Jeffrey, I. (1981) *Photography: A Concise History*, London: Thames & Hudson.

Jenkins, R. V. (1975) *Images and Enterprise: Technology and the American Photographic Industry*, 1939 to 1925, Baltimore: Johns Hopkins University Press.

Kaplan, E. A. (1987) *Rocking Around the Clock*, London: Methuen.

Katz, E. and Wedell, G. (1978) *Broadcasting in the Third World*, London: Macmillan.

Kerr, P. (ed.) (1986) *The Hollywood Film Industry*, London: Routledge & Kegan Paul and British Film Institute.

Kindem, G. (ed.) (1982) *The American Movie Industry*, Carbondale: University of Southern Illinois Press.

King, N. (1984) 'The sound of silents', *Screen* 25, no. 3, 2–15.

Kuhn, T. (1962) *The Structure of Scientific Revolutions*, Chicago: Chicago University Press.

Laing, D. (1985) 'Music video: industrial product, cultural form', *Screen* 26, no. 2, 78–83.

Lane, T. (1936) *The New Technique of Screen Writing*, New York: McGraw-Hill.

Lauretis, T. de and Heath, S. (eds) (1980) *The Cinematic Apparatus*, London: Macmillan.

Legrice, M. (1977) *Abstract Film and Beyond*, London: Studio Vista.

Levin, T. (1984) 'The acoustic dimension', *Screen* 25, no. 3, 55–68.

Lewis, P. (ed.) (1981) *Radio Drama*, London: Longman.

Lipman, A. (1985) *Video: The State of the Art*, London: Channel Four.

Mackay, A. (1981) *Electronic Music*, London: Phaidon Press.

Maclaurin, W. R. (1971) *Invention and Innovation in the Radio Industry*, New York: Arno Pres, reprint.

McLuhan, M. (1967) *Understanding Media*, London: Sphere.

McWhinnie, D. (1959) *The Art of Radio*, London: Faber & Faber.

Marion, F. (1937) *How to Write and Sell Film Stories*, New York: Covici Friede.

Marshall, S. (1979) 'Video: technology and practice', *Screen* 20, no. 1, 109–19.

—— (1985) 'Video: from art to independence', *Screen* 26, no. 2, 66–71.

Mathias, H. and Patterson, R. (1985) *Electronic Cinematography*, Belmont, Calif.: Wadsworth.

Metz, C. (1974) *Film Language*, New York: Oxford University Press.

Miller, J. (1971) *McLuhan*, London: Fontana/Collins.

Millerson, G. (1982a) *Basic TV Staging*, London: Focal Press, second edn.

—— (1982b) *TV Lighting Methods*, London: Focal Press, second edn.

—— (1983) *Video Camera Techniques*, London: Focal Press.

—— (1985) *The Technique of Television Production*, London: Focal Press.

—— (1987) *Video Production Handbook*, London: Focal Press.

Millington, B. and Nelson, R. (1986) *Boys from the Blackstuff: The Making of TV Drama*, London: Comedia.

Moore, F. L. (1984) *The Video Moviemaker's Handbook*, New York: New American Library.

Morgan, T. J. (1961) *Television*, London: Frederick Muller.

Morley, D. (1986) *Family Television: Cultural Power and Domestic Leisure*, London: Comedia.

Morse, M. (1985) 'Talk, talk, talk – the space of discourse in television', *Screen* 26, no. 2, 2–15.

Mowitt, J. (1986) 'The sound of music in the era of its electronic reproducibility', in R. Lappert and S. McClary (eds) *Music and Society*, Cambridge: Cambridge University Press, 173–97.

Mowlana, H. (1985) *International Flow of Information: A Global Report and Analysis*, Paris: Unesco.

Mulvey, L. (1975) 'Visual pleasure and narrative cinema', *Screen* 16, no. 3, 6–18.

Murdoch, G. and Janus, N. (1984) *Mass Communications and the Advertising Industry*, Paris: Unesco.

Murray, M. (1975) *The Videotape Book*, New York: Bantam Books.

Neale, S. (1985) *Cinema and Technology: Image, Sound, Colour*, London: British Film Institute and Macmillan.

Newall, B. (1982) *The History of Photography*, London: Secker & Warburg.

Nichols, B. (ed.) (1976) *Movies and Methods*, Berkeley: University of California Press.

—— (1981) *Ideology and the Image*, Bloomington: Indiana University Press.

Nisbett, A. (1979) *The Technique of the Sound Studio*, London: Focal Press.

—— (1983) *The Use of Microphones*, London: Focal Press, second edn.

Nordenstreng, K. and Varis, T. (1974) *Television Traffic – One-Way Street?*, Paris: Unesco.

Ogle, P. (1977) 'Development of sound systems: the commercial era', *Film Reader* 2, 198–212.

Owen, D. and Dunton, M. (1982) *The Complete Handbook of Video*, Harmondsworth: Penguin.

Pateman, T. (1974) 'Ideological criticism of television manuals', *Screen Education* 12, 37–45.

Percheron, D. (1980) 'Sound in cinema and its relationship to image and diegesis', *Yale French Studies* 60, special issue, 'Cinema/Sound', 16–23.

Phillips, W. (1986) 'Who really invented television?' *Broadcast*, special issue, 'Fifty years of television', 33–5.

Porter, R. and Teich, M. (eds) (1986) *Revolution in History*, Cambridge: Cambridge University Press.

Pratten, C. F. (1970) *The Economics of Television*, London: PEP.

Prince, G. (1973) *A Grammar of Stories*, The Hague: Mouton.

Proust, M. (1970) *Remembrance of Things Past: Volume Twelve – Time Regained*, London: Chatto & Windus.

Reich, L. S. (1985) *The Making of American Industrial Research: Science and Business at GE and Bell*, Cambridge: Cambridge University Press.

Reisz, K. and Millar, G. (1968) *The Technique of Film Editing*, London: Focal Press, second edn.

Ropars-Wuilleumier, M-C. (1980) 'The disembodied voice (*India Song*)', *Yale French Studies* 60, special issue, 'Cinema/Sound', 241–68.

Rosen, F. (1984) *Shooting Video*, Boston: Focal Press.

Rosen, P. (1980) 'Adorno and film music: theoretical notes on *Composing for the Films*', *Yale French Studies* 60, special issue, 'Cinema/Sound', 157–82.

—— (ed.) (1986) *Narrative, Apparatus, Ideology: A Film Theory Reader*, New York: Columbia University Press.

Salt, B. (1983) *Film Style and Technology: History and Analysis*, London: Starword.

Scharf, A. (1965) *Creative Photography*, London: Studio Vista.

—— (1974) *Art and Photography*, Harmondsworth: Penguin, revised edn.

Schickel, R. (1976) *Douglas Fairbanks: The First Celebrity*, London: Elm Tree Books.

Scholes, R. and Kellogg, R. (1966) *The Nature of Narrative*, London: Oxford University Press.

Shaw, J. (1986) 'Process work and community video', *Independent Media* 57.

Sklar, R. (1975) *Movie-Made America*, New York: Random House.

Smith, A. (1973) *The Shadow in the Cave*, London: George Allen & Unwin.

—— (1974) *British Broadcasting*, Newton Abbott: David & Charles.

—— (1980) *The Geopolitics of Information*, New York: Oxford University Press.

Sontag, S. (1978) *On Photography*, London: Allen Lane.

Staiger, J. (1979a) 'Dividing labor for production control: Thomas Ince and the rise of the studio system', *Cinema Journal* 18, vol. 2, 12–27.

—— (1979b) 'Mass-produced photoplays: economic and signifying practices in the first years of Hollywood', *Wide Angle* 4, no. 3, 12–27.

Statistics on Radio and Television, 1960–76 (1978), Paris: Unesco.

Swift, J. (1950) *Adventure in Vision*, London: John Lehman.

Taylor, R. (1979) *The Politics of Soviet Cinema, 1917–1929*, Cambridge: Cambridge University Press.

Thomas, T. (1973) *Music for the Movies*, South Brunswick: A. S. Barnes.

Tolson, A. (1985) 'Anecdotal television', *Screen* 26, no. 2, 18–27.

Tunstall, J. (1977) *The Media Are American*, London: Constable.

—— (1983) *The Media in Britain*, London: Constable.

Varis, T. (1985) *International Flow of Television Programmes*, Paris: Unesco.

Vaughan, D. (1974) 'The space between shots', *Screen* 15, no. 1, 73–86.

Wade, G. (1980) *Street Video*, Leicester: Blackthorn Press.

—— (1985) *Film, Video and Television: Market Forces, Fragmentation and Technological Advance*, London: Comedia.

Walker, A. (1978) *The Shattered Silents*, London: Elm Tree Books.

Wallis, R. and Malm, K. (1984) *Big Sounds from Small Peoples: The Music Industry in Small Countries*, London: Constable.

Walter, E. (1982) *The Technique of the Cutting Room*, London: Focal Press.

Watts, H. (1984) *On Camera: How to Produce Film and Video*, London: BBC.

Weis, E. and Belton, J. (eds) (1985) *Film Sound: Theory and Practice*, New York: Columbia University Press.

Willemen, P. (1976) 'Voyeurism, the look and Dwoskin', *Afterimage* 6, 40–50.

Willener, A., Milliard, G. and Ganty, A. (1976) *Videology and Utopia: Explorations in a New Medium*, London: Routledge & Kegan Paul.

Williams, A. (1980) 'Is sound recording like a language?', *Yale French Studies* 60, special issue, 'Cinema/Sound'.

Williams, R. (1974) *Television: Technology and Cultural Form*, London: Fontana/Collins.

Wilson, G. M. (1986) *Narration in Light*, Baltimore: Johns Hopkins University Press.

Winston, B. (1985) 'On Marshall McLuhan's television picture', *Sight and Sound* 54, no. 4, 258–63.

—— (1986) *Misunderstanding Media*, London: Routledge & Kegan Paul.

—— and Keydel, J. (1987) *Working with Video*, London: Pelham Books.

Wischmeyer, J. (1986) 'Independent video exhibition', *Independent Media* 59.

Wollen, P. (1982) *Readings and Writings*, London: Verso.

Wood, N. (1984) 'Towards a semiotics of the transition to sound: spatial and temporal codes', *Screen* 25, no. 3, 16–24.

Wyver, J. (ed.) (1982) *Nothing But the Truth: Cinéma Vérité and the Films of the Roger Graef Team*, London: Institute of Contemporary Arts/British Film Institute.

INDEX